THE BATTLE OF HURTGEN FOREST

Charles Whiting, the author, is Britain's most prolific military writer with over 250 books to his credit. He saw active service in the Second World War, serving in an armoured reconnaissance regiment attached to both the US and British armies. He is therefore able to write with the insight and authority of someone who, as a combat soldier, actually experienced the horrors of the Second World War.

by the same author

Vol. 1 *West Wall: The Battle for Hitler's Siegfried Line*
The story of Hitler's top-secret line of fortifications
which turned out to be Germany's last line of defence
in the final year of World War II

Vol. 2 *'44: In Combat from Normandy to the Ardennes*
Eyewitness accounts of the attack from the beachhead to the Wall

Vol. 3 *Bloody Aachen*
The first major battle for the most impregnable
part of the West Wall

Vol. 4 *The Battle of Hurtgen Forest*
The officially covered-up defeat of 12 US Divisions;
the lead up to the Battle of the Bulge

Vol. 5 *Ardennes: The Secret War*
The secret preparations for the 'surprise attack' in
the Ardennes – the US's 'Gettysburg of the twentieth century'

Vol. 6 *Decision at St Vith*
The decisive battle for the West Wall frontier town
that broke the back of the German assault

Vol. 7 *The Other Battle of the Bugle: Operation* Northwind
The unknown battle fought by the US 7th Army
– the 'Forgotten Army' – in Alsace

Vol. 8 *Patton's Last Battle*
Patton's major breakthrough in the West Wall,
before his fall from grace and his accidental death

Vol. 9 *Bounce the Rhine*
The British role in breaching the West Wall,
and the triumphant crossing of the Rhine

THE BATTLE OF HURTGEN FOREST

Charles Whiting

PAN BOOKS

First published 1989 by Leo Cooper Ltd, London
Revised edition first published 2000 by Spellmount Ltd, Kent

This edition published 2003 by Pan Books
an imprint of Pan Macmillan Ltd
Pan Macmillan, 20 New Wharf Road, London N1 9RR
Basingstoke and Oxford
Associated companies throughout the world
www.panmacmillan.com

ISBN 0 330 42051 8

1 3 5 7 9 8 6 4 2

A CIP catalogue record for this book is available from
the British Library.

Printed and bound in Great Britain by
Mackays of Chatham plc, Chatham, Kent

Dedicated to the dead young men and the old ones still alive who fought in the 'Death Factory' – the men of the 'Big Red One' (1st Division), the 'Ivy League' (4th Division), the 'Golden Arrow' (8th Division), the 'Bloody Bucket' (28th Division), and all the rest of those ill-fated divisions: to the P.B.I. – the poor bloody infantry.

List of Maps

1. The Hurtgen Forest — viii

2. The Western Front, September 1944 — 4

Contents

Introduction   ix

Part One: Into the Green Hell   1

Part Two: The Death Factory   71

Part Three: Dark December   145

Part Four: The Race for the Dams   211

Epilogue   269

Source Notes   275

Index   286

THE HURTGEN FOREST

Introduction

An ugly man cradling his shattered hand waited patiently with the rest of the wounded. "Not much you can do, Doc. Cut it off," he says. . . . The medics hide the severed hand under a carpet so that the others won't see it. . . . A full regimental colonel, wounded twice, sobbing with anguish, crawled on his hands and knees through the shattered trees, desperate to tell HQ about the slaughter taking place up there in the Forest. . . . A thirty-six-year-old sergeant, who had cried when he had first been ordered into combat, ran into his last attack and won the Medal of Honor posthumously. . . . The solidarity of the men at the "sharp end." Germans and Americans putting down their weapons in the middle of the Forest and drinking coffee together, not giving a damn about the Top Brass's war. . . . The regimental colonel wrung his hands together piteously when he heard the latest casualty figures—nearly twenty-five hundred killed and wounded out of a total of three thousand—and moaned "my magnificent command . . . *cut to pieces!*" . . . An ex-major of infantry, who after seeing the slaughter of his battalion up there in the Forest on Thanksgiving Day 1944 could never again eat a Thanksgiving dinner. "I would get up and go to the backyard and cry like a baby. . . . I passed up a helluva lot of turkey dinners that way."

Little of this terrible battle in the Forest was reported to the folks back home. The Army's censors kept a tight wrap on the many tragedies that happened in those grim and fire-shrouded valleys in that bloody winter of 1944–45. Few correspondents ever ventured into the woods. After the crazy, triumphant dash across France and the Low Countries and the hard slog to capture the first German city the U.S. Army encountered, Aachen, officially, the front had gone to sleep. The reports were of "penetrations," "limited patrol activity," "local skirmish and fire fights." There were few public accounts of the terrible, ever-mounting casualties; of the Army hospitals to the rear in Liège, Verviers, Metz, that filled with more and more "combat fatigue" cases, broken men who simply couldn't take the Forest anymore, and of the thousands and tens of thousands of men suffering from "trench foot."

Even later, when the slaughter was over, the accounts of that six-month-long battle, which was a major defeat for the U.S. Army, were neatly swept under the carpet and forgotten. In his *Crusade in Europe*, Eisenhower mentioned the battle only *once*, despite the fact that half a million of his soldiers were engaged in it at some time or other that winter. The official U.S. history of the era, *The Siegfried Line Campaign*, stated only that at a cost of "more than five thousand casualties per division," the Americans "had conquered a formidable forest barrier by frontal assault."*

The 1944 invasion of France, the breakout from the beaches, the surprise German counterattack in the Ardennes, the final reckoning with the Third Reich have all been exhaustively mulled over and written about. There are whole libraries of books on the subject; all of them were victories. Even the Battle of the Bulge became a victory in the end. But what of the U.S. Army's greatest defeat in Europe in World War II, the battle that most observers today feel shouldn't have been fought in the first place? What has been written about that terrible battle of attrition in that remote German frontier forest, that forerunner of the jungles of the Vietnam fiasco? Virtually nothing, then or now, because it was a defeat and, for obvious reasons, the Top Brass does not like defeats and discourages attempts at writing about them.

At the time, the few journalists who ventured up into the Forest called the slaughter taking place there "the Green Hell of the Hurtgen." There was a suitably dramatic ring about the

---

* Charles MacDonald, *The Siegfried Line Campaign*. Washington 1961.

phrase. The doughs who went into that forest to fight—and to die in the thousands—had another name for it. It was one that, for obvious reasons, was never publicized by the media back home during that gray, bitter winter more than forty-odd years ago now. They called it simply "the Death Factory"!

For that was what the fifty square miles of rugged, hilly woods lying on the Belgian-German border below the city of Aachen was. From September 1944 to February 1945, every two weeks or so, a new American division of infantry was fed into those dark green, somber woods, heavy with lethal menace. Fourteen days later the shocked, exhausted survivors would be pulled out, great gaps in their battered ranks, passing like sleepwalkers the "new boys" moving up for the slaughter. Seeing nothing, hearing nothing, muddy, filthy, unshaven, they had somehow escaped the Death Factory while all around them their comrades had died by scores, by hundreds, by thousands.

In the six months of the Battle of the Hurtgen Forest, eight infantry and two armored divisions, plus several smaller U.S. outfits, went into the Death Factory. In a matter of only fourteen days most of the rifle companies suffered up to 50 percent casualties. In the case of two unfortunate regiments, the 9th Infantry Division's 60th Regiment and the 4th Division's 22nd Regiment, the losses were a staggering 100 percent!

By the end, nearly thirty thousand young American soldiers died or were wounded there and many thousands more cracked and went down with combat exhaustion—unable to take any more. Company commanders refused to attack, battalions broke and ran away, even a regimental commander seemed to desert his outfit. By the time the battle had reached its high point, the Top Brass was relieving divisional commanders due to their apparent lack of drive and will to succeed.

To what purpose? The attack into the Forest was launched as a kind of flank guard for the assault of General "Lightning Joe" Collins's VIII U.S. Corps into the Reich. Even then it was totally unnecessary. The Forest could have been sealed off using the superior armor and air power at the disposal of the Top Brass.

The Germans defending it would have been left to rot on the vine. They would have posed no real threat to the American assault.

But the Top Brass was not prepared to admit defeat once they were committed to the attack into the Forest, despite a first abortive assault on the *Hurtgenwald*. The prestige of the U.S. Army was at stake, wasn't it? So, division after division was thrown into the perfectly useless battle, which served no tactical or strategic purpose. Later—much later—they rationalized and attempted to justify the tremendous waste of American lives: they had attacked to capture the strategically important dams beyond the Forest. But in the first four months of the six-month-long battle there was not a single mention of the Roer dams at any level. Most of the men who were to die there had never heard of the River Roer on which the dams were located.

Save for one lone divisional general, no one at the top ever protested this criminal waste of young American lives. Nor at home did anyone find out what was going on in that remote border country. In those days there were no Vietnam-type protest movements. Technology had not yet changed the public's perception of war. Television had not yet brought combat—in full color—right into people's living rooms the length and breadth of America. Few correspondents ever ventured into the combat zone. What little the general public learned of the battle was that it was a hard slog, but the "boys" were winning; American "boys" always did, didn't they?

How could the correspondents report otherwise? Even if they had been allowed to see that the Army was suffering horrendous casualties (in one case, a dead or wounded American for every yard of ground gained over a three-mile stretch), it would have been unpatriotic to report the facts back home. In those days, correspondents, however cynical and worldly wise, were American patriots. It would take Vietnam and Watergate before news-papermen really started to question seriously the military and political leaders of the country—especially in wartime.

So the generals got away with it: the longest single battle in the history of the U.S. Army for an objective that was not worth the death of a single American soldier. When they finally did perceive the real strategic target of this long, bloody battle, they failed to achieve their objective in time. As a result, sixteen thousand additional British and Canadian soldiers, dead and wounded, would be added to the already terribly high butcher's bill.

This, then, is the story of the Battle of the Hurtgen Forest, which the doughs called the Death Factory. It is not a pretty story, but in those days, forty-five years ago, with the world locked in the greatest war of all time, there were few pretty stories.

For us the Hurtgen was one of the most costly, most unproductive, and most ill-advised battles that our army has ever fought.

GEN. JAMES GAVIN,
Commander, 82nd Airborne Division, 1944–45

The German Command could not understand the reason for the strong American attacks in the Hurtgen Forest . . . the fighting in the wooded area denied the American troops the advantages offered them by their air and armored forces, the superiority of which had been decisive in all the battles waged before.

GENERALMAJOR VON GERSDORFF,
Chief of Staff, German 7th Army, 1944–45

The Hurtgen hurt . . . It was a living hell.

ARTHUR P. GOMEZ,
Pfc, 1st U.S. Infantry Division, 1944

PART ONE

Into the Green Hell

SOLDATEN DER WESTFRONT. *I expect you to defend the sacred soil of Germany . . . to the very last . . .* Heil Hitler!

FIELD MARSHAL GERD VON RUNDSTEDT,
Commander in Chief in the West, 1944

1

he Americans are coming!

For nearly a week now, the humble villagers of this remote border area had heard the muted rumble of the gunfire from the west coming slowly but surely ever closer to the river line that marked the border. Day by day, as they labored in the hot fields to bring in the harvest before it was too late, the drumroll of the heavy guns beat across neighboring Belgium, approaching nearer and nearer. At night in their blacked-out medieval villages set deep in the thickly wooded valleys, they could see the silent pink flashes on the western horizon broken here and there by the cherry-red flames of fires.

Now the great enemy bomber fleets, which for years had sailed overhead, aimed at the great industrial cities to the north, no longer seemed so harmless. As the massive silver "V's" glistening in the sun of a perfect September sky roared over now, they were abruptly threatening, no longer so remote; the bringers of sudden death to the city folk of the Ruhr. These old men, women, and children who were all that were left after five years of total war—for the young men had long gone, vanished in the wastes of Russia—knew it would soon be their turn too.

Farther South, the U.S. Thunderbolts and Lightnings and the RAF's Typhoons commenced their attacks on the border area, a sure indication of what was to come. The "Jabos," as the fearful peasants called them, came flashing down out of the sun, cannons pounding, angry purple flames crackling the length of their wings. They attacked individual targets on the ground below: the sweating peasants toiling in the harvest fields; the ancient locomotives with their fading legend (*Raeder*

3

THE WESTERN FRONT,
September 1944

0   10   20   30 Miles
0 10 20 30 40 50 Kms

Rijn

Rhine R.

Arnhem

Nijmegen

Maas R.

CHAZAUD

Wesel

Lippe R.

R U H R

Deurne

Venlo

Niers R.

Ruhr R.

DÜSSELDORF

Roermond

Maeseyck

Mönchen-
Gladbach

Roer R.

Erft R.

COLOGNE

Jülich

FRONT

Maastricht

AACHEN

Düren

Bonn

Sieg R.

LINE

HURTGEN
FOREST

LIÈGE

SEPTEMBER 11

Meuse R.

Münstereifel

Remagen

Sinzig

Huy

Malmédy

Blankenheim

Rhine R.

St. Vith

Mayen

A R D E N N E S

E I F E L

Mosel R.

ivet

Bastogne

WEST WALL

Wittlich

Bitburg

Bollendorf

Trier

Meuse R.

LUXEMBOURG

Nennig

Thionville

Saarlouis

*Rollen fur Den Sieg**) on their sides chugging in and out of the deep, wooded valleys, the plodding ox-carts; even horses, sending them careening and panic-stricken down the cobbled streets, manes ablaze, eyes wide and wild with unreasoning fear.

The Americans are coming.

On the fourth day of September that year, work stopped in the villages and hamlets of the area as, with the usual blare of brass and ruffle of kettledrums, the harsh-voiced, arrogant announcer in far-off Berlin snapped, *"Die Grossdeutsche Wehrmacht gibt bekannt!"*† It was the daily report on the fighting put out by the German Army. The worried peasants in their shabby blue clothing pressed closer to the pear-shaped "people's receiver," as the "Poison Dwarf"‡ had named it.

The news was bad, and for once Radio Berlin was not lying. The announcer stated that the "heroic defenders" were attempting to stop (but with little success) the advancing Americans on the River Meuse southeast of the French border town of Sedan, the site of one of Germany's greatest victories in the nineteenth century. Farther north, the "heroic defenders" had been unable to stop the enemy in Belgium. The Americans had now reached the western approaches to the great Ardennes Forest. It wouldn't be long now.

The first weary columns of peasants fleeing from the west, heavily laden with the pathetic bits and pieces they had managed to rescue, began to pass through the border villages heading for the safety of the interior. Four years before, these "settlers," as they were called, had ventured proudly to the west behind the victorious German Army, to "colonize" the newly captured territories of East Belgium and Luxembourg. There they had been given land and farms and told to put some new, Germanic spirit into the "border pack," make them realize they were of good German stock.§ Now

---

* Wheels roll for victory.

† The Greater German Armed Forces.

‡ Dr. Josef Goebbels, the Minister of Propaganda and Popular Enlightenment, known thus on account of his small build and vitriolic tongue.

§ Both these areas were originally German and are today still German-speaking.

they were fleeing from their recently acquired homes and farms before the wrath of the locals was turned against them.

The humble little people started to prepare for the invaders. They cleaned out their *Jauchewagen,* those wooden tubs on wheels drawn by lazy oxen that they used to transport the human manure from their privies to dung their narrow fields. The GIs with a wry sense of humor would later call the creaking, malodorous devices "the honeydew wagons." Into them they crammed whatever they considered to be of value, reasoning with peasant cunning that the *Amis* would never suspect the stinking barrels. Others sewed gold into the seams and lapels of their children's clothes—just in case they were separated when "it" happened. Even the kids knew what "it" was.

Everywhere they buried and prepared, laying in hoards of food: smoked sausage and ham, great stone jars of pickles and pickled eggs. They placed layer after layer of potatoes and carrots down in the cellars, each layer separated from the rest by fine white sand, and bundled up huge piles of crackling and brittle tobacco leaf that later would be sprayed with "Virginia odor," and deposited them in the barns for the shortages to come. Indeed, it was as if they had been thrown back in time three centuries to the days of the Thirty Years' War, and the Protestant mercenaries from the north were about to descend upon their remote villages, once again plundering, pillaging, and raping as they came.

The Americans are coming.

On Sunday, September 10, all the bridges over the frontier rivers, the Sauer and the Our, were ordered blown. The passages from nearby Belgium and Luxembourg had to be destroyed before the *Amis* reached them. Even as the defeated field-greys, lousy, weary, dejected, started to stream out of the Ardennes, the trails behind littered with their bloodstained feces (for they all had the "thin shits," as they called it), the engineers began to blow the bridges spanning the frontier rivers. They did not even wait for the survivors of the beaten Army of France to cross. Their haste was too great. The *Amis* were almost there.

"We were busy in the fields," one eyewitness from the border village of Berscheid recalled many years later, "trying to get in the last of the harvest before it was too late. Suddenly there was a tremendous crash from the other side of the border. It was the first boom of the *Ami* cannon from Luxembourg. That first shot was followed moments later by a series of explosions, one after another, as they blew up the bridges the length of the River Sauer."[1]

Another eyewitness, Hermann Puetz, recorded in his diary that dramatic September: "There was nothing of a peaceful Sunday about this day. American *Jabos* flew up and down the Sauer shooting up anything that they thought was a worthwhile target—soldiers, civilians, vehicles, cows. We sought refuge in a *Westwall** bunker camouflaged as a weekend house. About two we were ordered into the cellars. They were going to blow up the bridge near us. Afterwards we went out to see the damage and to our surprise we saw that there was one span still standing on the Luxembourg side of the river, with half a dozen German soldiers standing on it, staring at us, wondering what to do next. Not for long, though. Suddenly there was a rending sound and the rest of the bridge went thundering into the water, taking with it the screaming trapped soldiers."[2]

The Americans are coming!

On the following Monday, "the golden pheasants"—as the Party bosses were called, due to their love of uniforms and gold braid—and their hangers-on started to appear everywhere in the border villages of the "Red Zone," the area running the length of the frontier now endangered by the approaching *Amis*. With them they brought a proclamation signed by Grohé, the National Socialist *Gauleiter* of the Aachen-Cologne region. In the melodramatic fashion of the time in that cruel, jackbooted republic, he announced: "When the foe reaches the German positions in the West, he must be met with fanatical resistance . . . The eyes of our children exhort us to resistance to the last breath, with every available means. We must expect that all forward positions

* The German name for the Siegfried Line defensive system.

in the west of our fortifications and also villages within the fortifications will soon become combat areas. Therefore, the Führer has ordered the evacuation of the cities and villages located in the above-mentioned combat area."[3]

The locals were dismayed. They had not anticipated that they would be forced to flee their homes for a second time. Five years before, at the outbreak of war, they had been ordered to evacuate the "Red Zone" and had spent months in the Protestant north, where they had felt unwelcome among people who did not share their religion or even understand their native dialect. Now they were expected to do it once again. *"Wu as dann de nei Waff?"* an old woman using the thick dialect of the area was reported to have called out in the village of Koerperich. *"De Führer lesscht doch net!"** But there was no new V-3 or any other "wonder weapon" to stop the advancing Americans. So it was that they prepared their "treks," as they called the refugee columns, as they had done back in September 1939. This time virtually all order and certainty had vanished. Everything was confusion and chaos.

Despite their bombast and arrogance, the "golden pheasants" themselves were visibly nervous and inclined to overreact, throwing constant nervous glances at the wooded heights to the west from whence the invaders would come. The thunder of the guns was getting ever nearer, and overhead a massive bomber force from the RAF droned threateningly, as Bomber Harris's men flew to launch yet another devastating raid on Darmstadt. Time was running out rapidly.

Hurriedly the oxen were spanned. Carts were piled high with precious possessions, topped with mattresses or thick down quilts in a pathetic attempt to stop the bullets and shrapnel from the *Jabos* that might be theirs on the morrow. It seemed as if the whole of the Eifel was disgorging a century's accumulation of anything on wheels: carts, coaches, funeral hearses, wheelbarrows, bikes, prams, and pushcarts. The frantic peasants, urged on by their brown-clad masters, prepared to flee before the invaders.

---

* "Now where is the new weapon [promised by Hitler]? The Führer does not lie."

"We knew they were there already on the opposite side of the River Our," the then 12-year-old Hannalore Thomas-Weiss remembers many years later. "From up on the heights above our village of Gmünd, we could see something moving among the trees on the Luxembourg bank and hear the noise of their vehicles on the road beyond. I remember well how I burst into tears when my mother showed them to me just before we fled. They were the dread *Amis,* come to do . . . I didn't know what.

"I little realized then that ten years later I would be married to one of them and living in Chicago. But *then* I was frightened, awfully frightened. Now I know, of course, that on that Monday the world was about to change, not only my little world, but the world of everyone in Europe . . . for the rest of the twentieth century."[4]

And then they were gone. The long, miserable, pathetic columns disappeared into the glowing darkness, the oxen and skinny-ribbed old nags straining under the loads. Behind them the peasants left the empty villages, so hastily abandoned. Like thieves in the night the handful of ragged, demoralized field-greys stole into the cottages and barns still warm from the animals, to wait, tense and expectant, for the *Amis* to come across the river.

It was the second week of September 1944.

The Americans had arrived!

First Lieutenant Vipond, Executive Officer of Troop B, 85th Reconnaissance Squadron of the U.S. 5th Armored Division, had told S. Sgt. Warner W. Holzinger that he'd better hurry if he wished to claim the credit of being the first enemy soldier to enter Germany since the time of Napoleon nearly a century and a half before. From Strasbourg to Aachen, American troops were approaching the border of the vaunted Thousand-Year Reich. As the shadows started to race down the tight wooded valley of the River Our, Sergeant Holzinger decided to stick his neck out and take his little patrol across, where hours before 12-year-old Hannalore Thomas-Weiss thought she had seen the *Amis* and had burst into tears.

The little stone bridge across the river just outside the Luxembourg village of Stolzemburg had been blown up the day before. After a dry summer the water of the river was shallow and sluggish. Crouched in the cover of the trees on the Luxembourg bank, the four Americans and the French interpreter who made up the patrol could see the bottom of the Our quite easily.

Holzinger went in first and started to wade across, carbine held at the high port position. Cpl. Ralph Diven, T/5 Coy Locke, Pfc George McNeal, and the Frenchman, Lieutenant Lille, followed. Their gazes were fixed apprehensively on the steep, heavily wooded slope on the German side. Nothing happened. All was silent save for the continuous rumble of the heavy guns of the barrage, the background music of total war.

Together they climbed out of the water and crossed the narrow winding road on the German side. Almost immediately they stumbled across the first bunker of the famed Siegfried Line, cunningly cut into the hillside to cover the bridge. It was empty.* Apprehensively, they ventured a little farther up the hillside through the firs and found another three pillboxes. They were empty too, and had been so a long time, or so it seemed. Germany, or at least its frontier, had been abandoned to the invaders.

The five tense young men venturing onto enemy soil for the first time finally struggled almost to the top of the hill to find yet another score of pillboxes of the Siegfried Line—all empty, with thick dust on the floor as if there had been no one inside them for years. Around one some local farmer had built a chicken coop, which Holzinger thought had been there a considerable time.

Now it was getting dark. Holzinger felt no desire to linger any longer in the middle of the Siegfried Line, empty though it was. He and the others stumbled down the height as the sun started to sink over the hill. Hastily, the little patrol splashed back across the Our and doubled back to their scout-car.

Thirty minutes later an excited Holzinger was reporting what he had seen to Lieutenant Vipond. Sixty minutes after that the

---

* For those interested in such things, it is still there.

news was hurrying up the "channels" to no less a person than Gen. Courtney Hodges, the commander of the U.S. First Army, to which the 5th Armored Division belonged. That same night, Hodges's HQ issued a statement couched in the dry, unemotional prose of the Army. It read:

"At 1805 hrs on 11 September, a patrol led by S. Sgt. Warner W. Holzinger crossed into Germany near the village of Stolzemburg, a few miles northeast of Vianden, Luxembourg."

For the first time since 1814 an armed enemy soldier had set foot on German soil in wartime. Staff Sergeant Holzinger had returned to the land of his forefathers as a conqueror to find the defenses abandoned. It seemed there was nothing to stop the Americans now.

That evening and the following morning, more and more outfits started to slip across the frontier between Trier and Aachen, entering a strangely quiet and seemingly undefended Germany. A patrol of America's premier infantry division, the First (known as "the Big Red One"), crossed near Vaals, Holland. Lene Nellesen, who had a war-blinded husband and two small children, watched fearfully there as a big, black American armed with a tommy gun advanced upon her. "Don't shoot please," she called hesitantly in English. "There are children here." Slowly the black man lowered his weapon and said casually, "Nice day for a war, eh?"[5]

A little farther south, in the German hamlet of Schmithof, Pastor Welter was confronted by a patrol from the 3rd Armored Division. In his robe, with the Host in one hand and a briefcase in the other, the frightened priest tried to tell the suspicious *Amis* that there were no German soldiers left in the village. Their hard looks did not relax. Desperately the priest tried again in French. This time they understood. Indeed, two of them bent on one knee and crossed themselves in front of the Host. An officer pushed his way through the throng. He thrust out his hand at the priest and said, *"Guten Tag, Herr Pfarrer."* Then he said heartily in a mixture of German and English, "Nice to be in Germany again."[6]

The first general crossed, driving his jeep through the shallow waters of the Our. Later, big burly Tubby Barton, whose 4th Infantry Division would be decimated twice before the year was out, boasted that he had been the first Allied general to cross into the Third Reich during the war. With him went his men of the ill-fated 22nd Infantry Regiment, closely followed by the soldiers of yet another infantry regiment that would be wiped out twice by the end of 1944: the 109th Infantry Regiment of the 28th Division. They brought back with them from the Third Reich peaked German caps, some marks, and a symbolic packet of German earth to show that they had been there. Perhaps to this day it holds a place of pride in some suburban front parlor—if its possessor survived to take it home to the States.

The first correspondent who ventured across the border was Robert Dunnett of the BBC. He reported, "I never expected to set foot on German soil so quietly. The first Germans we saw were an elderly couple standing on the roadside in front of the first house in the town. They looked at us without either a smile or a frown. Farther into the town people were at their garden gates. Every house flew a white flag. Everybody carried something white—even if it was only a handkerchief in their hand. Some of them waved and smiled. A girl came running out of one house with a basin full of plums and reached up to the Americans in the turrets of their tanks. There were children dressed in their best clothes, waving handkerchiefs in one hand and clutching their toys in the other. The people looked well dressed, well fed, and certainly not either angry or afraid."[7]

Another correspondent, American this time and looking like a khaki teddy bear in his uniform, thought the first Germans encountered unpleasant to look at: "ugly women and squatty ill-shaped men," who came sidling up to him and the soldiers bearing bottles of schnapps and drinking some themselves to prove the stuff wasn't poisoned.

Ernest Hemingway, working for *Collier's*, had been following the progress of Tubby Barton's 4th Infantry Division (in particular, its 22nd Infantry Regiment) ever since the fall of Paris. As the regiment crossed the frontier, intent on its first encounter with the Germans on their own soil, Papa Hemingway set about organizing a dinner for the regimental staff, as the heavy machine guns chattered frantically to the east. He shot the heads off a small flock of chickens with his .45 and then sent one of the "ugly German women" off to pluck and fricassee them.

Some time later Colonel Lanham, the commander of the 22nd Infantry, short, wiry, and something of a writer himself, and his three battalion commanders arrived to eat the first meal to be consumed on enemy soil. "All our booty drunk up," Hemingway noted in his diary. "Teague sends for some wine. Supper of chicken, peas, fresh onions, carrots, salad, and preserved fruit and jelly for dessert."[8]

To Colonel Lanham, in retrospect, the dinner eaten that night in the border hamlet of Hemmeres seemed the happiest meal of a long and bitter campaign—indeed, of the whole war. "The food was excellent, the wine plentiful, the comradeship close and warm. All of us were as heady with the taste of victory as we were with the wine. It was a night to put aside the thought of the great *Westwall* against which we would throw ourselves within the next forty-eight hours. We laughed and drank and told horrendous stories about each other. We all seemed for the moment like minor gods and Hemingway, presiding at the head of the table, might have been a fatherly Mars delighting in the happiness of his brood."[9]

It was the last happy night. Within weeks Col. Buck Lanham would be lamenting to a suddenly somber Papa Hemingway, "My magnificent command [has] virtually ceased to exist." By the end of November 1944, the 3,000-strong 22nd Regiment would have suffered 2,678 casualties, 85 percent of its original strength—lost a dozen miles from where they now celebrated so happily. The name of the place? *Der Hurtgenwald.*

But that was yet to come. Now, in the second week of September, the American Top Brass was jubilant. They had destroyed the German Army in France and had gained a toehold in Germany 233 days ahead of the schedule laid down in England before the Invasion. There was a problem, of course, occasioned by the rapidity of their great sweep across France into Germany. They had outrun their supplies. The order went out to the various forward units that for the time being, with the supplies being trucked two and three hundred miles from the Invasion beaches, they would have to ration gas and ammunition, even food.

Predictably, flamboyant General Patton, commanding the U.S. Third Army, ignored the order. Gen. Courtney Hodges, who commanded the U.S. First Army, a stolid plodding infantryman whose last taste of combat had been as an infantry captain in 1918, was inclined to obey the Supreme Commander's order, but he had not reckoned with the fiery, restless temperament of one of his corps commanders, who everyone said (behind his back) ran the First Army.

This was Gen. Joe Collins, a dynamic 48-year-old (he looked ten years younger) who had gained the nickname "Lightning Joe" by his flamboyant handling of the 25th ("Lightning") Infantry Division in the Pacific, and who now commanded Hodges's VII Corps. He felt that the Germans were nearly defeated, and it would take only one last effort for the First Army to break through to Germany's last natural barrier, the River Rhine.

That second week of September, he wrote to his wife: "*Somewhere in Germany!* . . . How is that for a heading? . . . So far we have received no resistance from the civil population. In the first German town we occupied (Rótgen) the acting burgomaster told our Civil Affairs people that the Nazis had all fled, that the people who lived there were primarily interested in their homes, that we were there as a conquering army, and that they were ready to receive orders. Many homes had white towels, undershirts, or pillowslips stuck on poles in the yards or hung from windows in token of submission. The Nazis had told the people we would burn their homes, though returning German soldiers had assured them that we would not. They are so relieved that we are not molesting them that I feel sure that this side of the Rhine, at least, we will have no real fears about guerrilla warfare behind us . . . Thus far we have had no sniping and no acts of sabotage and I am hoping that no underground resistance will be attempted."[10]

The letter mirrored exactly Collins's thinking. The German Army west of the Rhine was defeated. So far Eisenhower's fears that, now that they were defending their own soil, a German underground resistance would spring up had not yet materialized. Why stop, then? Keep on going toward the Rhine until the supplies of gas gave out. Only then would the First Army need to halt. "Don't stop men when they're moving," he protested hotly to Hodges. Instead he suggested that the army commander should let the troops pass the fortifications around Aachen, the first major German city in the path of the First Army, and *then* pause so that fresh supplies could be brought up from the Normandy beaches. Wouldn't Hodges authorize a "reconnaissance in force," to commence on September 13, 1944, which would breach the Siegfried Line before the Germans had time to put troops into the fortifications?

In the end, Hodges backed down. In spite of the supply difficulties, he told Collins to go ahead with his "reconnaissance in force," but warned him that if he ran into solid opposition and failed to achieve a "quick penetration," he was to halt and wait for further supplies. Collins gave him that Irish grin of his, but said nothing. He had his go-ahead. That was all that mattered. Once he started his reconnaissance, he would soon develop it into a full-scale attack. Then he'd let General Hodges worry about keeping his VII Corps supplied with the necessary.

But there was a problem. As a young officer Collins had not served in France in World War I, but he had read of the problem of the Argonne Forest that had menaced Black Jack Pershing's left flank during the great American offensive of September 1918, exactly twenty-six years before. Now he was to drive into the Reich with his 80,000-man-strong VII Corps, with a similar stretch of forest just over the border menacing his right flank.

Starting some five miles south of Aachen, it was a collection of several woods extending fifty square miles within a triangle formed by the cities of Aachen, Duren, and Monschau. One of these woods was called the *Hurtgenwald*, which name the Americans later gave to the whole area: a name that since the war has been adopted by the Germans themselves. Unwittingly therefore, these tens of thousands of young Americans who would come to fight and die there would name a part of Germany, and the name would last long after they had been forgotten.

From southwest to the northeast through the Forest two ridges point toward the Roer. On the northern ridge lie the small townships of Hurtgen, Kleinhau, and Grosshau, with the ridge itself extending some two miles. The southern ridge extends from Lammersdorf to Schmidt, townships which were then completely unknown outside the area even to the Germans themselves. Between these two ridges is the deep gorge of the little, but fast-flowing, River Kall.

The terrain, tough enough already, had steep, wooded heights reaching up 1,000 feet and packed with firs and fast-flowing little streams racing through the tight valleys. But for the attacker, the Hurtgen Forest was made even more difficult by the German fortifications: concrete pillboxes and bunkers fronted by "dragon's teeth," with interlocking fields of fire, concrete stumps to stop the advance of tracked vehicles, and extensive minefields filled with the dreaded "Schu" mine, which couldn't be detected using the mine detectors of the time, and "bouncing Bettys," known more crudely by the troops who suffered them as "deballockers." These crude devices, with a series of metal balls that exploded to about waist height, had devastating results when detonated. One survivor said many years later: "We called it a 50-50 mine. The name was derived from your chance once you trod on it. If you hit it with your right foot, the rod flew up your right side. If you hit it with your left, you'd end up singing tenor!"[11]

To guard the right flank of his main attack, Collins proposed to send an American force into the deep Forest to root out the second-rate German division (at first, in September, the 353rd Infantry Division, and later, in October, the 275th Division) that held it. No one was ever able to figure out why, then or now.

For by sending troops into the forest, Collins lost the mobility and superiority that his tanks and aircraft had given him so far. Among the thick, tight rows of trees his fighter-bombers, Shermans, and artillery hardly made themselves felt, while the shelter afforded by the same woods and their network of bunkers lent strength to the at first irresolute defenders.

It was a fatal mistake, perhaps the greatest one made by the Americans in the eleven-month campaign in Europe. It was condoned by all the Top Brass, right up to Supreme Commander General Eisenhower himself, none of whom got within ten miles of the actual fighting in the dark, bloody maws of the Hurtgen Forest. It was a mistake compounded by the various divisional commanders, who really knew what was going on. They saw their divisions going into the forest to fight, on average, for two weeks before being pulled out of the line—decimated. These divisional commanders lost half their men, yet not a single commanding general ever registered a protest. Dutifully and obediently they sent their handful of veterans and large numbers of callow replacements to an almost certain death (if they were infantry) without once objecting to the futility of the exercise.

Week in, week out, month after month, the slaughter went on from 1944 right into 1945. It would become perhaps the greatest bloodletting in the history of the U.S. Army in Europe in World War II. Yet in the final analysis, the six-month-long battle for what was to become known as the Green Hell of the Hurtgen did not affect the course of the war at all. The slaughter of America's youth there was totally and absolutely unnecessary. As the commander of the 82nd Airborne, Gen. "Slim Jim" Gavin, whose division was to take part in the last of the Hurtgen fighting, would say contemptuously after the war, it was "a battle that should not have been fought."[12]

2

During the spring and summer, the U.S. 9th Infantry Division had covered 450 miles in a rapid and victorious advance across France and Belgium. On a cold and hazy Wednesday morning, September 13, 1944, they crossed into the Reich coming from the Belgian city of Eupen. The men were eager and confident, as befitted the soldiers of a veteran division that had fought in North Africa and Sicily since November 1942. Besides, the opposition was light, even nonexistent. Within twenty-four hours they had penetrated through the outer defenses of the Siegfried Line to a depth of six miles.

But on Friday the fifteenth, the resistance started to thicken. After capturing 400 prisoners the previous day for a handful of casualties, the leading battalion of the 47th Regiment was attacked by a battalion of German infantry marching into battle in columns of three. Staff Sergeant La Barr, in charge of a roadblock in the Forest, was the first to see the advancing men. In the poor dawn light he couldn't make them out, so he trained his carbine on the officer leading the column. Suddenly the German officer spotted the Americans. He grabbed for the machine pistol slung around his neck, but "that was the last time he reached for anything."[1] La Barr put the bullet right between the German's eyes.

The battle broke out almost immediately as the Germans rushed up tanks to support the surprised infantry. The Americans began to give ground in this their first battle on German soil. A huge sixty-ton Tiger tank rumbled up to halt outside the cookhouse of the 47th Regiment. The cook, T/4 Clarence Ed Combs, hurriedly dropped his meat cleaver and grabbed a bazooka. Even a cook couldn't miss at that range. The whole side of the Tiger caved in as the bazooka round struck the metal with a great ringing clang. The five-man crew of the tank staggered out dazed, and with faces blackened, only to be shot down mercilessly by Combs. The men of his company reportedly sighed to a correspondent afterward, "What a man. If he could only cook!"[2]

It was the kind of crude, heavy-handed humor that characterized the reports of the first battles on the fringe of the Hurtgen Forest. The American soldier was more than a match for the German, they maintained, and when the chips were down, rear-line personnel such as cooks, even sick men, would willingly join the battle. One such was an officer suffering from an acute attack of appendicitis when the German counterattack came. As the 9th's after-action report, which went through channels right to the First Army and then to the War Department in Washington itself, put it: "[the officer] was lying in a roadside ditch awaiting the arrival of the ambulance to evacuate him. Several of the enemy passed over him, one even stepping on him and continuing on. He waited for the last one of the enemy patrol to approach and took him prisoner. When last seen, by Lt. Robert F. Hodges, he was hobbling down the road, bent double with pain, with his German prisoner in front of him."[3]

It was the sort of devil-may-care bravery, tinged with humor, that the Great American Public expected of their soldiers. Sitting over their bacon and eggs at breakfast, they wanted news from the war front in Europe that was snappy and optimistic, and the Top Brass's PR men gave them exactly that.

For months now American forces had been "sweeping, racing, storming forward at a great rate against shattered, battered, reeling enemy soldiers." Now that they were in Germany the PR talk continued, with the Allied troops always "victorious" or "triumphant." Headlines such as "Germany's Volkssturm made up of old men, stomach cases, cripples with glass eyes, and wooden legs" made awfully good, encouraging reading that September. The public was amused. Surely the Krauts were scraping the bottom of the barrel now? Hitler's vaunted Thousand-Year

Reich would have to collapse soon. The war would be over by Christmas.

The men at the sharp end on that dark frontier, the poor bloody infantry, were *not* amused. As one of them commented to the *Yank* magazine reporter on the headline above, "I don't care if the guy behind that gun is a syphilitic prick who's a hundred years old—he's still sitting behind eight feet of concrete and he's still got enough fingers to press triggers and shoot bullets!"[4]

By September 17, the fight to penetrate into the outer fringes of the Hurtgen Forest had developed into a ding-dong battle for the 9th Infantry Division, in particular its 60th Regiment. Roadblocks, pillboxes, and thick minefields held up the advance of the infantrymen down the narrow trails that led into the Forest, and there were persistent, bitter German counterattacks. As the divisional history of the 9th melodramatically put it, "German harassing patrols and heavy artillery backed the Nazi effort to eject the American invaders from the soil of Hitler's *sacred Fatherland*. Blood flowed down the hills and ravines . . . as possession of key points see-sawed back and forth between the battle fortunes of American and German infantry and heavy firepower."[5] Now German real estate on the remote frontier began to become expensive. Gains began to be measured not in miles, but in yards.

On September 22, two days after Cardinal Francis J. Spellman had held the first communion service on German soil for the men of the 9th, the division's leading battalion suffered the most devastating barrage they had ever experienced. It was a massed concentration of seventeen 150mm howitzers, nine 105mm howitzers, many 120mm and 80mm mortars, as well as several huge 210mm rifles.

For fifteen minutes the earth reeled and quaked as the startled, frightened, ashen-faced infantrymen cowered in their damp foxholes. The soil and pebbles shot up to the gray sky in whirling black mushrooms, and the firs snapped like matchwood as great chunks of red-hot shrapnel cut through the air. Then, as abruptly as it had started the terrifying barrage ceased, leaving behind a loud echoing silence.

Not for long. In the trees, the whistles shrilled. There were hoarse exultant cries in German and the rattle of tank tracks. Then the Germans rushed to the attack—a whole regiment of them. Within the hour, the defenders' right flank was overrun as radio communications failed on all sides. The battalion headquarters was threatened. The hard-pressed defenders appealed desperately right up to the divisional commander, General Craig, for help. He ordered the 60th Regiment's 3rd Battalion to stand by. Still the Germans pressed home their attack. For a while Staff Sergeant William D. Clark, though wounded in both legs, managed to hold them off. Another NCO, Sgt. Albert Moses, risked his life to make a 150-yard dash to bring 1,000 rounds of badly needed ammunition back to his platoon. Half an hour later he was killed trying to drag his wounded commander to safety under a hail of intense fire.

A cannon company was overrun by the Germans and their howitzers captured. The situation was serious, and the artillerymen and some nearby engineers were forced to grab their rifles and fight as infantry. Craig threw in a counterattack: a complete tank battalion, the 746th, and self-propelled guns from the 899th Tank Destroyer Battalion. They went into action with a will and the Germans broke, the steam going out of their attack, though they continued to savagely shell the defenders.

That first counterattack seemed to symbolize the ever-hardening German resistance. Now, the American infantry and the combat engineers went into action using packs of dynamite or flamethrowers strapped to their backs as the only means of overcoming the pillboxes and strong points that were everywhere in the forest and along the mudbound trails. Time and time again the attacks bogged down when the infantry ran into mines, and the engineers risked their lives as they tried to clear them under machine-gun fire, crawling forward doggedly through the goo on their stomachs, prodding with their bayonets for the deadly little devices, which were so often booby-trapped.

In one case, after edging their way through yet another minefield, the engineers of the 15th Engineer Combat Battalion were confronted by a pillbox defended by forty very stubborn Germans. For twelve hours the engineers bombarded the single pillbox, one of thousands in the forest, using 24 pounds of dynamite, 400 pounds of TNT, 18 Teller mines,* and bringing direct, short-range fire from artillery and bazookas to bear on it. Only then did it finally surrender: its occupants, smoke-begrimed, totally deaf, shaking like leaves, staggered out to collapse with total shock in the mud.

Pillbox fighting in the tight confines of the trees and trails was something new to the Americans. Even the engineers, as one of them, Cpl. Frederick Griffin, admitted at the time: "We didn't know exactly how much demolition to use at first. The first time we put twenty packs of tetratyl inside and let her go. She just went up into the air, turned a half flip and came down. After that we used less and less . . . When we were in a big hurry, we sometimes blew up only certain ones so that we'd break the chain and they couldn't cover each other even if the Krauts did get back. Lots of these pillboxes weren't manned and we never knew which was which, especially if the infantry bypassed them. That bothered the hell out of us, because when we're loaded with tetratyl like that and a shell lands anywhere near us, there isn't enough left of us to make even a good memory."[6]

However, in the Hurtgen *all* the pillboxes were manned, and before the fighting finally died out temporarily in the Forest, the 15th Engineer Combat Battalion would not only have lifted 1,352 mines and defused some 100 booby traps, they would also have neutralized 125 fortified pillboxes under fire. The engineers and the infantry were paying the bloody butcher's bill for the war in the Forest. In both outfits, the 15th and their friends of the 9th Infantry, casualties started to mount, as German resistance thickened by the hour.

When the casualties had become horrendous, worse than the Division had suffered in all its combat career in North Africa, Sicily, and France, it was decided at the top to give the 9th a rest. Colonel Gibney's 60th Infantry Regiment, which bore the brunt

---

* A German anti-tank mine.

of much of the fighting, suffered in the end almost a 100 percent turnover in combat personnel since September 1, 1944! The Hurtgen had beaten the brave young attackers on the first attempt to take the Forest. It wouldn't be the last time.

"The enemy seemed to be everywhere," one of the men of the 9th complained afterward, "and in the darkness of the thick trees and the confusion, the firing seemed everywhere."[7] A battalion commander declared bitterly, "If anybody says he knew where he was in the forest, then he's a liar!"[8]

The survivors of the 9th who came out of the Forest to rest and refit were understandably bitter, confused, and not a little frightened by what they had just undergone. One sergeant reported, "The forest will stink with deadness long after the last body is removed. The forest will bear the scars of our advance long after our scars have healed and the Infantry has scars that will never heal."[9]

In the Hurtgen the regulation foxhole was useless unless it was covered with logs and sod, as the Germans' foxholes were. For here, shells didn't explode on the ground, with the deadly shrapnel erupting upward; instead, they exploded in the air on contact with the trees. The lethal "tree bursts" showered the men cowering below with red, gleaming, razor-sharp pieces of metal. Nor was it any use throwing yourself on the ground when tree bursts were exploding all around. To do so only exposed more of the man's body surface to the lethal metal. Although it took a lot of nerve to do so, it was the only way to survive: During the bombardment the soldier had to stand upright, sheltered by a tree—and pray.

Night movement was out of the question. Both sides had itchy trigger fingers, and often their positions were only separated from one another by a score of yards. After darkness men shot first and challenged afterwards. The men of both sides cowered in their gravelike holes at night praying for the first ugly light of dawn to come, not daring to get out of their pits, carrying out their natural functions where they squatted. Better defiled than dead.

Casualties were a problem. To evacuate them at night was virtually suicide; even skilled, fit messengers took their lives in their hands during the hours of darkness. So they lay there in their misery and squalor in the mud and the makeshift bunker clearing-centers waiting for a favorable moment for evacuation. Often they were never taken away and died where they lay. Six months after the 9th Infantry Division first went into the Forest, General Gavin of the 82nd Airborne came across "dozens of litter cases, the bodies long dead. Apparently, an aid station had been established near the creek and in the midst of the fighting it had been abandoned, many of the men dying on their stretchers."[10] As the fighting intensified ever more, both sides asked for—and received—truces so they could evacuate those who were broken in body and in mind.

Now in the Hurtgen Forest a new illness made itself felt in great numbers for the first time, reaching almost epidemic proportions, attacking not only enlisted men and junior officers, but company, battalion, even regimental commanders. Due to conditions in the Hurtgen, men were often cut off for hours, even days at a time, separated from their comrades by the terrain and the trees. The strain was considerable and for some people unbearable. As even the official history of the 9th Division, *Eight Stars to Victory,* admits: "With adverse weather conditions and the impossibility of continued and accurate artillery or air support, many soldiers felt as if they were fighting in the dark. Each infantryman, moreover, was on his own. More than at any other time GIs and officers experienced the tension and strained nerves that make men victims of *combat fatigue.*"[11] Even battalion commanders would crack up, begin to cry, and refuse to fight.

"We moved to a patch of small pines," one of them recalled afterward, "and they must have pinpointed our command post because they threw in a six-hour barrage right on top of us. Me and this buddy of mine were in the same hole with only a little brush on top and I remember I was actually bawling. We were both praying to the Lord over and over again to please stop the barrage. We were both shaking and shivering and crying and praying all at the same time. It was our first barrage.

"When it stopped both of us waited for a while and then we crept out of the hole and I never saw anything like it. All the trees were torn down and the hill was just full of holes. They hit everything—even the battalion aid station. Every officer got hit except one.

"They sent me back to an aid station for a while and I guess they treated me for shock or something. Then they sent me back to my outfit. Everything was just as cold and slimy as it was before and the fog was so thick you couldn't see fifteen yards away.

"And it was the same shells, the same goddamn shells. Soon as I got there, the Jerries started laying them on again. They started laying them all over the road and I tried to dig in and then I started shaking and crying again. I guess I must have banged my head against a tree or something because I lost my senses. I couldn't hear anything. I don't remember exactly what happened, but I was walking down the road and I remember seeing this soldier crawling out of a tank with both arms shot off. I remember helping him, and then I don't remember anymore. I guess I must have gone off my nut."[12]

The time had not yet come when the problems of combat fatigue and what General Arnold called "intentional evasions of further combat service" were to be major headaches for the Supreme Commander. But the day was not far off when Eisenhower would visit a field hospital and blow his top when he discovered that the patients it contained were all combat fatigue cases or men who had deliberately inflicted wounds upon themselves to avoid combat.

So the survivors of the 9th Infantry Division came out of the line—for a while. Now it was almost winter, and the wooded ridges where they had fought and died were wreathed in a cold damp fog in the morning. In the valleys below, where they lived in the medieval half-timbered houses that huddled together as if fearful of what was soon to come, it rained: a cold, gray, persistent drizzle which turned the fields into quagmires and rutted the tracks so that they soon became impassable, unless they were constantly worked upon by the engineers.

Here they waited doggedly, bemused and wrapped in a cocoon of their thoughts and apprehensions, while the battered regiments received replacements by the score, the hundred, and in the end, by the thousand. The smart ones found somewhere to get undercover: a barn, a cottage, a farmhouse smelling of boiled white cabbage, animal droppings, and human misery. When the October sun shone fitfully at noon, weak and yellow, they'd take their shoes and socks off and wiggle their stiff frozen toes in the mild warmth.

They lived for mail call and hot chow, sleeping much and trying to blot out the past and the dread future. They sweated out their turn for a hot shower (a tent in the middle of a muddy field) and stood in the blessed spray of water for as long as they were allowed, rubbing their skinny bodies with soap, trying to get the stink and weariness out of their limbs for at least a few minutes. If there were no showers, then they returned to the methods of their childhoods during the Depression: a tin bath in front of one of the local potbellied stoves, with the squad lining up to take its turn until the water was cold, scummy, and gray.

But whatever they did during that time "out of war," all of them knew, to the greenest rookie, that a new offensive in the Hurtgen Forest was about to start soon. The evidence was on all sides in the border villages where they rested. There was a flood of new men and equipment to replace the losses of September. The tank support companies trundled up to be parked under camouflage in the mud-churned fields, and waited for the call to spit fire. The field hospitals, the medics, and row upon row of empty cots waited for the broken bodies to come.

In the fall of 1944, the veteran war correspondent Ernie Pyle, who, after two years on active service, would himself be killed in action before the war was over, wrote: "The Ninth is one of our best infantry divisions." It was indeed, for it had been in action since February 1943 when its artillery had helped to stop Rommel's Panzers after the defeat of the Kasserine Pass. Thereafter it had seen some hard fighting in Sicily and had landed in France shortly after D-Day. It had performed well at the siege of Cherbourg on the French coast and then played a key role in the breakout from the beachheads.

It wasn't a flamboyant division that was always in the headlines. It had no real nickname like Hell on Wheels or the Bloody Bucket, no vainglorious title conceived by an eager-beaver divisional PR man to bolster the morale of innocent, nervous cannon fodder. Unlike the Big Red One,* the best known of all World War II U.S. infantry divisions, it had no calypso-singing PR man, who so roused Papa Hemingway's ire and scorn (one wonders why—he was no slouch when it came to personal publicity).

Even though the 9th Division was not well known, it was a fighting outfit consistently more successful in combat than many of those featured so often in the newspaper headlines back home. By the end it would be in battle a total of 304 days and suffer 23,277 combat casualties, always gaining its objective—with one major exception. It never succeeded in achieving its objective in the Hurtgenwald.

In retrospect, one wonders why the difficulties experienced on the fringe of the Forest in September, coupled with the tremendous number of casualties, did not bring into question for the Top Brass the feasibility of the entire Hurtgen operation. Why was it that Gen. Louis Craig, who had taken over command of the Division back in August 1944, did not raise some objection to the new plan of attack proposed for his 9th Division? By now he already knew the immense difficulties facing any attacker in those dense, well-defended woods.

General Craig was a middle-aged, somewhat heavy-set man with rather sad eyes who had seen active service in World War I but (like so many of his contemporaries) had seen none since. At the time of Pearl Harbor, as a lieutenant colonel he must have been contemplating a slippered retirement somewhere in the sun, somewhere it was cheap and he could afford to play a gentle round of golf in the afternoon. Suddenly there was a war on and

---

* The 1st was the only wartime division to have a movie made of its exploits, Sam Fuller's *The Big Red One*.

the U.S. Army, which in 1939 had not been much bigger than a wartime corps, started to expand at a tremendous rate. Craig, like the rest, abruptly found himself jumping up the ladder of promotion, commanding a battalion, a regiment, a division, responsible for the destinies of 15,000 young men who were half his age.

In four short years he was an officer whose activities were reported in major stateside newspapers and whose life-style had changed dramatically. Suddenly he and the rest (from the Supreme Commander Eisenhower with his mistress down through the 5,000-strong headquarters, housed in a French château) were conscious of their position, their rights, their public image. They were the first commanders to fight a war against the background of "instant communication," surrounded by skilled, critical journalists and radio reporters who didn't mind flattering the egos of these hitherto obscure men, though they weren't impressed by them.

Eisenhower himself wrote later: "The morale of the combat troops had always to be carefully watched. The capacity of soldiers for absorbing punishment and enduring privations is almost inexhaustible so long as they believe they are getting a square deal."[13] During the campaign he was constantly annoyed by the callous indifference of some commanders to their men. More than once he passed convoys of open trucks taking infantrymen up to the front, with the men huddled and frozen in back because no one had ordered the covers raised. He saw troops bivouacking in icy tents while their officers enjoyed warm substantial shelters nearby.

His mail, too, was full of complaints from ordinary soldiers about their treatment. On November 6, 1944, Eisenhower wrote to all his subordinate commanders detailing some of these complaints, an endless catalogue of beefs: "officers' food is better . . . men out of the line never get passes, officers go everywhere . . . officers get whisky rations, men in the line don't even get cigarettes, etc., etc."

General Craig and all the rest of the divisional generals who were to follow him into the Forest knew the state of their men and how morale fell almost to zero once they had commenced fighting in the Green Hell of the Hurtgen. Yet, as we have seen, no protest was ever registered by Ike's generals who led the attacking soldiers. No one at the top ever seemed to realize exactly what kind of horror the average infantryman faced there. In his *Crusade in Europe,* Eisenhower mentions the battle only once, stating: "The weather was abominable and the German garrison was particularly stubborn, but Yankee doggedness won through. Thereafter, whenever veterans of the American 4th, 9th, and 28th Divisions referred to hard fighting they did so in terms of comparison with the Battle of the Hurtgen Forest which they placed top of the list."[14]

In fact, nothing was learned from the 9th's previous foray into the fringe of the Forest, and nothing was done. Dutifully, the planners went ahead with their preparations for the next attack. They decided that the initial objectives for the Division would be the villages of Germeter and Vossenack, with a southward drive over the high ground beyond the Germeter-Hurtgen road. The attack would continue through the Hurtgen Forest and have as its final aim the clearing and seizing of the Schmidt-Steckenborn ridge.

On paper and on the sand tables it all looked purposeful, planned for—"tidy," as the staff officers liked to boast in their farmhouses and châteaux well to the rear. "Objective X, Deadline Y, Zero W," everything taken care of down to the last detail. Nothing was overlooked. It was impossible that anything could go wrong on "the day." The 60th Regiment, and, to its right, the 39th Regiment of the 9th Division, would go in to clear the Forest on a three-mile front, while the Division's 47th Regiment would secure the left flank and carry out day and night patrolling. If necessary, the 47th could supply the reserve in any emergency; but of course there would be no emergency.

Elegant staff officers with their strikers (servants), custom-made uniforms, and titled mistresses had not considered for one instant that the 9th's infantry was not trained for forest warfare;

whereas their German opponents had had plenty of experience of that kind of combat in the tundra and endless forests of northern Russia and Finland. Nor had they calculated the problems that would occur when it came to supplying the two regiments in the Forest where each regimental sector had only one narrow trail, which could easily be cut off. Tanks would also be unable to support the infantry; there was no room for them to maneuver on the trails, and once the infantry succeeded in reaching the open ground, dominated by the next ridge held by the German infantry, they would not be able to move without tanks. Above all, the planners had not taken into consideration that all control would be lost once the infantry entered the Forest.

The firs in the Hurtgen were so thick that they interlocked. The advancing infantry would be faced with a solid mass of dark, impenetrable green. At the level of a crawling man there was room, so that it was as if the individual soldier were entering a dark green forbidding cave that immediately cut him off from his fellows. In these caves regiments lost battalions and battalions lost companies. Even at the company level it would be difficult to maintain control. In the end it came down to squads of men fighting on their own, cut off in a claustrophobic green little world without support of tanks, aircraft, or artillery.

There were thickets in the Forest where two battalion command posts operated for three days without knowing that thirteen Germans and two anti-tank guns were firing in between them! "Four thousand yards from the German lines," one infantry battalion executive reported grimly later, "and we had to shoot krauts in our own front yard . . . The engineers bridged the creek and before they could finish their work they had 12 Germans sitting on a hill two hundred yards away directing artillery fire on them by radio."[15]

This was to be the *real* battle of the Hurtgenwald. The planners, who would never be near the sharp end where the fighting took place without benefit of maps and sand tables, could not imagine it.

So the 9th went up once again. Laden like pack animals, faces flushed with the strain and bent under their loads, they slogged through the ankle-deep mud with the heavy guns rumbling threateningly in the distance. It was raining as usual, and as they took over the battered positions now held by the 4th Cavalry Group, there was none of the usual coarse joking, Bronx cheers, and calls of "you'll be sorr-ee!" Both the men in the line and the relief were too weary. Somewhere they had been told that October 2, 1944, they could send in their votes to APO 9. The fighting men overseas could now post their ballot in the first wartime election, but most of them weren't interested in whether President Roosevelt, who had once solemnly promised that no "American boy" would ever go overseas to fight in World War II, was elected or not—their minds were elsewhere. Faced with the prospect of imminent death, the United States—or the "ZI"* as they called it—seemed a million miles away. Their only duty this wet dreary day, with the German spandaus already hissing fire at a rate of 1,000 rounds per minute, was to survive. Democracy was just another fancy word used by the feather merchants back home who could not even begin to conceive the kind of life they led out here.

Within twenty-four hours the relief was accomplished and they were dug in, the guns thundering, fitful evil red flames springing up on the horizon every now and again. As they waited in their holes each man was prey to his own doubts, fears, and little hopes. Their average age was between 19 and 24. They were a cross section of American society from college boys to farmers. Few of them were volunteers for the service, but most of them had answered the President's "greetings" willingly enough. Now all of them, the handful of veterans and the "wet mouths"† alike, felt that their country had abandoned them to a soulless military machine. Once again they were doomed to fight over impossible terrain for an unobtainable objective which, in the final analysis, had no strategic or tactical value whatsoever.

The actors were in place. The drama could begin.

---

* Zone of the Interior.

† Name given to raw replacements.

3

Dawn. October 6, 1944.

Fog shrouded the silent wooded heights of the Hurtgen. Up there were the Germans, but there was no sign of them among the dripping, somber firs. There was no indication that there were hundreds of young men in field-grey waiting in their earthen bunkers and concrete pillboxes. The Forest might well have been completely deserted.

Down below all was activity as the minutes ticked by rapidly to H-hour. In front of the 9th's positions NCOs had spread the silken identification panels. Now they and the assault infantry crouched in their holes expectantly, nerves ticking electrically, minds racing. All of them, veterans as well as "wet mouths," made some sort of preparation for what was soon to come. One had hung himself with extra bandoliers of ammunition. Another had placed a steel shaving mirror in his left breastpocket. He had heard of a guy in another outfit whose life had been saved in this manner when a slug had hit him. Another soldier had filled his canteen with whiskey stolen from an officer's drink allowance. A few prayed—but not many.

The tension began to mount swiftly. To the rear there was the rumble of tank tracks. In the sodden fields just behind the waiting infantry the artillerymen started to elevate their guns. More ambulances drove up and the medics got out to watch the infantry with curiosity, hands cupped around the glowing ends of their cigarettes. A jeep came bumping, bouncing, and skidding down the rutted trail, carrying a staff messenger bearing something for the forward battalion commanders. In spite of the morning cold, the hands of the young men in the holes tensely gripping their weapons started to grow sticky and wet with sweat. It was almost time now.

With startling suddenness, as the sun began to burn off the fog, the massed Thunderbolts came zooming in at treetop level. The spirits of the infantry rose immediately as they flashed by, fat-bellied and squat, all gleaming silver. Someone cheered silently. Then the planes were screaming down on the German positions. Dark black, lethal eggs started to tumble from their bellies in crazy profusion. In an instant all was noise, confusion, and sudden death.

Time and time again the pilots of the Tactical Air Force roared in to drop their deadly load, diving steeply to pinpoint their targets, and then, while the gaping infantry held their breath, leveling out at the very last minute when a crash seemed inevitable. The whole horizon was aflame with huge mushrooms of thick black smoke, flecked by bright red flame rising into the morning sky. Within thirty minutes seven squadrons of fighter-bombers (84 planes) had come zooming in to hit the Germans, who were taken completely by surprise.

Now it was the turn of the waiting artillery. The entire weight of the 9th Division's guns, supported by three additional battalions of artillery, came into action. The noise was ear-splitting, and it took the breath away from the awed infantrymen. They automatically opened their mouths to prevent their eardrums from shattering as the blast struck them across the face like a blow.

For exactly three long minutes the artillery blasted away, while the infantry gasped and fought for breath. There followed a five-minute silence as the echo reverberated around the circle of burning hills. Suddenly the guns opened up yet again, hoping to catch the surviving Krauts struggling out of their shattered, smoking pillboxes. For another two minutes the sweating artillerymen, ankle-deep in gleaming, smoking, yellow shell cases, blasted the German position. Then the whistles shrilled and the noncoms and officers yelled that old, old frightening order, "All right, men. On your feet. Follow me!"

Six thousand men of the 39th and 60th Infantry regiments clambered out of their holes in trepidation and started forward into the trees, bayoneted rifles held across their chests, bodies tensed and leaning forward slightly as men do when they advance against a high wind. It was 11:30 A.M. The great attack on the Hurtgen had commenced. Back in divisional headquarters General Craig's G-2 felt confidently that "should a major breakthrough occur, or should several penetrations occur, the enemy will begin a withdrawal to the Rhine River, abandoning his Siegfried Line."[1] It was a pious hope.

The Germans were waiting for the 9th. The men of the German 942nd Infantry Regiment and the 275th Fusilier Battalion thrust their weapons through the slits of their bunkers and pillboxes and waited for the Americans to come within range. They fired almost immediately on the advancing men, who were unprotected and exposed as they filtered through the firs in groups and who had broken into platoons and squads.

To the northeast the 39th Infantry's progress very quickly slowed to a snail's pace. The obstacle course of pillboxes, roadblocks, and tied-in field defenses were overwhelming and the infantry started to take heavy casualties. On all sides the cry went up: "Medics!" Bodies littered the ground; men refused to move without orders. Noncoms threatened and cajoled, officers pushed on desperately, taking with them those who were still prepared to fight. But the attack was bogging down.

It was little better in the 60th Infantry's sector. At first, the Go-Devils moved off at a good speed, but when the Regiment's 2nd Battalion was within one thousand yards of its objective it was struck by a hail of small arms fire and joined almost immediately by the obscene howl of the feared German multiple mortars. Great fingers of black smoke roared into the sky, followed the next instant by the baleful howling of the mortar shells. Men fell screaming everywhere—bodies ripped apart by the huge shards of jagged metal.

The Regiment's 1st Battalion fared little better. It ran into an extensively wired and mined area. Men ripped and tugged at the barbed wire that dug into their uniforms and clothes, pulling themselves free in a frenzy of despair only to stumble onto the deadly prongs of the devilish devices buried just beneath the earth that shattered their feet and turned their lower limbs into a pulp from which the blood oozed or spurted in a scarlet jet, the bones gleaming in the redness like polished ivory.

Meanwhile, the Regiment's 3rd Battalion was launching a diversionary attack to relieve the situation and to take the pressure off its two sister battalions where, in one company alone, the hard-pressed infantry had already suffered a staggering 50 percent casualty rate. But it, too, soon ran into severe opposition and bogged down with heavy casualties.

As that terrible October 6 progressed, it was clear that the planners back at divisional headquarters had got it all wrong from the start. Although the 9th's artillery fired five thousand rounds that day and the TAC Air Force flew fighter-bomber attacks all the while, these bombardments had little effect on the enemy dug deep in the earth or protected by concrete bunkers. From the start the battle had become an unsupported, infantry slogging match, man against man, machine gun and rifle against machine gun and rifle, with the advantage on the German side. Impervious to artillery and aerial attacks themselves, the Germans could direct their fire on the attackers at will, spraying them with those deadly tree bursts, which in one battalion alone knocked out one hundred men, one eighth of its effectives, even before the real attack had started.

The confused battle started to die down that night and aid posts to the rear filled up rapidly with wounded men. Soon two thousand men were being air-evacuated *daily* from the First Army's front, back to England—and they were only the serious casualties. Those in the know calculated that it was costing the 9th Infantry Division exactly one man lost for every square yard of ground captured. In the Hurtgen Forest, the 9th was bleeding to death—rapidly.

Field Marshal Gerd von Rundstedt, the aged German soldier who had created so many victories for his country and who was now bitter, resentful, and given to cognac, called him contemptuously "der Bubi-Marschall" ("the Boy Marshal"), a man who had sold his soul to Hitler in order to gain personal advancement, and von Rundstedt hated the Bohemian Corporal with a passion. The man referred to was Field Marshal Walter Model, who was now in charge of the front to which the Hurtgen Forest belonged.

Model was a loner and a ruthless commander much hated and feared by his subordinates. He readily sacked army and battalion commanders with all the relentless drive of a small man with too much power. At fifty-three he affected a monocle like the aristocrats who had commanded the old Prussian Army from which he had emerged after being twice badly wounded in World War I. But Model had none of their aristocratic reticence, charm, and discretion. Rather, he was direct, outspoken, and coarse in speech and appearance with a jowly, somewhat gross face. During the second week of October 1944, a Colonel Wilck, defending what was left of Aachen, asked to be allowed to withdraw. Model signaled: "Fight to the last man. If necessary, have yourself buried under the ruins!"[2] That was that.

In the fall of 1944, Model was exactly what Hitler needed to bolster the sagging front in the west after the terrible defeat of the *Wehrmacht* in France. Model was not interested in politics and did not attempt to interfere in affairs of state as had his fellow field marshals von Kluge and Rommel, both of whom had been forced to commit suicide because of it. Most of all, Model managed to keep his nerve—his will to fight intact, despite the fact that the enemy was at the gates of the Reich in both west and east. He was a fighter, the Führer's Fire Brigade, as his admiring frontline soldiers called him. They regarded him as one of them, "a front swine" who had no time for the staff, "the rear echelon stallions." He was the commander who had always managed to save the front, whatever the circumstances.

He saved the Russian front from disaster five times, advancing from a corps commander in 1939 to an army group commander in the process. Once, in January 1942, when the German Ninth Army had reached the end of its tether under severe pressure from the Red Army, Model had appeared at the Army's headquarters. He appeared without ceremony, a small tubby man with a fur-collared greatcoat that reached down to his ankles, old-fashioned earflaps over his ears, and the inevitable monocle screwed into his left eye.

The staff officers present had quickly clicked to attention. Model did not appear to notice. He slung his coat on a chair, cleaned his monocle (it had steamed up immediately as he had entered), stalked over to the situation map on the wall, glared at it for a moment, and announced: "Rather a mess."

Thereafter he rapped out a series of orders while the staff officers gaped at him in openmouthed awe. Where was he going to get the strength to carry out his instructions?

Finally Colonel Blaurock, the Ninth Army's Chief of Staff, had ventured, "And what have you, *Herr General,* brought us for this operation?"

Model looked at him calmly, then answered with one word: "*Myself!*"[3]

It was typical of the man. He knew that the days of Germany's almost limitless reserves of manpower were over. What resources there were had to be husbanded carefully, especially now in October 1944, when Hitler was already planning a major counterblow against the Western Allies that might well change the whole course of the war. First-class soldiers and top-quality equipment were in short supply. He would have to defend the western front, and in particular the current hot spot, *"der Hurtgenwald,"* with what he could scrape together: police battalions, convalescent companies, training units, stomach battalions.* He would use anything and anybody that could move, be fired, hold a rifle, or fire a machine gun.

At the end of September he had stopped the Anglo-American airborne attempt to "bounce the Rhine," as Montgomery had called it, and had wiped out the British 1st Airborne Division at Arnhem, using two shattered SS divisions to do so. Now his

---

* Men with stomach wounds or stomach problems were grouped together in special battalions so that they could all be fed the same light diet.

handful of riflemen in the Hurtgen were faced with a well-equipped American division, plus two battalions of tanks and self-propelled guns, and obviously, the *Amis* would follow up any breakthrough they made there with all the other divisions they were keeping in reserve. He knew that there were plenty of them from his intelligence sources, "the sleepers" that the retreating German Army had left behind in Luxembourg and Belgium.

Now he had to stop Hodges's men. Accordingly, he summoned one of his few reserve units, the two-thousand-strong *Kampfgruppe* (Battle-Group) *Wegelein*. The *Kampfgruppe* consisted mainly of officer cadets, the cream of the *Wehrmacht*. In the German fashion the group was named after its commander, Colonel Wegelein, an old and very experienced soldier who had been in the Army for nearly a quarter of a century.

In the German Army there were no "sixty-day wonders" as were most of the shavetail lieutenants who now commanded the 9th's infantry platoons: college men recruited straight into OCS and trained, ready to be shipped to the front, within ten weeks. In the *Wehrmacht,* all potential officers who had previously attained the rank of corporal while serving as enlisted men were sent to the front for six months to prove themselves. After this *Frontbewährung,* as it was called, they went to officer school to be trained in the duties of an officer and gentleman. Consequently, they knew well what the life of the ordinary *Landser** was like. In addition, they had all seen active service before they were allowed to command men in battle.

The use of these young officer cadets was a calculated risk for Model. He could ill afford to lose such fine young men with the Army crying out for infantry officers. But Field Marshal Model had always been prepared to take risks and would continue to do so until that day not far off when, surrounded and cut off, with only one remaining staff officer to support him, he declared defiantly: *"A German field marshal does not surrender!"* Whereupon he blew his brains out.

---

* The German GI.

Model did not consider long. He ordered his staff to ensure that *Kampfgruppe Wegelein* was sent to the Hurtgen front immediately. Once there Colonel Wegelein was to lead his young officer-cadets into an all-out attack against the *Amis*—and rout them.

For four long bloody days the 9th's two regiments had been battering against the German defenses, their casualties mounting all the time. In the green confusion of the woods, whole platoons were cut off and killed or captured by German infiltrators. Engineers, right up front with the infantry, were lifting mines by the hundred. On one area, they estimated there was a Teller mine every eight paces for *three* miles! In one narrow firebreak they found five hundred of the deadly devices.

Together the infantry and engineers fought desperately to clear the way ahead while under fire all the time. They looped primacord onto a rifle grenade and then fired the grenade. As it soared forward, carrying with it the length of the primacord, they waited tensely, hoping the latter was going to cover the length of the path to their front. Then, when it had landed, they touched the primacord off and ducked as mine after mine exploded.

Others resorted to even more primitive methods. They threw ropes around the logs of the many roadblocks and yanked them, hoping to explode any mines or booby traps fixed there. But the only sure way to clear the route was for the engineers and infantry to go down on their knees and probe the earth with their bayonets or Number 8 wire to uncover the mines, which were everywhere and came in all sizes and shapes.

There were box mines, which had to be detected from the side because they exploded at a mere two or three pounds of pressure. And there were huge, round Teller mines, intended for vehicles, each one cunningly booby-trapped with a "matchbox" detonator beneath a two-leafed metal device containing a power spring. If the mine was lifted without the "matchbox" being detected, then the Teller exploded right in the man's face. There were harmless little round mines, no larger than an ointment box, scattered on the surface of the earth in the thousands, but they were still large enough to blow a man's foot off.

In that terrible second week of October, all was horror, mutilation, and sudden, violent death in the Hurtgen. The 9th started to bring up tanks to try to help the infantry advance, but they were of little use. Firebreaks offered the only sizable maneuver areas for the thirty-ton monsters. But soon the tankers learned that firebreaks were potential death traps; they packed the tanks and tank destroyers in so tightly together that they were easy marks for the German artillery.

Time and time again, the Shermans would have just gotten into position when there would be a sudden vicious hail of fire. Tree bursts would pepper the sky above them, scything down the men standing up in the "unbuttoned" turrets, or crashing into the side of the tanks with the great hollow boom of steel striking steel. In one case, for example, the tank destroyers of the 899th TD Battalion fought across one single thousand-yard-long firebreak *six* times, losing vehicles to enemy action all the time. In the end, the few survivors managed to cross it for good and found themselves firing at the enemy over open sights—they were that close. So the bloody slogging match went on and on with grim inexorability.

Back home no one knew anything of what was happening at the front in Europe. The war was nearly over, wasn't it? On Columbus Day, October 12, 1944, the same day that America's most senior soldier arrived at the front from Washington to find out exactly what was happening in the Forest, the main news in the media was totally and utterly remote from the war. On that day, according to the papers, thirty thousand screaming teenagers tried to storm New York's Paramount Theatre. Inside, four thousand of them had already taken their seats for the "great event."

They had brought sandwiches and Hershey bars with them to sustain them over the long wait so that they would not be forced to leave their precious seats. Others, it was reliably reported afterward, peed in their pants rather than go to the toilets; they knew they'd never get back to their places if they left them.

They were the lucky ones. Another huge mob of teenagers outside was weeping, screaming, throwing fits of hysterics, and so frightening to Mayor La Guardia that he declared a state of emergency in New York. Two hundred detectives, seventy patrolmen, fifty traffic cops and four hundred reservists, plus twenty patrol cars, were hurriedly rushed to the area around the theater in an attempt to control the crazy kids.

In the middle of the U.S.'s third year of war, what was the cause of this mass hysteria that made little girls in bobby sox smash store windows, fight policemen, and overturn cars in the first recorded instance of what was to become an everyday occurrence in our own time—unthinking violence and vandalism at a pop concert?

The cause was a skinny Italian-American singer from Hoboken with greasy hair and blue eyes, who looked as if he were suffering from an advanced case of malnutrition. Between performances of the long-forgotten movie, he crooned to his drooling teenage fans, "Only the Lonely."

The prime mover of the first pop concert riot was Frank Sinatra, whose draft board had exempted him from military service due to a supposedly damaged eardrum, though it never seemed to affect his musical pitch. The exemption did cause some misgivings among the Top Brass, but a quick five-thousand-dollar contribution to FDR's 1944 election campaign had helped to quiet the protests coming from the direction of the Department of War. Besides, a Sinatra endorsement brought votes—lots of them.

So while Sinatra crooned and bobby-soxers rioted and wet their pants, three thousand miles away, in a war that was as remote from New York as if it were being fought on the moon, hundreds of other teenagers in Craig's 9th Division were preparing to fight, even to die in the Forest, for an unthinking America. Of course, by now the Top Brass was worried by the lack of progress and the ever-mounting losses. Heads began to roll at the divisional headquarters of the 9th. The assistant divisional commander had gone; the colonel commanding the 9th's 60th Regiment had departed too. The Division's Chief of Staff had followed him. He had been replaced by the "athletic and affable" 30-year-old commander of the 34th Field Artillery, an experienced soldier who had fought in North Africa, Sicily, and France. His name was Col. William C. Westmoreland, who was fated three decades later to have his own Hurtgen in Vietnam.

These cosmetic changes did not satisfy America's most important and feared soldier (even Eisenhower, the Supreme Commander, called *him* "sir"). On that same Columbus Day that Sinatra caused his sensation in faraway New York City, General George C. Marshall, the U.S. Army's Chief of Staff, a stern, austere, remote man of iron self-discipline and transparent honesty, and before whom Eisenhower trembled, descended upon General Craig's Headquarters in Germany. Even the President stood in awe of him. Once Roosevelt let it be known through an intermediary that he would like to call the Chief of Staff by his first name, George. Marshall sternly discouraged the proposal. "It would," he said to the intermediary, "be utterly out of character for me."[4]

Today we do not know what Marshall said to Collins (who was present that day) or to Craig. But an officer like Marshall, who had planned Black Jack Pershing's battles for him back in 1918 and who was widely regarded throughout the U.S. Army as being of the highest intellectual caliber, must have seen that there was something wrong with the battle currently being fought in the *Hurtgenwald* with such high losses.

Perhaps the craggy-faced army commander spotted something his subordinate officers had overlooked. *Life* magazine had informed its readers that the Battle of the Hurtgen Forest was taking its place in American military history beside the classic struggles in the Wilderness during the Civil War and those of the Argonne Forest in 1918. The comparisons were apt and surely could not have escaped a man like Marshall, who was so well versed in American military history.

When two armies confront each other with approximately the same numbers, weapons, and tactical skills, as was the case in the Wilderness, the Argonne, and the Hurtgen, the defender is invariably at an advantage and can hold out, inflicting tremendous casualties on the attacker, until he decides he no longer wants to hold and defend the terrain in question.

Marshall must have also realized that the U.S. Army was already deeply involved in the Hurtgen, and that the Forest had no real strategic importance. They had been fighting there for a month and had taken a tremendous beating. Could they simply abandon the action now and leave the Forest to the Germans? *Wasn't the prestige of the U.S. Army involved?*

Marshall, whose whole life had been devoted to the Army, knew that they could not withdraw from the Hurtgen now. As a professional officer he was rightly jealous of the Army's reputation and prestige. He also realized that his and his subordinate commanders' professional reputations were at stake. All of them, without exception—army commanders, corps commanders, divisional commanders—desired fervently to keep their records unblemished; all of them wanted to go down favorably in the history books. Only a handful of them would admit later that they had made a single error during the whole course of World War II. (Patton, for example, grandly admitted to a mere *two*!)

Marshall had urged the previous August that there be fewer written records. Some documents, he maintained, should be preserved, but only under lock and key. "For example," he wrote, "references in historical writings to the bitter discussions which have arisen from time to time over various plans of campaign, allocations of material etc. . . . will be highly inadvisable in the future."[5]

Marshall was fond of pointing out that his former chief, Black Jack, still held documents pertaining to World War I and refused to release them to the historians. Hadn't Washington and Franklin both insisted on complete secrecy about what took place in the discussions of the American Constitutional Convention back in the eighteenth century? In short, in Marshall's considered opinion, America's generals should close ranks for the sake of their own reputations and the prestige of his beloved Army. There would be no public washing of the Army's dirty linen either during or after the war.

Whatever the cost, the battle for the Hurtgen would continue. The attack would no longer be considered as merely an assault to protect Lightning Joe Collins's right flank. Another reason would have to be dreamed up to explain and justify the great blood-letting in the Death Factory. In due course, the Top Brass would "discover" that the dams beyond the Forest on the River Roer produced electricity for Germany's great Rhenish cities. More important, they controlled the floodwaters of the Roer. If the enemy decided to release these waters, he could flood the Rhenish plain and bar any further American progress. Surely, then, an objective of this nature was of the greatest strategic importance.

According to the statements made by senior American commanders long *after* thousands of young Americans had been killed and wounded in the Forest, they had always known that the dams had to be captured. Following the war General Bradley wrote: "It might not show in the record, but we did plenty of talking about the dams."[6] A First Army report, written in *February 1945,* says that the attack on Schmidt in the Hurtgen was "a preliminary phase of a plan by V Corps to seize two large dams on the Roer River."[7]

In his autobiography, written thirty-five years after the event, General J. Lawton Collins states that "in the light of subsequent developments, there seems to have been no excuse for the lapse in intelligence with respect to the potential threat to our operations posed by those dams if they should be destroyed or their flood-gates opened."[8]

According to Lightning Joe in 1979, apparently the only responsible officer to note the danger was the 9th Division's G-2 Major Jack Houston, who remarked in his G-2 report, dated October 2, 1944: "Bank overflows and destructive flood waves can be produced [on the Roer River] by regulating the discharge from the various dams. By demolition of some of them great destructive waves can be produced which could destroy everything in the populated valley [of the Roer] as far as the Meuse and into Holland."[9]

Six days later (again according to Collins) the chief engineer of XIX Corps wrote to his commander: "If one or all dams were blown, a flood would occur in the channel of the Roer River that would reach approximately 1,500 feet in width and 3 feet or more deep across the entire corps front . . . The flooding would probably last from one to three weeks."[10]

Nobody at the top seemed to take the dams seriously till *after* the war, or at the earliest, in February 1945. It was certain, however, that the officers who actually did the fighting in the Hurtgen never heard anything about the dams. Col. Carl L. Peterson, whose 112th Infantry Regiment of the 28th Division was soon to be shot to pieces in the Forest during the first week of November 1944, recalled afterward that the dams *"never entered the (planning) picture."*[11]

Lt. General Everett S. Hughes, Eisenhower's womanizing, hard-drinking crony of the campaign in Europe, once lamented, "God, I wish we could forget our egos for a while!" But the truth was, Eisenhower's generals could not. Throughout the eleven-month campaign, mistake after mistake was made and subsequently hushed up by the generals for the sake of the prestige of the U.S. Army and their own egos. From the disaster of Omaha Beach right through the surprise German counterattack in the Ardennes, from Patton's costly raid to rescue his son-in-law in Hammelburg Prison Camp to the total reversal of Allied strategy, which changed the face of postwar Europe, due to the Top Brass's mistaken belief that there was something called the "Alpine Redoubt" in the German Alps, the generals would not admit mistake or failure. Everything had been planned in advance and had gone "according to plan."

So it was with the Hurtgen Forest battle. Even as disaster after disaster struck the hard-pressed young men of the 9th Division in a completely pointless campaign, the Top Brass was preparing to bring in more troops to capture those fifty square miles of perfectly useless German real estate.

In World War I, the French commander in chief, Marshal "Papa" Joffre, once remarked cynically about the cost of the war in the trenches: "It takes fifteen thousand dead to train a major general."* Well, in the case of the Hurtgen Forest in 1944, it would take considerably more dead young Americans than that to convince America's major generals that they were simply throwing good money after bad. In the final analysis, some never learned. Thirty years later, U.S. generals who had once been majors and colonels in the Death Factory were still throwing away the lives of their young soldiers in Vietnam with the selfsame careless abandon in order to achieve objectives that were equally unimportant. They had forgotten nothing and had learned nothing from their own experiences in the Death Factory.

---

* The size of a French infantry division at the time, which was usually commanded by a major general.

4

As if some god on high was reluctant to throw light on the crazy war-torn landscape down below, dawn came slowly, hesitantly. In the shattered positions of the 9th's 39th Infantry Regiment, the weary unshaven men stretched their stiff limbs or crept furtively out of their damp holes to attend to the calls of nature. Cupping the glowing end carefully, here and there a man drew nervously on the first cigarette of a new day in hell, for there were snipers everywhere among the trees. Others chomped mechanically on another tasteless C ration. They had been in the Forest six days, and now they wisecracked to one another: "After five days up there you talk to the trees. On the sixth day you start getting answers back."

The day grew lighter. Here and there a noncom or officer came through the trees and issued orders for the coming day in a whisper. They always whispered now, as if there was a Kraut hiding behind the very next tree, and they didn't want to attract attention to themselves, for attention could mean sudden death. Most of the men had become passive and apathetic, but a few men started to clean their weapons, while others primed grenades for the day's new battle.

Smoke started to rise slowly behind them where the cooks were attempting to prepare a hot meal, and there was the creak of handcarts sloshing through the ankle-deep mud of the trail. It seemed like any other morning in the Green Hell of the Hurtgen: cold, damp, and boring, with the prospect of more violent action to come.

A whine. A groan. A sound like a diamond being scratched along a piece of glass. Then the frighteningly familiar, baleful shriek of the German multiple mortar was heard. Fingers of black smoke poked their way up into the leaden sky, and suddenly, all was chaos and confusion. The rockets ripped great steaming holes in the earth like the work of gigantic moles. They snapped the trees, flinging their crowns high into the air, and sent huge shards of jagged metal hissing lethally to all sides.

The survivors said later that the barrage seemed to last for hours. In truth, it took only a matter of minutes. But it sufficed to sever communications, knock out several gun pits, and force the men of the 39th to cower at the bottom of their holes, the gravel and earth pattering off their helmets like heavy rain on a tin roof. To their front the whistles shrilled. Hoarse voices cried commands in German, and then they came streaming out of the trees in their camouflage jackets, firing from the hip as they came. *Kampfgruppe Wegelein* was attacking!

Attacking along a wooded plateau, the officer-cadets swiftly enveloped the first overextended battalion of the 39th it encountered. The jubilant enemy poured down the Regiment's main supply trail, heading toward Germeter. Colonel Bond, the 39th's commander, realized immediately what the Germans intended. Their move was "aimed on the left rear exposed flank and designed to cut off the 3rd Battalion that had crossed the Germeter-Huertgen road and had patrols in the far edge of Vossenack."[1]

Bond reacted correctly. Although his 2nd Battalion was yelling for help, he concentrated on getting the 3rd Battalion to carry out one of the most difficult tactics in the book—to turn around completely and attack to its rear. If the 3rd Battalion made a mess of it, the resultant confusion might well be followed by panic and flight. A worried Bond knew that there were no regimental reserves; even the divisional reserves consisted solely of a portion of the 9th's reconnaissance troop and a platoon of light Honey tanks, not much to stop the thrust of two thousand highly trained, combat-experienced German officer cadets.

All that terrible Thursday, Colonel Bond sweated it out, as the battle raged back and forth, with hardly any news coming out of the Forest. What did come out was not very encouraging. Nothing was able to stop the Germans!

Then the inexplicable happened; the Germans failed to advance farther than the east-west trail leading into Germeter. Enemy prisoners later said the decision to stop was due to a failure in communications. Others said that they were just as lost in the Forest as were the Americans. At the moment, however, Colonel Bond thought his regiment was fighting for its life.

A battalion command post up front had been virtually overrun, and the men were split up in little pockets, fighting back as best they could. Wide-eyed and pale-faced stragglers streamed back with tales of woe. "The Krauts are just behind us . . . We haven't a chance . . . they're everywhere . . . The Krauts are coming. . . ."

On the following day Colonel Bond ordered the remaining able elements of his badly hit regiment to counterattack *Kampfgruppe Wegelein*. At dawn they would go in—dawn on Friday, the thirteenth of October.

Unknown to a worried Bond, however, Colonel Wegelein, stalled on the Germeter-Hurtgen road, was having problems of his own. He had lost five hundred men in the first attack, his second-in-command had been badly wounded, and now he had received a surprising order from his superior, General Schmidt, who commanded the German 275th Infantry Division. "With immediate effect," as the jargon of the military had it, he had to return all officer-cadets to Division. He told himself wearily as it began to grow dark that Thursday and the thunder of the guns was muted that he would lose half his force. Any further offensive action was completely out of the question. The mood of the German colonel, who had been in the Army since 1921 and had spent five years in combat, was understandably gray and somber. Perhaps it explains what he was going to do on this Friday the thirteenth.

The 39th's attack started without pep or élan. The men were just too groggy and punch drunk from seven days' hard fighting in the Forest. Despite the weakness of Wegelein's position, held now by a mere five hundred men, the Americans advanced very slowly. The Americans, of course, had also been weakened by the terrible losses of the previous week. One company had only two platoons left: one consisting of 12 men, the other of 13–25 men out of the original 120. It was typical of the whole regiment. Yet reduced as it was to about one third of its original strength, the 39th still outnumbered the Germans by two to one.

The Germans fought back valiantly, making the Americans pay dearly for every foot of ground gained. They ambushed an American company and two full platoons went tamely into the bag, hands in the air, frantically crying probably the only word of German they knew, "*Kamerad!*" Another group of attackers ran into a minefield and the Germans mowed the attackers down mercilessly as they tried to extricate themselves. For both sides were too punch-drunk to show mercy. They were slugging it out like two old-time bare-knuckle fighters, punching each other to death.

Then something strange happened, something which impressed both sides despite their appalling weariness. Indeed, it was an occurrence that is talked about even now, all these years later, whenever veterans of the 39th Infantry Regiment or the German 275th Infantry meet and discuss the "bad old days."

Oberst Wegelein decided "to go for a walk" together with his adjutant and his pet dog, a large German shepherd. For reasons which no one has ever been able to explain, he sauntered right up to his frontline position. First Lieutenant Bernd Marzhauser, one of the last of his men to see him alive, reported later: "My position in a patch of shattered woodland had the disadvantage that it was directly under the observation of the Americans and I knew the enemy was using snipers. As the Colonel, plus his adjutant and the dog, started to come through some pines to our rear, I shouted very loud and clear, 'Take cover, Herr Oberst! You are observed by the enemy . . . There are snipers!'

"But despite this warning he continued for another fifteen meters while his adjutant fell to the ground to take cover. Next moment the Colonel stumbled and fell, shot by a sniper. Because of the danger of the situation we weren't able to pull him in. That night a patrol sent out to do so found he had gone and assumed that he had been taken prisoner. Indeed, they called to us they had taken the Colonel captive and shouted we should stop our senseless resistance."[2]

In fact, Colonel Wegelein had been spotted and promptly shot by an NCO of the 39th's Company E. But what had prompted this old and experienced soldier to go for a walk around the front line with his dog and allow himself to be shot so purposelessly? Was he, too, sick of the senseless slaughter of the Green Hell and had courted death as a way of ending the misery? Or had he simply lost his way?

The Wegelein attack fizzled out in the end, but by the time it was all over on Saturday, October 14, the steam had also departed completely from the 9th's drive into the Hurtgen. The Division went on the defensive, improving positions, laying mines, and using fire to determine the position of the enemy in the shattered trees. Patrolling continued all the time, however, for General Craig would not admit that his division was a spent force.

Future painter Kin Shogren, then a staff sergeant in the infantry, recalled over forty years later that although the drive had stopped, they still lost "between one quarter and one third of our troops each day, so that there was a constant turnover of company personnel. If a rifleman lasted three days, he was a veteran."[3]

But the weather, as well as the enemy, was a problem. Now it had become consistently bad with freezing temperatures and constant rain, sleet, or snow. Sergeant Shogren, one of the few survivors, remembers once taking out an extended patrol that was cut off by the Germans for some time so that the men had to crouch in the freezing Forest for many hours. When the sergeant managed to successfully bring back his men, it was found that every single one of them was suffering from frostbite of the feet and hands.

Trench foot became epidemic as well, causing as many casualties as the Germans. After standing for days in the freezing water of their foxholes without changing their socks or shoes, the men found their feet turning gray, puffy, and wrinkled, the skin peeling off in long smelly layers once the socks were taken off. To the rear, entire hospital wards were filled with moaning infantrymen, their feet bared, each toe painted a dark purple, with little bits of cotton wool separating their grossly swollen toes.

Pfc Noble Gardner remembers coming out of the line and finding he couldn't feel his feet; they were dead. "So I just sat down and I took off my shoes for the first time in two weeks and my feet looked blue and frozen. I started to rub them but I was too tired and I fell asleep. When I got up the next morning my feet were like balloons, so red and swollen that I couldn't get my shoes on. And when I tried to walk it was like somebody giving me lots of hotfoots and sticking needles in my feet.

"They kept me in the hospital for about ninety days before they let me go. But some guys had it lots worse. Some guys had big black blisters and a couple of guys had to get their feet cut off. The doc says you get that from not changing your socks when your feet are wet. Christ, what the hell you gonna do when you're living in a hole for two weeks and the water's up to here and Jerries are shooting at you and you can't go no place! Christ, I'm lucky I'm here at all."[4]

Food was another problem. Hot food was a rarity. The men in the line lived off C and K rations. C rations consisted of six cans: three light cans and three heavier ones. The light cans contained biscuits, some kind of powdered drink like instant coffee, cocoa, or lemonade, and a small pack of sugar, two cigarettes, and a piece or two of hard candy. The heavier cans contained meat and beans, stew, beef hash, meat and spaghetti. These six cans were a soldier's ration for one day, each meal being made up of one light can and one heavy one.

Any additional source of food was welcome, even if it meant turning a blind eye to the activities of the enemy. In the case of the 47th Infantry, they had a working agreement with the Germans opposite them not to attack a certain house, the cellar of which was packed with cheese—*and beer!* Situated in no-man's-land, the house was visited during the day by the American patrols and at night by the Germans, both groups alternately drawing their "rations" there. As there was enough cheese and beer to go round, neither side fired on the other until one day, as the Americans were drawing their rations at the house, the Germans opened up on them with mortars (perhaps they had a new hotshot commander). That did it! As *Stars and Stripes*, the Army newspaper, told it: "The Americans furious with the display of poor sportsmanship rearranged the furniture and that night the house, cheese, beer, and Jerries went up in smoke."[5]

But the bitterness and hardness of the fighting in the Hurtgen precluded most attempts at tolerance that is often common to opposing infantry. Frequently, infantrymen feel more comradeship and understanding for their enemy counterparts than for the canteen commandos behind the line, the feather merchants, or the rear-echelon stallions, as the Germans called them, who had sent them up to this death trap. *"One* man in the line and *five* to bring up the Coca-Cola," as the GIs cracked bitterly.

Both sides booby-trapped and ambushed relentlessly, taking an atavistic, savage pleasure whenever they caught the enemy off guard, "with his skivvies down," as the infantrymen liked to say. A forward observer with the 951st Field Artillery, which was supporting the 9th, Lieutenant Kelch recalled after the war: "One day our phone line went dead and a couple of linemen went out to find the break. I don't even remember who it was, but one of them was jerking the line up out of a ditch along the road looking for a break, and there were two Jerry grenades tied to the cut wire. The other lineman said his eyes were as big as baseballs. I doubt that myself, but they were big. Luckily, the pegs pulled up instead of the grenade pins, however, and everyone had a laugh out of the deal. The Jerries were full of cute tricks . . . Never a dull moment."[6]

But the Americans were not averse to cute tricks themselves. That same artillery battalion heard the sound of the Germans chopping wood every evening after dark and the rattle of their horse-drawn chow cart coming up to feed the hungry infantry. So Captain Thrasher of the artillery borrowed some mortars and "got a hit on the chow court . . . and the cans rattled for twenty minutes afterward . . . We used to help the Jerries to chop their wood too. These mortar sections always had fifty rounds to spare. Some fun!"[7]

Indeed, so warped had the fighting men become in that Green Hell that their sense of humor had become brutal, almost crazed. One day Lieutenant Keate of the 951st Field Artillery was commanding a party manning a roadblock in the Forest when he spotted movement in the nearby bushes. He snapped a command. His machine gunners opened up. There was a scream of agonized pain. Moments later, as the chronicler phrased it in the tough, cruel, unfeeling prose of the time: "They [the Americans] went out to see what they got and found a wounded Jerry officer and a girl dressed in an American officer's coat. She was a slick chick, but a slug had nipped her military career in the bud. Questioning disclosed that the German officer had a sketch showing all our road blocks and machine gun posts and the girl was supposed to be a come on. In between times she kept the boys from getting homesick. However, a .50 caliber slug has no conscience. This officer followed the girl a little too close to our outpost. It only goes to show. If you know what I mean."[8]

There were cruel men in the Forest, crazy men, cowardly men, and some who were outstandingly courageous: men who were prepared to risk or sacrifice their lives to save those of their fellows. One such courageous man was 31-year-old S. Sgt. Herschel F. Briles, a veteran of the fighting in Africa, who had already won the Bronze Star for valor. He belonged to the 899th Tank Destroyer Battalion, which was supporting the 9th.

At this time his strength was being sapped by another attack of the malaria he had contracted in Africa in 1943. His skinny body was racked by chills and fits of violent trembling, followed by hot waves that sent the blood rushing to his face. He felt bad.

All the same, when one of his tank destroyers was hit and started to burn, its frantic driver trying to escape and succeeding only in bogging the stricken vehicle even deeper in the mud, Briles didn't hesitate. He sprang out of his own tank destroyer and ran quickly two hundred yards across the muddy field, arms working like pistons, going all out, while the enemy sprayed the ground all around him with heavy artillery and machine-gun fire.

He lowered himself into the turret of the burning tank, the slugs howling off its steel sides, and pulled out one and then two wounded, burning soldiers. If that wasn't enough, he extinguished the flames and then ordered up another tank destroyer. With the enemy firing all they had at the bold soldier, he calmly had the battered vehicle towed away.

On the following morning Briles drove his tank destroyer straight into an advancing wedge of German infantry, scattering them in panic. Up in the open turret of the big lumbering vehicle, he manned the machine gun himself, spraying death and destruction to both sides. In the end the Germans gave up. Fifty-five of them dropped their weapons and held up their hands, yelling, *"Kamerad,"* urgently.

Later that day another of his tank destroyers was hit and began to burn. Just like the Sherman tanks, which were called Ronsons by their crews (after the cigarette lighter) because they caught fire so easily, the tank destroyers often blazed on the impact of a shell. *Twice* more Briles braved heavy enemy fire in order to drag wounded crewmen to safety, and once more insisted on salvaging the stricken tank destroyer. He certainly deserved the Congressional Medal of Honor, his country's highest award for bravery.

But of the dozen or so young Americans who won that award in the Green Hell of the Hurtgen, Staff Sergeant Briles, the veteran, was one of the very few to live and tell his tale. Young Pfc Carl V. Sheridan, who was eighteen and had been in the Army only seven months when he won the Medal of Honor, didn't. He was a bazookaman who blasted the way free for 35 men, what was left of his company of 120, in an attack on a fortified building.

A door barred any further advance and the bold young man was down to his last rocket. He worked his way forward alone, knowing that he had to make it count. Then he fired at point-blank range. The door flew apart in a burst of angry red flame. A smoking hole appeared that was large enough to charge through.

His blood roused now, Sheridan dropped his useless bazooka and drew his pistol. He waved it and cried to the men cowering against the wall to his rear, "Come on, men, *let's get them*!"

Pistol in hand, he rushed forward into the hole. There was a burst of enemy fire and Sheridan went down, dead before he hit the ground. He would also be given the Medal of Honor, though the brave youngster would never know it. He was dead, killed in a purposeless battle before he had begun to live.

For most of the infantry that fought in the Hurtgen there was little opportunity for such outstanding bravery. Death came to them anonymously—a shell "with their number on it," a sniper's bullet, a burst of machine-gun fire from an unseen gunner, yet another lethal tree-burst, a mine. The days blurred into one long, never-ending fearful misery. No one was later able to recall the separate days. Each dripping dawn among the shattered firs brought new cannon fodder, bug-eyed replacements, who stared at the dirty, unshaven vets as if they were creatures from another world, which they were in a way. Complete with neckties and new uniforms, the new men were assigned to their companies and squads—only to die before even knowing the name of the units they belonged to. "Don't send us any more replacements," the veterans stated cynically, "we can't keep up with burying 'em!"

All was cold, wet misery. The long interminable nights were particularly terrible. Pfc Don Lavender recalled after the war, "The dark of night in the forest was almost beyond description. A man couldn't even step out of his foxhole to relieve himself with any certainty that he would find his way back again. Trees less than five feet away were not visible. It was not possible to throw a grenade at night without the fear that it would bounce off a tree and come back again into the foxhole. Resourceful GIs overcame this problem by placing stones on the edge of the hole in daylight so that they could tell by the direction of a safe throwing lane in the dark."[9]

The days were little better. As Lavender recalled afterwards, it always seemed to be raining "and we were so well soaked that we couldn't find a dry match among us . . . During the dull, damp hours of the day, we gathered in small groups talking of anything that would get our thoughts away from our unpleasant situation. We frequently dwelled on rumors that we were to be relieved. The miserable weather and the apparent hopelessness of the situation led to a morbid feeling. The men who smoked cigarettes as they talked were never sure if they were to finish the one cigarette they were smoking, finish another pack or carton, or live to smoke at old age."[10]

On October 24 those rumors became truth. The 9th Infantry Division, "a tired group of fighting men," as the divisional history calls them, were ordered relieved. Their casualties had been enormous. For a gain of exactly three thousand yards on a three-mile front, the 9th had suffered 3,836 casualties! This meant that they had had a man wounded or killed for every yard of German earth gained. For the Division as a whole, the casualties were calculated as 30 percent. In reality, this was *not* the true figure. The Top Brass was "cooking the books." As the Division's 47th Infantry Regiment, some three thousand strong, had not been fully engaged in the battle (because of its lack of losses, it would remain in the Forest), the true figures were much more shocking. The 60th Infantry Regiment, for example, had suffered an almost 100 percent turnover in combat personnel since September 1, 1944—a truly appalling figure!

On that day the first elements of the 28th Infantry Division, the Keystone Division as it was called, started to move into the Forest. As they were swallowed up among the black shattered trees, they were shocked by what they saw. All about them lay the waste of battle: empty ration cases, heaps of yellow shells, unearthed mines, belts of used ammunition, and bodies. The somber-faced men of the Graves Registration Units still moved among the bloated, mutilated corpses that now stank, slinging them on the backs of their trucks like so many logs of wood.

As one eyewitness reported it, "The clean shaven files of the 28th were met by other files emerging from the forests, bearded men in torn and caked uniforms, stumbling along like sleepwalkers. Their eyes were bloodshot and held the unmistakeable look of those who had fought on a battlefield. They had seen death in many forms."[11]

It was not an encouraging reception for the new boys, and the GIs of the 9th, now departing for the rest camps of Belgium, did nothing to cheer the men of the 28th up. There was none of the usual banter of such occasions. The men of the 9th were too morose, too haggard and worn for that. They stumbled out of their positions glassy-eyed and staring. Even though the 9th had to hike five miles through the mud to reach their waiting truck, it didn't worry the survivors. *They were out!*

The 28th Infantry Division had a proud record. The Pennsylvania National Guard outfit could trace its origin back to George Washington's time. Three of its artillery batteries had fought with him back in the eighteenth century, and the 28th had been the first militia unit in the States to adopt the name "National Guard" (from the French term *garde nationale* of the French Revolution). Elements of the 28th had fought in the War of 1812, the Mexican War, the Civil War, the Spanish-American War, the Philippine Insurrection, and the First World War.

On February 17, 1941, Roosevelt had federalized several National Guard divisions, including the 28th Division, and for the first time since 1918 the Division was not starved for equipment and supplies. For two years the Division trained in the States and provided cadres for the establishment of other units while maintaining the nucleus of the old outfit, friends and neighbors from the "Keystone State" (which gave it its nickname), until finally in October 1943 it sailed for the United Kingdom. There the Division trained for another nine months until it went into action in the boscage country of Normandy.

Their first taste of combat shocked some of the 28th's officers, who were really too old and too set in their ways, militarily speaking, for the task of leading men into action against first-class soldiers, as the Germans were. Heads rolled rapidly. At the top, the commanding general, Maj. Gen. Lloyd Brown, was replaced one month after the Division entered combat because higher command was not satisfied with the 28th's performance. His successor, Brig. Gen. James E. Wharton, lasted only a matter of hours. The unfortunate commander was shot through the head by a German sniper while visiting one of his regiments and died almost instantly.

A commander now arrived to take over the Division who would set his stamp on it for the remainder of its fighting career. His name was Norman Cota, a craggy, overweight general of forty-seven, who looked older, and who possessed the reputation of being tough, very tough.

Unlike most of his contemporaries, save Patton, he came from a relatively rich family and attended Worcester Academy before being nominated for West Point at twenty. Here he gained his nickname, "Dutch," though he hadn't a drop of German blood in him. He graduated in 1917, but like Bradley and Eisenhower, didn't go overseas. It wasn't until November 1942, when he was forty-five years old, that he ever heard a shot fired in anger—after a quarter of a century in the Army.

Thereafter his promotion was rapid as he soldiered in North Africa with the 1st Division, "the Big Red One," before being sent to Britain, where he served with British Combined Operations until finally he became the assistant divisional commander of the 29th Infantry Division. The 29th had become nervous and had acquired a morbid fear of action and casualties, for it had been too long in England—two years to be exact. Its men cracked, "We've been in England so long that our job won't start till the war is over. They're going to have us wipe the bluebird shit off the White Cliffs of Dover!"*

The men of the 29th were sadly mistaken, at least those of its 116th Infantry Combat Team, which Dutch Cota led. For on D-Day Cota took it ashore in company with his old division, the Big Red One, to assault the beach at Omaha. The night before, Cota, a veteran by now, had told his officers, "You're going to find confusion. The landing craft aren't going to be on schedule

---

* A pun on the popular song of the time, with its "bluebird flying over the White Cliffs of Dover . . . Just you wait and see."

and people are going to be landed in wrong places. Some won't be landed at all . . . We must improvise, carry on, not lose our heads."[12]

Bloody Omaha, as it was called afterward, proved Cota right. There was total confusion and mass slaughter of the assault infantry. As one of the two general officers on the beach, Cota saved the day. He saw a Ranger battalion, which had gone to ground under the hail of German fire, stalled behind a fortified hill. Angrily he bellowed at them, "You men are Rangers! I know you won't let me down!"[13] They didn't. They stormed the hill and took it. The advance from the body-littered beach could continue.

Later, his citation for the Silver Star and the Distinguished Service Order, the second highest British award, pinned on personally by Montgomery, stated that "Norman Cota penetrated inland on this D-Day, to a point the American front line as a whole would not reach until two days later."[14] One month later, again in the forefront of the attack, Cota won the Purple Heart when he was wounded in the attack on St. Lô, plus a second Silver Star.

In short, Dutch Cota, the commander of the 28th Infantry Division, was a brave man who had actually shed his blood in action—unlike so many of his fellow generals, who sent their men to their deaths with such easy consciences in World War II. *He* knew what life was like at the sharp end. He had none of the usual American general's belligerent swagger. He was a quiet, modest man, with keen gray eyes, who could chuckle softly over a joke. At the same time he was a professional soldier through and through. He stood no nonsense from his soldiers. Nor did he believe in "combat fatigue" and popular psychology. As he told the writer William Huie after the war, "I didn't pay much attention to psychiatry at first, but I began giving it some thought there in England when I heard them referring to combat fatigue as a 'disease.' " Later in Normandy he studied a doctor interviewing some men who had run away from the line giving as an excuse "combat fatigue." "Have you had enough?" he'd ask them. "Yeah, Doc. I've had all I want." "Do you want to go back up to the line?" "No, Doc. I've had enough."

Cota exploded. He told the doctor, "These men aren't suffering from any *disease*. Nothing's wrong with most of them that a few hours rest won't cure."

Cota thought it was more important to "teach men traditions and obligations. Whenever I spoke to men under my command, I put it as simply as I could: 'Men, for every right that you enjoy there is a duty that you must assume. You've heard a lot of talk about rights. Now you'll hear a lot about duty.' "[15] And of course, General Cota was right. If an army is going to fight successfully, its men must know that they can't just drop out of combat when it suits them. They have an obligation to their outfit, their commander, and their country.

But a commander has an obligation to his men, too. Toward the end of October, as the 9th was being pulled out of the Hurtgen, Cota was told by his corps commander, General Gerow, that on November 5, General Collins's VII Corps would launch its main drive on the Rhine. In order to again protect the right flank of this drive it would be necessary for Cota's 28th Division to capture the Hurtgen township of Schmidt, which controlled the road network. This road network would provide "additional lateral supply routes for VII Corps." Therefore, the 28th would have to accomplish their mission by November 5—an impossibly short period to take over from the 9th, to plan, and then to execute the task, especially when Cota already knew the difficulties and casualties that the 9th had suffered in an advance of a mere one and a half miles through the Forest.

Afterward Cota stated that he had had "grave misgivings" about the whole operation. He admitted that the terrain over which he was to fight worried him. The Germans dominated the high ground, being dug in on each of the hilltops leading toward Schmidt. Yet he did nothing, save to point out to Gerow, the corps commander, and to Hodges, commander of the First Army, the dangers of attacking at a point where the Germans "looked right down the throat" of the assault force. When Gerow and

Hodges did not respond to his objection, Cota went ahead with his plans for the attack.

Although he knew all the difficulties, he reckoned he had a gambler's chance of success. At one point before the attack, he said that the 28th would take Schmidt if he "had to use every medic in the division."[16] It was a vain boast. The men of the Bloody Bucket Division, as they would soon call themselves,* would need every medic they could lay their hands on to aid the thousands of wounded in a bloodletting that was going to be even greater than that of the 9th.

Cota's officers were not so sanguine as their commander. Some observers who talked to them just before the attack found them with little hope. "None of the officers . . . was in the least bit optimistic. Many were almost certain that if the operation succeeded, it would be a miracle."[17]

Gen. Dutch Cota did not notice, even as his division prepared to attack from a position that one member likened to a "bloody finger pointing into Germany surrounded by the enemy on three sides."[18] Orders were orders. They were there to be carried out. Soon thousands of his young men would die suddenly and violently in the Forest because Dutch Cota did not question those orders from above. As for the general, he would die peacefully long afterward—in bed.

---

* From the divisional insignia, which was shaped like a bucket.

5

As the fighting on the First Army front died away everywhere—the 28th Division would soon be the only First Army division engaged in combat—the battle-weary infantrymen licked their wounds, absorbed the thousands of replacements, and if they were lucky had a spell of R & R, "rest and recreation." Most of them had to be content with what was offered behind the front or in the towns such as Verviers, Herve, and Liège, immediately to the rear of the First Army's line. These places had rest centers with beds that had sheets on them and Red Cross clubmobiles with well-meaning ladies handing out doughnuts and free java. There were movies, such as *Fanny by Gaslight* and Crosby and Hope in *The Road to Casablanca,* USO shows with the crooners singing "What a Difference a Day Makes" and "Straighten Up and Fly Right", and Marlene Dietrich, "the Kraut," as Hemingway called her, supposedly risking her life just behind the front,* singing in her husky seductive manner à la *Blue Angel.* But those million-dollar legs were carefully concealed now by khaki slacks.

Doughnuts, clean sheets, and showers were naturally fine. But for young men whose life expectancy in the infantry was exceedingly limited, something else was needed—*women!* They would have put it more directly then, and definitely more crudely. They wanted sex. They wanted a chance to forget, however fleetingly, what waited for them once they returned to the front. They wanted to prove their masculinity for perhaps one last time before it was blotted out for good.

---

* She was still a German citizen and, therefore, technically a traitor.

So for the lucky ones there was the pass for Paris: seventy-two hours they were going to devote entirely to getting gloriously drunk and then getting laid. That fall, thousands of young Americans from the line, their pockets bulging with back pay, for they had had little to spend it on during the preceding months, their packs heavy with goods to sell on the black market, rolled into Paris, or "gay Paree," as they and their fathers called it, ready to "make whoopee."

As soon as they fell out of the backs of the trucks that had brought them, they headed for the various leave centers that provided them with hotel accommodations and maps of the tourist sights. But the only tourist sight most of the happy, horny young men wanted pointed out to them was Place Pigalle, Pig Alley to them. For it was there, they knew, they'd find the "action" they craved.

They weren't disappointed. Pig Alley swarmed with whores, professional and amateur. There were young women of all shapes and sizes, ugly and pretty, in dyed rabbit-fur jackets, too-short dresses, and wooden wedge-heel shoes, their bare legs painted brown with the seams carefully drawn in with an eyebrow pencil (for nylons cost a fortune on the black market in Paris). There were companies, battalions, regiments of eager and ready women waiting to latch on to the young soldiers with their bulging wad of bills and to hurry them to their shabby little rooms in order to relieve them of some of that money. At night some of them didn't even have time to do that. The sexual encounter would be completed swiftly in the darkness of a blacked-out doorway or under one of the Seine's bridges. The GIs, with good-humored cynicism, called it a "knee-trembler."

Naturally, these ladies of the night, after servicing the German Army for four years, and now doing the same for the American, were not the healthiest of female specimens. The result was that many of those young GIs returned to their outfits with a little souvenir of gay Paree. The VD sufferer's plight was unenviable. He was treated harshly by both nurses and doctors, for the brass was unofficially classifying VD as almost a self-inflicted wound. The front was crying out for bodies, and VD was stopping the flow. The unfortunate victim's rear was pumped full of the new wonder drug penicillin for forty-eight to eighty-six hours (a shot every three hours day or night) until he had dried out. Then the "pox doctor" would subject the patient to the "umbrella," a much feared treatment in which a razor sharp catheter was inserted into the urethra to clear away any possible lesions. Thereafter, the unfortunate soldier was cured, but he would be, as the GIs put it, "pissing urine and blood in six different directions" for several days to come. That fall the United States Army sent 606 men, the equivalent of a battalion daily, to the "pox hospitals." Pig Alley was not very popular with the generals!

Drunkenness among the men on furlough was a much more serious problem. The men whored. They got drunk. They fought. Their tempers were short, and after the line their nerves weren't so good. They were quick, very quick, to take offense.

Discipline was strict in Paris and the other big cities behind the lines to which the GIs went in search of pleasure—it had to be. The Top Brass, who had their headquarters in these great continental cities, was very conscious of the public image of the American Army. On November 5, 1944, Kay Summersby, Eisenhower's chauffeur-cum-mistress, noted: "General Betts reports that disciplinary conditions in the army are becoming bad. Many cases of rape, murder, and pillage are causing complaints by the French, Dutch, etc." The next day she noted again that Eisenhower's Chief of Staff had "discussed with him [Eisenhower] the discipline of the 101st and 82nd Airborne Divisions. It is bad, numerous cases of rape, looting. Strong measures will have to be taken. E. suggests that there should be a public hanging, particularly in the case of rape."[1] The fact that the Supreme Commander was prepared to humiliate two of his finest divisions by the spectacle of a nineteenth-century-style public hanging showed the extent of the disciplinary problem that fall.

Thus it was that the MPs (the French called them snowdrops), in their white helmets, cross straps, and gaiters, wasted no time with troublemakers—drunk or otherwise. A club across the back of the skull and into the paddy wagon they went, straight to the nearest guardroom to sleep it off. They remained there for only a short while. Riflemen were urgently needed at the front. Minor crimes committed by drunken infantrymen were usually ignored and they were shipped back up the line in short order. Another taste of line duty would soon take the "piss and vinegar" out of the troublemakers, the authorities reasoned.

At the end of this short time out of war, most of them did go back of their own volition. Pockets empty, heads aching, some taking back with them a still undiscovered souvenir of gay Paree, they tumbled into the waiting trucks from Division and tamely allowed themselves to be transported to the front. The war machine would swallow them up again in its ever-greedy paws and it would be good-bye to the obliging "mamselles," the "canteen commandos," the "feather merchants" of the COMZ, the rear echelon. But not for all of them.

For some of them the fleshpots of these great European cities proved too tempting. Others stayed out of fear of what was to come and a sense of outrage at the way the COMZ men lived, while they were expected to lay their lives on the line every single day for a few dollars and a couple of cans of C rations. By Christmas 1944 there were an estimated twenty thousand American deserters in Paris alone—a good-sized infantry division of able-bodied men who had voted with their feet and "gone over the hill."

By the end of the war it was estimated that there were forty thousand deserters who were later apprehended by the United States Army. (This figure does not include men who overstayed their leave or went AWOL from training camps behind the line.) Most of these were tried by lesser courts, but 2,864 were arraigned before a general court-martial and received sentences ranging from twenty years to death. Of these death sentences a mere 49 were approved by the convening authority. Yet only *one* death sentence was carried out.

*   *   *

Between 1864 and 1953 the United States was to shoot only one citizen-soldier. His name was Eddie Slovik, a timid, under-sized 25-year-old who had done time for minor offenses. The men who shot him were his fellow citizen-soldiers of 28th Division's 109th Infantry Regiment, whose motto was "Let the citizen bear arms." The man who ordered that shooting was Gen. Norman Dutch Cota.

Slovik, together with a Private Tankey, first refused to fight in August 1944 when he had been landed at Omaha. After coming under their first shelling, Slovik and Tankey decided that war wasn't for them. As Slovik confessed in the statement he made after his second desertion in Germany in October: "They were shelling the town and we were told to dig in for the night. The following morning they were shelling us again. I was so scared nerves and trembling that at the time the other replacements moved out I couldn't move. I stayed there in my foxhole till it was quiet and I was able to move."[2]

For the next few weeks Slovik and Tankey stayed with—of all things—a Canadian Provost company, cooking and foraging for the Canadian military police. Then, in October, the two of them decided to give themselves up. In the confusion of that first week of October, with the Division licking its wounds after the first battles of the German frontier, they were accepted as having been lost somehow or other and no charges were pressed. Both of them were posted to the 109th's Company G at Rocherath on the Belgian-German frontier. Tankey decided he would fight and lasted exactly a month before he was wounded in the Hurtgen, which kept him in a hospital for most of the rest of the campaign.

But Slovik told Captain Ralph Grotte, C.O. of Company G, straight off that he was "too scared, too nervous" to fight with a rifle company. Grotte ignored the frightened outburst. He posted Eddie Slovik to one of his platoons and told him to stay there. But Slovik stayed with the platoon for only a matter of hours. Tankey spotted him leaving: "Eddie walked right past me with-out looking at me. He started walking down a little hill, fast. I ran after him fifty or a hundred yards, caught up with him, grabbed him by the shoulder and stopped him."

"Come on back, Eddie," Tankey said. "You don't want to do this."

"He just looked at me, dead serious. 'Johnny,' he said, 'I know what I'm doing.' He jerked away and kept on going."[3]

One day later Slovik turned up again at Rocherath with a written confession on a piece of green paper stating that he had told his C.O. he would run away if "I had to go out there again," and now he had done so. It was almost as if the timid ex-con *wanted* to be punished!

On October 26, Slovik was sent to the divisional stockade at the German village of Rott, which was also Cota's divisional headquarters, set up in a red brick *Gasthaus*.* It was full of petty military criminals from the 28th and the usual collection of goldbricks bucking for a court-martial so that they could stay out of the firing line. There these young men who wouldn't fight were quite happy to receive sentences of up to twenty-five years' imprisonment; most of them reasoned that once the war was over they'd be released immediately in some sort of general amnesty. Six months was the most they thought they would serve.

Perhaps Slovik thought he too would escape so lightly. One of his guards there in the divisional stockade, Sgt. Edward Needles, remembered after the war how one day Slovik was present when two of the men of the 28th came out of their court-martial. "They were as happy as hell. 'How much didja get?' Slovik hollered at 'em.

" 'Twenty years,' they hollered back and they seemed happy.

" 'I'll settle for twenty years right now,' Slovik said. 'How long you think you'll have to stay in after the war is over?'

" 'Aw, maybe six months,' " one of the kids said.

"That's how it was."[4]

But Eddie Slovik had not reckoned with General Cota and the Hurtgen.

---

* For those interested in such things, the inn is still there in much the same shape as it was in 1944.

The slaughter to come for the 28th Infantry Division and the disastrous effect it had on the morale of the men of the Bloody Bucket would ensure that there could be no other sentence for Slovik, the reluctant rifleman, but death—*pour encourager les autres*.

As October neared an end, General Hodges, the commander of the U.S. First Army, set a date for the main attack on the Rhine by Collins's VII Corps, which was going to be assisted by the men of Simpson's Ninth Army to the north. He ordered the 28th Division from Gerow's V Corps to kick off its attack on Schmidt at the very latest on November 2, three days before the main assault. To give the infantry added strength, Hodges told Gerow he could use a combat command from the 5th Armored Division to assist the 28th. Despite what was said about the Roer River dams *after* the war, there was no mention either at the top, in First Army Corps HQ, or at the bottom, in Cota's HQ, of these dams as the final objective of the new drive into the Hurtgen. The only objective given to Cota and the commander of the 5th Armored's combat command, reserve CCR, was the township of Schmidt.

Nor was there any change in the strategy of the attack. It was to follow the same route as that of the ill-fated 9th Infantry Division: Germeter, Vossenack, across the Kall River gorge to Kommerscheidt and finally to Schmidt. Indeed, the Top Brass made so many decisions in advance that Cota was left with little freedom to make his own decisions or to use his own initiative. As a result, the 28th Infantry Division was expected to attack across three high ridges, which could be held successfully by a few hundred determined defenders, under German observation from the heights all the time. Once again the men would be attacking through the Green Hell, the thick woods of the Hurtgen.

There was only one difference. Intelligence had discovered what was virtually a cart track, the Kall Trail, linking Vossenack and Germeter. This cart track, parts of which did not even show up on aerial photographs, was to be the 28th's main supply route and one which Cota hoped to use to bring up his tanks. It was going to be a pious hope.

Adding to the 28th's difficulties was the weather, which had now taken a turn for the worse. It had started to rain—a cold, relentless drizzle. If that were not bad enough, the Hurtgen was swathed in fog and mist, which precluded aerial support for the third attack on the Forest. Desperately, Cota pleaded for time. Twice Hodges allowed Corps Commander Gerow to postpone the assault. But on October 31, from his headquarters in far-off Spa, Belgium, Hodges decreed that the 28th Division would attack, regardless of the weather, on November 2.

The die was cast. Hodges, Gerow, and Cota had decided the fate of over four thousand young men. There was no escape for them now. They were going to attack into the Forest, enter what they were soon going to call "the Death Factory."

PART TWO

The Death Factory

Silent cannons, soon cease your silence.
Soon unlimber'd to begin the red business.

WALT WHITMAN

6

Dawn. November 2, 1944.

It was typical weather for this time of the year in what the GIs already called "the Awful Eifel": cold, damp, and gray with the mist curling itself in and out of the shattered, dripping pines. Frozen snow lay on the ground. Beneath it lay the iron-hard bodies of hundreds of 9th Division men who had still not been picked up. Pfc Bob Graff recalled long afterward how, as he had entered the line, "another guy took me back in the woods to a blanket, pulled it back, and showed me a man laying there with a hole in his back, already moldering. I thought of this guy's family with him layin' there. That was my first contact with what combat was all about."[1]

There was no time now to reflect about the dead and the futility of combat. The time for thought was over. The moment of truth and violent, unreasoning action was nearly upon the fourteen thousand young men of the 28th Division, most of whom were green replacements.

At eight o'clock precisely, the heavy, brooding dawn silence was broken by an awesome ear-splitting roar as the whole of the divisional artillery, plus support from other outfits, thundered into action, pouring twelve thousand shells into the enemy positions. This was the western front, circa 1918, all over again. The enemy was being softened up for the coming infantry assault.

Cowering in their pits and bunkers as the earth shook and trembled beneath them, the field-greys knew what was coming. As soon as the bombardment had ceased, the *Amis* would come surging forward to be mown down by the German machine guns, just as their fathers had been at Château-Thierry and in the Argonne during World War I. But the *Landsers* were in for a surprise. As the bombardment ceased, leaving behind it an echoing silence and a transformed landscape, a lunar surface of great smoking earthen pits, the *Amis* didn't come in a great surging, cheering khaki mass. Was this a new tactic? the puzzled Germans asked themselves.

It wasn't. The Brass was playing it safe. They were waiting for TAC air to arrive and begin strafing the German positions, but the mist was too thick and the planes didn't arrive. (When they did arrive that afternoon, their most notable attack was on an American artillery outfit where the "American Luftwaffe," as it was soon to be called, succeeded in killing and wounding twenty-four American artillerymen.) Colonel Strickler's 109th Regiment finally started to slip into the trees at nine o'clock without the support of the fighter-bombers, hampered more by the trees than the enemy.

It was little different on Colonel Peterson's 112th Infantry's front. Its 2nd Battalion, under the command of Lieutenant Colonel Hatzfeld, made a successful attack from Germeter and captured Vossenack and were digging in leisurely to the northeast of the village under the gaze of the Germans on the ridges at Brandenberg-Bergstein and the one extending from Kommerscheidt and Schmidt.

Only on the front held by Colonel Seely's 110th Infantry did the attackers run into serious trouble. No sooner had the two assault battalions risen from their holes than they ran straight into a well-directed hail of machine gun and mortar fire. The barrage stopped them dead. The men went to ground almost immediately, with great gaps torn in their ranks. Young Earl Fuller saw his first sergeant die in that abortive attack: "He had been a lieutenant in World War I but had stayed on as an NCO. All summer he had said the war would end in November. It did for him."[2]

Now the regimental aid station, code-named Honeymoon (although there was nothing sweet and loving about what was going to happen there over the next few terrible days), was flooded with casualties. The harassed medics quickly sorted out the wounded and wrote morphine dosages on their foreheads, asked the wounded if they had taken their sulpha wound tablets, and cut the bloody, torn uniforms from those due for immediate surgery. Steadily the heap of amputated limbs began to grow behind the makeshift hospital and the air was thick with the cries and moans of those who were suffering. The Death Factory was living up to its reputation.

As casualties mounted alarmingly, the officers and NCOs tried desperately to rally their shaken soldiers. By threatening, pleading, and cajoling they tried to make them move in platoons this time, hoping to infiltrate the enemy positions through the massed rows of barbed wire covered by mines and machine guns. Some tried. But not for long. The spandaus opened up again immediately. Men died screaming on the wire, and hung there like sodden bundles of rags for days to come. Others carrying satchel charges for blowing up the wire were hit and disintegrated in a welter of sparkling white bone and scarlet gore. Some simply couldn't take it.

As communications broke down, so did discipline. Men left the line, first in ones and twos, then by the dozen. These were the first cases of combat fatigue. One ex-artilleryman, who had been sent into the line without any infantry training whatsoever, was found sobbing and trying to dig a foxhole with his bare hands. His buddies tried to restrain him, but he wouldn't have it. They finally took him back to the rear by force. There he disappeared into one of the rest centers, set up by General Cota, for that strict disciplinarian was determined that there weren't going to be any further Eddie Sloviks in *his* division. Cota was in for a surprise, a great surprise.

As darkness started to fall over the battlefield, the 110th Regiment was fighting to maintain its original positions, several companies having retreated back to the start line, pounded by the gleeful Germans. Losses were high. In some companies they had lost two-thirds of their strength without having achieved a single objective. Other companies arranged local truces to retrieve grievously wounded comrades who lay moaning in no-man's-land. General Cota would have been furious, but individual soldiers took it upon themselves to stop the firing. The Americans watched in silence while the wounded were brought back under the gaze of their enemies, who stood at the entrances of their bunkers, with their rifles at the port.

Even stranger things happened on the 110th's front that terrible night. Two hours before midnight RAF bombers began to drone overhead heading for targets deeper in the Reich. Almost immediately the German defenses sprang into action, and down below young Jack Colbaugh, an artilleryman, thought it was definitely a very weird and frightening feeling to see the tracer bullets fly around at all angles and listen to that terrifying noise of machine-gun chatter in the darkness.[3]

Two planes were shot down before midnight, and from one of them Pilot Officer Walter MacKay and Pilot Officer Albert Howe of the Royal Air Force parachuted into the unknown. They did not know whether they were dropping into enemy-held territory or their own. Fortunately for them they landed in the positions held by the 110th, where they were challenged by Private Spike Malloy from Brooklyn. He demanded the password from the two RAF officers. Obviously they didn't know it, and for a little while they were pushed around by the boy from Brooklyn until finally they persuaded him to call his superiors. He did so, telling the man at the other end of the line at the company command post, "Dere are a coupla guys here speakin' broken English. We tink dere Germans." That was about the only funny thing to happen to the 110th that night.[4]

On the following day, however, things started to get better for the 28th. A company of tanks neutralized Kommerscheid and had the Germans cowering in their holes. As the tanks' 75mm cannon poured down the fire, two battalions of the 112 Regiment forded the swift-flowing Kall River and started for the key town of Schmidt. To everyone's surprise, the lead battalion, commanded by Lieutenant Colonel Flood, was in among the shattered half-timbered cottages of the place before the Germans were aware they had arrived. Though persistent snipers still hindered the Americans, the energetic Lieutenant Colonel Flood was soon organizing the place for defense. He was here, there, and everywhere, siting machine guns, having his men lay mines, and deciding where the strongpoints were to be set up.

But as only his battalion had reached the Schmidt ridge, Flood realized that he could not form a continuous perimeter. He would have to defend the place in the German style, using what they called "hedgehogs," a series of outposts with no defenses in between, but which were mutually supporting. Flood was realistic enough to know that the Germans wouldn't take long to counterattack (they never did). Schmidt was a key road center. Without it the Germans were cut from their bunker line up around Monschau. They had to have it back!

But what if the Krauts brought up tanks? Apart from the battalion's bazookas, they had no other anti-tank weapons, nor had any American tanks succeeded in crossing the Kall. It was now vital that the Kall Trail should be opened up and tanks sent in. Time was running out fast!

But if Flood was worried, the staff was jubilant. It had been surprisingly easy. The Division had captured its primary objective within forty-eight hours. As night descended over the Forest like the shadow of a giant crow, Schmidt was firmly in American hands. Congratulations started to pour in. What the 9th had failed to do in two weeks, the 28th had done in two days! Corps commanders all along the American line in Germany and Holland began to telephone their best wishes and congratulations. Whatever reservations Dutch Cota had had before the operation now vanished. He wrote that he started to feel like a "little Napoleon." It had been easy, all too easy.

With no particular sense of urgency that night of November 3–4, 1944, engineers began to check out the last of the Kall Trail. They knew Schmidt had been captured, and they did not feel any great need to rush the check. Just before dark the first company of tanks set out to follow the engineers. As the tanks, heading up to relieve the infantry in Schmidt, strained and groaned their way up the Kall Trail, the commanders cursing and bitching, knowing that one false move would cause the loss of a twenty-thousand-dollar vehicle, the C.O., a Captain Hostrup, realized he was running into trouble. The trail was getting narrower and narrower. Furthermore, the left shoulder, which dropped sharply to the gorge below, was beginning to crumble alarmingly under the weight of his tank.

He gave up finally, and ordered his driver to reverse. He was not going any farther, he told his C.O., Lieutenant Colonel Ripple, by radio, until the engineers strengthened the Trail. Ripple agreed. So Hostrup's tanks huddled together like frightened primeval monsters on the trail, while the enemy artillery went to work on them, hitting the Shermans repeatedly, gouging great gleaming silver marks on their metal hides but not succeeding in knocking one of them out.

All that long anxious night, the engineers higher up on the Trail labored away, expecting to be attacked by the Germans at any moment, sweating over their picks and shovels, until at five on the morning of November 4, the officer in charge signaled that the track was clear.

Hostrup didn't hesitate. He ordered Lieutenant Fleig in the lead tank to take up his platoon. With a roar, the 425 HP engines burst into noisy life. The dawn air was suddenly filled with the cloying stench of gas. Then they were rumbling forward. Not for long. Almost immediately there was a muffled roar and a bright sheet of scarlet flame beneath Fleig's tank. It rocked and came to a sudden halt, one track falling behind the Sherman like a severed limb. The tank had gone over a mine!

Hostrup fumed. Grimly he ordered Fleig to get the wrecked tank out of the way at once. Fleig bolted for the next Sherman. Desperately he edged it around the crippled vehicle, but it was no use. It started to slip alarmingly in the mud and loose earth. Suddenly it stuck. Angrily the driver gunned the engine. A wake of flying earth rose behind it. To no avail—it was well and truly stuck.

Fleig did manage to get three tanks up the Trail, which was now effectively cut by their own vehicles, and reach the first of the infantry, some of whom cried openly when they saw the Shermans. Hurriedly the infantrymen told Fleig where the Germans were, adding, "There's a lot of Heinies with lots of tanks over there." Fleig promised, "I'll do what I can, boys," and then he was off, not realizing that he was on his own. There'd be no more armor coming up the Kall Trail this day. The fate of Schmidt was sealed.

At dawn the German artillery started the softening up. Shells began to fall to the front of Schmidt, and then the enemy began "walking" his fire throughout the village. Suddenly the frightened, weary men of the 112th's 3rd Battalion, which had captured the place the day before, could hear the squeak and rumble of tanks. Here and there in the cold morning mist, they could spot enemy soldiers slipping in and out of cover, coming toward them. The long expected German counterattack had commenced!

They came in with a dozen tanks and about 150 men. Desperately Lieutenant Colonel Flood, commander of the 3rd Battalion, asked for artillery support. Nothing came. Disdainfully the Mark IV tanks rolled right over the mines the defenders had set the day before. Here and there the infantry attempted to knock them out with their puny bazookas. The rockets simply bounced off the Mark IV's tough hides like glowing Ping-Pong balls. The tanks rolled ever nearer, the long overhanging cannon swinging back and forth like the snouts of predatory monsters, trying to sniff out their prey.

The men of Company King started to break in panic. One whole platoon began to move back without orders. Flood knew that if K withdrew, the whole flank of his Love Company would be exposed to the enemy. He and his officers tried to rally the men, but the sight of those seemingly unstoppable tanks had unnerved them too much. There was no holding them. Some were so panicked that they abandoned their wounded comrades, ignoring their piteous pleas for help. Others fled into the woods, right into the arms of the waiting Germans.

Slowly the messages of dismay started to filter up the chain of command. Peterson, the regimental commander who had served with the 112th since 1916 and had once known every man in the outfit by name, passed on the bad news to Cota.

Cota was bewildered. Was it only one company that was retreating or the whole battalion? Hurriedly he sent Colonel Lockett from the 112th to investigate. Lockett never made it. His jeep was ambushed and he was captured. All was chaos and confusion. Everywhere troops were streaming back from Schmidt in disorder. Officers tried to stop them, to no avail. They were "bugging out."

Everything now started to go radically wrong for Cota's 28th Infantry Division. The sense of panic and hopelessness was infectious, as the wide-eyed, ashen-faced stragglers from the shattered 3rd started to come through the next village, Kommerscheidt, held by the 112th's First Battalion. The defenders began to grow nervous and apprehensive. Officers and noncoms tried to hold the fugitives, kicking and striking them. More than once an officer drew his .45 and threatened them, but as S. Sgt. Frank Ripperdam reported later, "There was no holding them. They were pretty frantic and panicky."[5] In the end only some two hundred were coerced into staying in the line at Kommerscheidt; the rest fled into the woods.

The first to flee when the German tanks made their appearance at two that afternoon were the men who had been bullied into fighting once more. It was understandable. The sight of those gray monsters rolling forward into the beleaguered village was too much, but unlike the situation at Schmidt, the defenders of Kommerscheidt had Lieutenant Fleig's three Shermans.

Now the latter bravely rolled into action, although outnumbered by more than three to one. Fleig's Sherman made a direct hit almost immediately, and with a roar a Mark IV went up, the German crew clambering out frantically and running to the rear. Fleig spotted a Panther whose sloping armored glacis plate*

---

* The frontal plate of a tank.

made it virtually unstoppable from any frontal attack. He was undismayed and fired two rounds of high explosives at it. The shells rocked the tank back on its sprockets but otherwise did no harm. However, the German crew panicked and fled. Fleig knocked out five German tanks, and the armored attack fizzled out. It was not surprising that the admiring infantrymen, who thought the young lieutenant had saved them, called him "General Fleig." But General Fleig's little victory was the only one that the 28th secured that bitter November Saturday.

Still Cota remained sanguine. That night he prepared a new order for the battered 112th Infantry, which would be transmitted the following day. It read, in part, "It is imperative that the town of Schmidt be secured at once. Task Force R under the command of Lieutenant Colonel Ripple is attached to your command . . . It is imperative that no time be wasted in getting this attack under way . . . I again caution you that men defending road blocks or a terrain feature must dig in . . . Great care will be exercised to prevent any recurrence of the episode of the 3rd Battalion."[6]

The Top Brass was breathing down Cota's neck now. No less a person than Eisenhower, accompanied by Hodges, Collins, and Gerow, was to visit him on the morrow, and Cota wanted to be seen doing something decisive when Eisenhower arrived from his chateau HQ outside Paris. Of course, the plan was absurd: a couple of battered battalions, supported by whichever of Ripple's tanks could get up the Kall Trail, were to attack elements of a German infantry division and the famed 116th Panzer Division, The Greyhounds, that had been in the forefront of the fighting ever since Normandy. A harassed Colonel Peterson knew it was absurd.

On receipt of the order he hastily sent a Lieutenant Simon back to Cota at Rott with his comments—two badly shaken battalions and seven tanks weren't enough. Cota was determined to carry the attack through, and he sent his assistant divisional commander, General Davis, personally to see Peterson. Those outside the regimental command post heard them arguing. Peterson wanted to hang on to Kommerscheidt first. When the time came, *then* he would attack Schmidt. Davis wouldn't have it. He *ordered* Peterson to attack on the morrow.

Meanwhile, the Germans changed their tactics. While a desperately unhappy Peterson prepared reluctantly to assault Schmidt, they turned their attention to the Kall Trail. That same evening they infiltrated the vital supply route. A lone jeep churning its way through the mud, past the wrecked tanks, ran straight into a German patrol. They came slipping out of the trees like gray wolves and opened fire. Tracer zipped lethally through the darkness. The officer in charge screamed, "Shoot, man! *Shoot!*"

"I can't, Lieutenant," his driver cried back. "I'm dying right here!"[7]

Throughout that long tense night reports came flooding back to divisional HQ that the Germans were infiltrating the Trail. The chief engineer, Colonel Daley, angrily ordered, "Get every man into the line fighting."[8]

But it was Ripple's tanks, making their way to help Peterson's counterattack, that first ran into the Germans in strength just as they were emerging from the Trail. There they were hit by elements of the Greyhounds' reconnaissance battalion. A dingdong tank battle started. Solid glowing AP shot hissed through the darkness. There was the crackle of machine-gun tracer. Like crazy fireflies, it zipped back and forth. At regular intervals there was the hollow thud of a shell hitting a tank, followed a moment later by the cherry-red flicker of flames or the tremendous whoosh of an engine exploding. By dawn that lunar landscape was littered with burning, shattered tanks. There were only six American tanks and three tank destroyers available for the attack on Schmidt.

In the meantime, Peterson's third outfit, Colonel Hatzfeld's 2nd Battalion, which was dug in on the exposed Vossenack ridge, started to have trouble. Even before the Germans came the men were shaky and nervous. Some were crying as if brokenhearted. Others just slumped apathetically and had to be ordered to eat their rations. The battalion commander, Colonel Hatzfeld, sat on a box in his cellar command post, apathetic, motionless, silent, face buried in his hands, a broken man who no longer seemed to care what happened.

That the Germans would come at dawn was a foregone conclusion. There was a short, intense artillery barrage and then they were advancing through the fields. A company broke. It grabbed its gear and made a run for it. Another company commander, seeing his flank exposed, now ordered his men to move back. Panic broke out. Nothing could stop the retreating soldiers. They were all heading for the rear.

"It was the saddest sight I have ever seen," Lieutenant Condon of Company E reported later. "Down the road from the east came men from F, G, and E Companies: pushing, shoving, throwing away equipment, trying to outrace the artillery and each other, all in a frantic effort to escape. They were all scared and excited. Some were terror-stricken. Some were helping the slightly wounded to run, and many of the badly wounded, probably hit by artillery, were lying in the road where they fell, screaming for help. It was a heartbreaking, demoralizing scene."[9]

As yet, however, not a single German had penetrated Vossenack. The frantic staff officers who tried to stop the rot pointed this out to the fleeing men. But they wouldn't stop to listen. "Yet it is no use pointing this out to the panic-stricken fugitives," Capt. James Nesbit, the battalion personnel officer, explained later. "Those we saw were completely shattered . . . There was no sense fooling ourselves about it. It was a disorderly retreat. The men were going back pell-mell."[10]

Some did stay and wait for the German attack. They waited in the ruins as the rain began. The hands that gripped their weapons were wet with nervous sweat, and the men jumped at the slightest sound, their nerves ticking electrically. The Germans were out there; they knew that. When, for God's sake, would they finally put an end to this terrible suspense and attack?

Manfred Otten, a German infantryman on the opposite hilltop, had dug himself in that afternoon and was observing Vossenack, which he remembered from the days of his youth. He was appalled by what he saw. "It was a valley of horror. Bloody and moaning soldiers, shattered woods, bombed meadows . . . For the first time I realize—Death lurks here. And then at five o'clock on the morning of the seventh, the order was passed down the length of our line of foxholes: *FERTIGMACHEN ZUM ANGRIFF!*"[11]* They were coming.

At the rear, fearing another disaster such as the one that had taken place at Schmidt the previous day, the staff worked feverishly to send reinforcements to Vossenack. Colonel Hatzfeld had now been evacuated suffering from combat exhaustion. It was clear to Cota and General Davis that if a battalion commander had succumbed, then the state of his men must indeed be terrible. New blood was needed, but there was little available. Hastily, a battalion of engineers was sent forward. Back at Germeter the dressing station was combed for men able to hold a rifle. A twice-wounded lieutenant volunteered to take some seventy slightly wounded men to Vossenack, but by the time he reached there, most of the "volunteers" had vanished.

But there were still determined men, prepared to sell their lives dearly, sheltered in the ruins of Vossenack, as the Germans edged their way slowly forward, their uniforms smeared with mud and soaked black with the pelting rain.

"Our losses must have been terrible," Rifleman Manfred Otten remembered later, "because there was only a sergeant and a handful of men, including me, left when we were given the order to search through Vossenack as far as the church."[12]

There, through a shell hole in the wall, the sergeant spotted an American tank. *"A panzerfaust,"* he yelled urgently to Otten. *"Los!"*

Hurriedly the latter raced through the smoking rubble and rain to fetch the German equivalent of the bazooka, a one-shot weapon that had more hitting power than the American weapon. Minutes later the NCO took careful aim and slammed a rocket

* Prepare to attack.

right into the side of an unsuspecting American tank at forty meters' range. The tank began to burn immediately.

"Eine neue Panzerfaust her!" he cried triumphantly to Otten.

This time the sergeant wasn't so lucky. Just as he prepared to fire at another U.S. tank, he was spotted. There was a burst of angry machine-gun fire. The NCO screamed. He reeled back, his face looking as if someone had tossed a handful of red jam at it. He tumbled down the stairs and fell dead in the ruined church, his arms extended like some field-grey Jesus on the cross.

In the end, neither side made progress in that terrible shattered village filled with death. Both the infantry and engineers (who still wore their hip boots, they had been committed so hastily) and the men of the 116th Panzer Division were worn out. As the rumble of the guns died away that awful day, the combatants, Germans and Americans, sank into an exhausted torpor, lying in their holes in the rain like dead men. All around them the village lay in ruins. Dead men sprawled among the smoking masonry on every side in the extravagant postures of those done to death violently. Here and there a man whimpered in pain or cried softly to himself as if heartbroken, like a child who could not be comforted. A few (the fortunate ones) fell into an exhausted sleep, snoring harshly, out to the world, while the raindrops dripped off the edge of their helmets.

Try as they may, some couldn't sleep, haunted by the memories of the day. The few remaining officers, in particular, brooded on what had happened. For they knew that nothing like this had ever happened to an American army before. Twice in two days, a battalion of a regiment whose traditions went back to the Civil War had broken and run for the rear. The men had fled in scores. Officers had run with them too, throwing away their weapons in their unreasoning, overwhelming fear. Even a battalion commander had succumbed to combat exhaustion.

No one felt the shame more than Colonel Peterson, who had served for twenty-eight years both in peace and war with the 112th. His regiment was shattered, and he knew that his men had run away. He felt he had been given unreasonable assignments by a commander who never visited the front and had no idea of just how terrible conditions were up at Schmidt, Vossenack, and Kommerscheidt. Now with the battered survivors and Colonel Ripple's handful of tanks he was supposed to attack Schmidt—yet another impossible objective. He brooded and brooded, mulling over the rumor that there was already a new colonel at divisional HQ ready to replace him. Thus, at this lowest moment in his whole life, the ex-mining engineer received a call from Cota to report to divisional headquarters immediately. It was the last straw. Handing over command to Colonel Ripple, he set off with one companion for Rott. When he got there, he was determined to give General Norman Dutch Cota a piece of his mind.

7

As Peterson moved off in the rain in his jeep, it was clear that his 112th Infantry was a spent force. Even as he did so, the man he had appointed to take over, Colonel Ripple, ordered his Company C to set off for Kommerscheidt. But the company commander and his men seemed too dazed to understand. Colonel Ripple tried to lead them to the village himself. But they refused, and in disgust the tank colonel told them to stay where they were.

The sight he had just seen steeled Colonel Peterson's resolve. Cota *must* be told what really was going on down the line! He nudged the jeep driver and urged him to greater speed. Behind him German artillery started to fall on Kommerscheidt, the enemy's next objective. Before nightfall the demoralized Americans would be driven from the burning village, the entire staff of the ill-fated 1st and 3rd Battalions of the 112th Infantry Regiment killed, wounded, or captured. Disaster was about to overtake the 28th.

But a brooding, angry Colonel Peterson did not know this, nor the fact that a Colonel Nelson was already attempting to make his way to Kommerscheidt to take over command of what was left of the 112th. (He would make the attempt four times before he finally got through, only to find the village in enemy hands.) Peterson and his companion, Pfc Gus Seiler, concentrated on getting down the Kall Trail, aware already that there were Germans lurking in the shattered trees on both sides. The two men and the driver hoped that the driving rain and the mist would conceal their progress through the thick gray mud down to the river below.

They were out of luck, however. Coming round the second elbow bend in the Trail, they came under heavy small-arms fire. Slugs hissed lethally through the air, whining off the rock face and slicing the branches off the firs. The trio hastily abandoned their jeep and bent double, made a run for it with bullets stitching the mud at their feet. They managed it, and now Colonel Peterson experienced the suffering of the men who had tried to supply his regiment over the Trail. There were abandoned Weasels* everywhere, some of them filled with the dead. There were also dead Americans sprawled on the Trail itself, two of them crushed to a bloody pulp, probably by a tank. Swiftly, the three of them pulled these bodies to the edge of the Trail and hurried on, followed by another burst of enemy machine-gun fire.

Now Peterson decided they would be safer in the trees themselves; they stood out too much on the Trail. At his command the other two plunged into the Forest, heading south, hoping to ford the Kall River upstream. They were in luck. Avoiding small parties of Germans who were everywhere in the trees, they managed to ford the river, only to run into more small-arms fire on the other side.

This time they were not going to escape so easily. A firefight broke out in the confused mess of the shattered trees. They succeeded in killing two of the German attackers, but they were hit almost immediately by mortar fire. Peterson yelped with pain as something burned in his left leg. He had been hit, but he didn't know it at the time. He thought the painful irritation was caused by a piece of metal still left in the leg from World War I.

Their progress was slowed as Peterson started to limp badly. The third soldier volunteered to act as point. He soon disappeared, leaving Peterson and Seiler to their fates. The two of them began to crawl through the Forest. Suddenly there was the high-pitched hysterical burr of a German machine pistol. Seiler

---

* Small tracked supply vehicles.

moaned and collapsed, blood spurting from a series of red buttonholes abruptly stitched the length of his side. Peterson put an ear to Seiler's chest; there was no sound. He was dead and had died saving the colonel unwittingly, his own body acting as a shield.

Another mortar barrage came hurtling down as Peterson crawled on along, his face lacerated by twigs, his hands black with mud and dirt. This time the colonel felt a burning pain in his right leg. He cursed and tried to move on, standing up this time. To no avail. The limb was useless. He started to crawl again, gradually becoming weaker and more confused, alone, it seemed, in the middle of the whole of the German Army.

He recrossed the river, and as he pulled himself out, he spotted three Germans. He held his breath and hoped they wouldn't see him. Two passed, without noticing him, but the last man did. As Peterson automatically pulled the trigger of his burp gun, his vision blurred and he saw the Germans as through a mist. The Germans fled and Peterson continued to crawl on his lone odyssey, dragging his useless right leg behind him.

What thoughts must have gone through his mind during those long hours, with seemingly every man's hand against him? Did he think of those long summers before the war when he and his fellow National Guardsmen were the forgotten men: fools or bigots, grown men playing soldier? Or was it the good times, when they got together after usual deadly dull weekly training session for a few beers and chats about the old days in the trenches? Now all those men, the old boys who had served with him in France, and the kids, who had joined back in the depressed thirties when the Guard had served as a free social club, had all vanished. What had taken twenty-four long years to build up, the proud 112th Infantry Regiment, had been wiped out in four short days in that terrible Death Factory.

Half out of his mind and praying for salvation, Colonel Peterson blacked out for a while. When he came to he heard American voices. Weakly he called for help, but no one came. Instead, more shells started to fall all around him. He crawled on and crossed the River Kall once again. Now everything was vague and confused as he continued on. He saw two Germans sitting on the road that ran along the river. They didn't seem to notice him. Some Americans came along and took them prisoner. He called to them. Instead of helping, they dropped to the ground and took up a firing position. When no enemy bullets came, they walked off with their prisoners.

Peterson gave in. He lay on the ground waiting for death. Periodically he called weakly, *"General Cota . . . Colonel Peterson . . . General . . ."*

Finally he was found. An engineer corporal gave him a shot of morphine and strung the very weak officer to a plasma bottle; thereupon he was transported to the rear on a stretcher. But he was still determined to see Cota, despite the fact that he had been wounded twice and was suffering from exposure. At the divisional aid station, he demanded to see the commanding general. Hastily Cota was summoned and was appalled by what he saw—a senior colonel who looked like a ragman, dirty, unshaven, red-eyed and virtually incoherent with rage and exhaustion. According to his own statement later, he knew of no message recalling Peterson to the divisional CP. He assumed that Peterson had abandoned his shattered regiment to its fate. Tired, upset, and living off his nerves after the events of the last few days, big tough Dutch Cota, the hero of Bloody Omaha, fainted clean away.

General Cota had good reason to be at the end of his tether and in a highly nervous state that day. The 28th's attack into the Forest had gone disastrously wrong. His 112th Regiment was a spent force, its casualties running into thousands. His 109th had scarcely gotten farther than its start line, although it had now been fashioned into Task Force Davis under the personal command of the assistant divisional commander, General Davis, and his 110th was in little better shape. The Top Brass was breathing down his neck and had ordered the 2nd Ranger Battalion and the 4th Division's 12th Infantry Regiment to his support, trying to patch up the mess before the 28th collapsed totally.

When Colonel Peterson confronted him from his stretcher that day, Cota had privately admitted to himself that he could not win the Battle of the Hurtgen Forest. But he knew what the prestige of the United States Army meant to Eisenhower and the Army Group commander, Bradley. The latter had often stated proudly that the American Army never gave up ground that it had "bought with its own blood." But was there any hope of recapturing the three lost villages of Schmidt, Vossenack, and Kommerscheidt?

In his despair he turned to General Davis, who, unlike himself, had actually been up front three times in these last horrific five days and knew what the morale of the survivors was like. What should he do about what was left of the engineers, tankers, and infantry beyond the Kall Trail that had been cut by the Germans? Should Task Force Davis (the 109th Infantry) try to break through to them? Or should he order a general withdrawal across the Kall?

Davis told him that the Trail was definitely lost to the 28th. "Fire is keeping up and is right across it and below it . . . It comes from every direction."

Cota frowned. "I recommend that we pull in," he said, knowing that his decision was not going to be liked at all at higher headquarters.

"I concur," Davis agreed.

"Can I tell General Hodges that?" Cota asked warily.

"You can tell him that," Davis snapped impatiently.[1] He knew the true situation of the Division. Time was running out if they were going to save it from extermination.

But the Top Brass were not prepared, at first, to let Cota withdraw. Corps Commander Gerow still believed that something could be salvaged from the mess. He told Cota to "get the rest of your outfit back in some area and get them reconstituted."[2] Once that was done, Gerow thought the 28th, with support from a combat command of the 5th Armored Division, would be able to attack and recapture lost ground.

Again Cota wavered, obviously trying to please his superior, even when the situation was so desperate. He told Gerow that his division would be combat-ready "in about three days if replacements come through satisfactorily."[3] This, of course, was absolute nonsense. When the replacements in the thousands did come flooding in later, it still took three long *months* to make the shattered 28th combat-ready once more!

In the end, at a personal confrontation with Hodges, the First Army commander, at his command post in Rott, the latter gave Cota permission to withdraw over the Kall. But he *did* demand his pound of flesh. There would be no withdrawal in the Vossenack sector. In addition, Cota was to supply troops to the Fourth's 12th Regiment to help them with an alternate attack on the township of Hurtgen. Finally, Cota was to lend one regiment to the 5th Armored for an assault on Monschau. By now Cota should have protested, perhaps even threatened to resign. He did nothing of the sort. The general who felt his men had "obligations" obviously did not think he had any to them. The battered 28th was going to suffer and bleed another week.

On Wednesday, November 8, in a drenching rainstorm, the haggard, battle-worn survivors of the 112th and 110th Infantries, plus engineers and tankers who had supported them so loyally, began their withdrawal to the Kall. As darkness fell, every man was ordered to strip down to absolute essentials. All remaining equipment, including the three surviving tanks, was to be wrecked as silently as possible. The Germans were not to know that the Americans were retreating.

As the covering artillery began to thunder, the men slung greatcoats between poles to fashion litters and makeshift stretchers that would be used for taking the many wounded down the Trail. Then the last of the jeeps were destroyed and a tank rolled into place to serve as a rough-and-ready roadblock at the entrance to the Trail. The retreat could commence.

They were a pathetic lot: some 350 men with twenty walking wounded and thirty litter cases, moving off in small groups to avoid bunching, with Colonel Nelson leading and Colonel Ripple bringing up the rear. They set off, each man placing a hand on the preceding man's shoulder; the going was tough. In the van

Colonel Nelson had to proceed with his head lowered, using his helmet as a shield to prevent his eyes being gouged out by the branches of the shattered trees that blocked the Trail. Every now and again he paused to look up to see where they were going.

Somewhere Colonel Nelson had lost his compass. Now he kept his direction simply by instinct. Once he led his party into an open space that in the darkness he took for a lake. Hesitantly he stepped into the water, only to find that it was the glow of the night sky filtering through the trees. It was about then that the enemy began to mortar the rear of the long, miserable column. The men broke in panic, fleeing into the trees and abandoning their wounded, save for those being carried on the makeshift litters.

So Colonel Nelson found himself leading only a handful of men, while Colonel Ripple to the rear managed to collect eighty and continue the downward descent to the River Kall. Another party of fifty was led by the intrepid General Fleig and his C.O., Captain Hostrup. Somehow all of them managed to get through, although the litter-bearers were stopped and searched by the Germans before being allowed to continue.

Behind them on the three heights that had cost so many young American lives, they left scattered bunches of soldiers, many of whom were badly wounded, while others had not been notified that the Division was pulling out beyond the Kall. Some of these wounded were later allowed out under a flag of truce and escorted to their own lines by the Germans.

Others fought on to the very last. In one case, the Germans sent a captured clergyman, Chaplain Madden, to the positions held on the Kall Trail by what was left of the 109th Regiment's 3rd Battalion to ask the hard-pressed infantry to surrender. Twice the men of the 3rd refused. In the end the Germans themselves asked for a truce to collect their own wounded lying in the trees between the two positions. During the lull in the fighting the Americans succeeded in evacuating their own sorely hit men. Then they fought on.

*   *   *

But Cota now had to pay the promised price for the privilege of being able to withdraw his men over the River Kall. Colonel Seely's two mutilated battalions of the 110th Infantry were hastily filled out with five hundred reinforcements. They were brought up in batches and broken up into twenties and tens to be assigned to platoons and companies in which they would die before they knew the names of their commanders. But even the five hundred could not completely fill the gaps in the battered battalions.

In Company C of the 1st Battalion, for example, there was only one officer, three noncoms, and nineteen exhausted enlisted men left when Seely's Regiment was alerted for action. Yet despite their fatigue and battle-weariness, "not one of the men offered any bitches or complaints," their company commander remembered, as they were ordered to move out once again.[4]

Their mission was to support the drive of the 4th Division's 12th Infantry Regiment in its attack into the so-called Monschau Corridor. The 1st Battalion of the 110th was to assault due north from Vossenack and seize some woods overlooking the township of Hurtgen. It was a tall order for the weary vets and the hundreds of raw replacements who were not briefed at all on what was expected of them because of lack of time. The weather didn't help either. It had turned freezingly cold with snow. Indeed, it had become so cold that two signalers were found frozen to death while repairing a wire on the morning of the attack!

But like cattle being led to the slaughter, the men of the 110th went into battle again, slogging through the knee-deep snow as the guns rumbled and thundered and the machine guns rattled. It was the last gasp of the dying regiment. Their main objective that first day was the line of pillboxes outside the village of Raffelsbrand.

Almost immediately they ran into trouble as they assaulted the bunkers, which were already spitting vicious fire at the attackers. One noncom recalls, "forging ahead against grenades, small arms fire, mortar rounds, and machine guns."[5] After losing several men, including an officer who was the platoon leader, the

American platoon succeeded in capturing the pillbox. Two hours later, however, they were back there, cowering behind its thick walls as the Germans counterattacked—and now they were down to exactly five men and the NCO.

It was the same everywhere. For five terrible days Colonel Seely's men attempted to break through the pillbox line at Raffelsbrand without success, and suffering tremendous casualties. By the time General Davis, who had come up front yet again to see what was happening, ordered the attack to end, Seely's 1st Battalion numbered 57 men left out of a normal strength of 870.

Col. James Luckett's 12th Infantry of the 4th Division, fighting with them, fared little better. They had, because of the crisis in the 28th, been flung into action without the slightest briefing. For three days they tried to make headway. On the fourth they were fighting for their very lives. Colonel Luckett hadn't liked Cota's plan right from the start. Now he protested, after three days of heavy casualties, that he wasn't getting anywhere. He requested Cota to give him further instructions. Bluntly Cota informed him to use "fire and movement" and continue the attack "at all costs." Reluctantly, Luckett accepted the order. It would cost him not only the lives of five hundred of his men, but also his command.

That day the frightening, big tanks of the 116th Panzer Division attacked the 12th Infantry. The Greyhounds caught the American infantry by surprise. Two companies were surrounded. Desperately Luckett formed a final stop line to the rear. Another two companies were surrounded, and casualties, as always in the *Hurtgenwald,* started to mount rapidly again. By dark on November 10, the luckless 12th Infantry was split into five isolated groups.

Escaping from one such pocket was Colonel Sibert, accompanied by some prisoners (who were helping him to guide a blinded young American) plus 12 wounded and six other unwounded men of the 12th. "Luck was not with us," he recalled after the war. "We flushed three Krauts out of a hole right on our path. We started them across a firebreak, a tank fired at us down the firebreak. The prisoners started to run, the patrolmen opened up on them with their tommy guns and the three Krauts were kaputt. Our men went so far as to run over and pump lead into their heads to stop their yelling. It made me a little sick."[6] Thereafter there was a lot of confused fighting at close quarters in the woods, and the colonel found himself alone with the blind soldier and the German prisoner who was guiding the latter. Suddenly "a shot rang out and the Kraut dropped down screaming. The blinded man yelled for me and I reached over and pulled him to me, but he stumbled. As he fell in my arms, two slugs were pumped into his back and he was dead. I took off across the firebreak, tripped, lost my helmet, and got shot as I went down. My tail was on fire! I grabbed my hat, set a new record for the 440 and dove back into my old hole out of breath."[7] Colonel Sibert's experience was typical of many that terrible day. For Luckett, his command divided in two, most of his advance positions surrounded, there seemed only one solution for his problem. Withdrawal! Under the cover of mist, which hung low across the damp snow, those of the 12th Infantry who could be reached started to pull out.

Colonel Sibert was one of the fortunate ones. The night before, "we really prayed. In the morning we found that God had answered all our prayers. It snowed during the night and the whole area was covered with fog—perfect for getting out."[8]

In a long cautious line, the tired infantry set out, taking their wounded with them, sneaking through the circle of German troops silently. The supply line that they used was littered with dead, Sibert recalled after the war. "The men that came out with me were so damned tired they stepped on the bodies—they were too tired to step over."[9]

The 12th Infantry Regiment was now burnt out. It had lost 1,600 men in five days of combat—half its strength. In the 1st Battalion alone the effective fighting strength of the three rifle companies totaled exactly 63 men and four officers. Only one medic was left alive in the whole battalion.

The men were hollow-eyed, drawn, trembling like ancient

alcoholics with a bad case of the DTs, and staggered back to the rear on legs that seemed made of soft rubber. Watching the survivors limping back that day, Army Commander General Hodges turned and murmured softly to one of his staff. "I wish everybody could see them."[10] But the man who succeeded in bringing them out received no mercy from the army commander. Hodges must have believed like Napoleon that there are "no bad soldiers, just bad officers." Colonel Luckett was immediately relieved of his command, just as Colonel Peterson before him. But the unfortunate Colonel Luckett would not be the last regimental commander to be relieved in that terrible fighting in the Hurtgen. There would be others. Even generals were fired in the end.

However, General Cota didn't get fired, despite the disaster that had been inflicted on the 28th Infantry Division. Perhaps Hodges and Gerow were aware of the fact that they were just as guilty as he was. On the same day that the 12th Infantry was withdrawn, 33 men of the 28th Division's First Battalion (the 109th Infantry) slipped exhausted into their own lines. They were the last survivors of a company that had been surrounded for five bitter days. Without drink or food, and with only the ammunition they carried on their own person, in snow and sleet, fighting from foxholes knee-deep in mud, they had battled against everything the Germans had been able to throw at them. They were also the last men of the shattered 28th Division to see combat in the Hurtgen.

The second attack on Schmidt had become the most costly American division-strength attack in the whole of World War II. In one regiment alone, the 112th Infantry, there had been 232 men captured, 431 missing, 719 wounded, 167 killed, and 544 nonbattle casualties, making a total of 2,093 out of the original 3,000 men who had gone into action two weeks before. For the Division as a whole, the losses were estimated at 6,184 casualties, a bloodletting of some 45 percent of the 28th's original strength. In reality, the percentage among the rifle companies, which bore the brunt of the fighting, was almost twice this figure. As the official U.S. history of the battle states: "[it] represented a major repulse to American arms."[11]

Still the Top Brass had not had enough of the Green Hell. The Hurtgen Forest exercised a seemingly fatal fascination for them. The prestige of the U.S. Army was at stake. Pointless as the battle was, they were not going to allow the American Army to be beaten there by the Germans, although it was clear to them, as General Gavin of the Airborne phrased it later, that the Hurtgen Battle had become "our Paschendale."* Now they were going to assault it with elements of two armored divisions, the 3rd and the 5th, a Ranger battalion, the 2nd Rangers, and infantry from the 9th (in the form of the 47th Infantry Division), 1st, 4th, and 8th Infantry Divisions, a grand total of 100,000 young Americans. This time they'd bulldoze their way through the damned Forest by sheer weight of numbers.

---

* The terrible slaughter of British troops at the place of that name on the western front in 1917.

8

In November 1944, the woman who was destined to become Ernest Hemingway's fourth and last wife, Mary Welsh, was staying at the Ritz Hotel in Paris, using it as a base for her war reporting and for her affair with Papa Hemingway. Both Mary Welsh and Hemingway, the writer-cum-war correspondent, were still married.

It was a good time for war correspondents, who were now being classified under that new fashionable title as "Very Important People." There were two-bottle lunches, excellent black-market food, unlimited supplies of captured German booze, and Marlene Dietrich in the same hotel, prepared to tell anyone who would listen that the gastronomic spelling of her name was "diet-rich."

There was always a party going on somewhere in the place, and when Papa wasn't singing his favorite French ditty, "Après la guerre finie," he might be found taking potshots at lavatory bowls with his .45 and flooding his room. It was whoopee in "gay Paree" all the time in those days.

It was about this time, just before the front in the Hurtgen flared up yet again, that Papa invited the officers of his favorite division to join him at the Ritz on a short leave. They were Colonel Lanham, commander of the 4th Division's 22nd Regiment, and his three battalion commanders, all "well-groomed, hair and hands and boots cleaned and polished," as Mary Welsh recalled after the war.

The champagne flowed, "the Hotel Ritz never ran out of it," and to Mary Welsh's dismay she began to notice that these originally so well-behaved young colonels of the infantry were starting to get drunk. By the time all of them went downstairs to eat in the presence of Mary's boss and co-owner of the *Time-Life* Group, Clare Boothe Luce, who was dining with an Air Force officer, "eyes were becoming a little bit glazed and speech a bit slurred."[1]

To her alarm one of the infantry colonels, who had been listening to Mrs. Luce praising the work of the Air Force before mentioning patronizingly that the infantry must be of some use, suddenly turned and said thickly, "You're darned right, babe. And don't you put your mouth on it!"

Mrs. Luce, all sweetness and light and still unaware with whom she was dealing, suggested, "The infantry—they pinpoint the advance, don't they?"

"Pinpoint!" the colonel exploded. "Sweet Jesus, you ought to read a book, you dumb broad!"

Mary fled, fearing the worst for her job. A little later Papa knocked at her door just as she had finished cleaning up where one of his friends had thrown up in the bathroom. She let him in reluctantly and he prowled around, "silently, glumly." Finally she said, "Well, I have to go to bed now. I'm tired, if you'll excuse me."

"You insulted my friends!" Hemingway blurted out abruptly. "All evening and without cease you insulted my friends! You could not have behaved more horribly."

That did it. Half drunk herself, Marsh Welsh snapped, "Your friends are drunks and slobs! They threw up all over my bathroom. They probably lost me my job. They drove Marlene away. They may be heroes in Germany, but they stink, stink, stink! But I DID NOT INSULT your boorish friends!"

Hemingway never did like women who talked back. He didn't hesitate one instant. He promptly punched her on the jaw.

Before the subsequent row finally petered out, Mary told her lover, who left in a huff, "Knock my head off, you coward. Why don't you knock my head off? Show what a big strong coward you are. Take it to the Twenty-second on a platter. Show 'em you won't let me insult 'em, you bully."[2]

Well, Papa refused to take her up on her offer. The rumors started to flood Paris that a great new offensive was soon to start in the Hurtgen, and that Hemingway's favorite, the 4th, was going to take part in it. Hemingway decided he would go up to the 22nd. Out of the experience would come the only novel that Papa would write about World War II.*

Thus, it was on the afternoon of November 15, 1944, one day before the great offensive would start, that Col. Tom Kenan looked out of his CP, a deep hole in a small clearing in the Hurtgen, to find a civilian staring down at him. His bulk, already large, was accentuated by the white German camouflage combat jacket the bespectacled civilian was wearing. Under his arm he carried a tommy gun, something correspondents certainly weren't authorized to carry.

"Hemingway," the newcomer introduced himself. "Ernest Hemorrhoid, the poor man's Ernie Pyle."[3]

All that night he talked and drank in Colonel Lanham's trailer, equipped with a German helmet, tastefully decorated, and used as a chamber pot. Lanham, the C.O. of the 22nd Infantry, was gloomy. He told Papa he didn't think he would survive the coming battle. Hemingway exploded. He told the thin, wiry Regular Army man that he was sick "of all this shit" about premonitions. The "Great Ernie Pyle," a man he didn't like, was always running off at the mouth about them. All the same Hemingway knocked on wood. Whatever he might say to the contrary, Hemingway was a superstitious man. Lanham would be right, too. Before this fourth push in the Hurtgen was over, virtually all of Lanham's "magnificent command," as he called it, would have vanished in the Death Factory. Soon the slaughter would commence once more.

Hodges's plan envisaged the use of two whole corps, Collins's VIIth and Gerow's Vth, for the attack. To the north in Lightning

---

* There was another young novelist present up there that winter, J. D. Salinger, but as far as is known that secretive man never wrote anything about his experiences there. The novel was *Over the River and Into the Trees.*

Joe's sector, America's premier infantry division, the Big Red One, with part of the 3rd Armored Division and the 47th Infantry Regiment from the 9th Division under command, would attack in three spots, with its right wing attacking through the Hurtgen. Here, too, the newly arrived 104th Infantry Division was wedged into the line so that the 1st and 3rd Divisions could narrow their front for the attack.

Farther south, Tubby Barton's 4th Division would attack directly into the Forest itself, followed by General Stroh's 8th Infantry Division and a combat command of the 5th Armored Division. It was a massive force attacking on a front of some thirty miles and supported by the whole weight of the Allied Air Force—providing the weather played ball.

But obstinately the weather refused to brighten. Each day dawned gray and raining. The great attack was postponed twice while a weary Army Group Commander Bradley fumed at his headquarters in far-off Namur, Belgium. As Bradley wrote at the time, "This can end the war—with air we can push through to the Rhine in a matter of days."[4] But still it rained and rained.

In her tent behind the lines, the first American woman soldier to be killed in Germany in World War II listened "to the steady even breathing of the other three nurses in the tent and thinking about some of the things we had discussed during the day. The rain is beating down on the tent with a torrential force. The wind is on a mad rampage."[5] Then, in the middle of the night, with the aid of her flashlight, she wrote a letter of appreciation to the *Stars and Stripes*. The frontline nurse, Second Lieutenant Slanger, wrote: "We have learned a great deal about our American soldier and the stuff he is made of. The wounded do not cry . . . The patience and courage they show, the courage and fortitude they have is sometimes awesome to behold. It is we who are proud to be here . . . It is a privilege to be able to receive you and a great distinction to see you open your eyes and with that swell American grin say, 'Hi-ya, babe!' "[6] But Lieutenant Slanger would never see the new streams of wounded soon to come from the Hurtgen. She'd be killed by a German shell before that letter was even published: another Army nurse KIA, joining those already killed in action in North Africa, Salerno, and Anzio.

By November 14, 1944, the Top Brass was getting desperate, as it continued to rain and the roads at the front disappeared in a sea of mud. Gen. Pete Quesada, the airman, swore grimly, "Our airplanes will be there with them if we have to crash land every one of them in a field!"[7] Hodges kept his opinion to himself, not commenting on the airman's remark, but the strain was beginning to tell. November 15 came. Still it rained and remained too overcast for the planes to fly the support operation.

Then, on the morning of the sixteenth, Hodges came down to breakfast at his HQ in Spa's Hotel Britannique, where a quarter of a century before German Field Marshal Hindenburg had told his kaiser there was no hope for Imperial Germany. With him was his bad-tempered chief of staff, General Kean. For once Kean's normal heavy sober mien was replaced by a bright grin. Hodges was grinning too. The staff sensed that there was something in the air.

Outside they could see through the former hotel's tall windows that the clouds had begun to draw. Suddenly the sun appeared. "Look at that ball of fire," Hodges exclaimed, "that's the sun!"

Around him his staff officers looked and laughed.

But as always Hodges, the plodding stolid infantryman, was cautious. "Don't look at it too hard," he warned. "You'll wear it out and chase it away."[8]

Still, as one who was present at that breakfast so long ago recalled, "But we couldn't keep our eyes off it . . . This was the sun and the sun spelt [sic] a chance. God, how pleased we were to see the sun!"[9]

The great attack, which might "end the war," could start. But none of those happy confident staff officers present at that breakfast could imagine, even in their wildest dreams, that within six short weeks, all of them would be fleeing Spa for their lives, with the point of the SS armored column only a matter of miles away.

* * *

At 11:30 that great morning, the first of the heavy bombers appeared over the battlefield: gleaming silver ships of the U.S. 8th Air Force based in England. A total of 1,191 bombers flew over the heads of the excited infantry to drop more than four thousand tons of fragmentation bombs on the towns to the rear of the Hurtgen Forest. Not to be outdone, Bomber Harris's boys of the RAF dropped more than five and a half thousand tons from 1,188 planes on the towns of Duren, Julich, and Heinsberg. Now, as the artillery started to thunder, the 9th Air Force bombers roared in, escorted by a thousand fighters. Behind them, the fast fighter-bombers of the TAC Air Forces came zooming in, bombing and machine-gunning, looking for targets of opportunity on the battlefield itself, cheered on by the excited, happy footsloggers. Surely, they told themselves, not a single Kraut could survive a pulverizing like that? How wrong they were. The German "stubble-hoppers" (as the infantry called themselves cynically) were well dug in—and waiting.

Now on this dry Thursday, with the horizon to the east a mass of smoke and flame where the bombers had carried out their lethal handiwork, the infantry started to move out: a long straggling line of young men in khaki coming out of their holes and hiding places along the thirty-mile front, apprehensive, confident, tense, relaxed, hopeful, fearful. Thousands upon thousands of them moved out, skinny young bodies leaning slightly forward, weapons at the ready in hands that were sticky with sweat, every sense acute, abruptly aware of the drama of the life they led. They knew, without a shadow of a doubt, that they were permitted to kill—and could be killed themselves. Suddenly they realized that their young lives could be predictably short, that someone up there, whom they would never see probably, was out to murder them. As soon as they stepped out of their cover, they became targets: simply anonymous human animals to be shot and killed without a second thought being given to the matter. German and American, the Mark of Cain was on them all.

Hemingway, who the night before had been sick of premonitions, sensed that death hung over them all. As he visited with Colonel Lanham, the 1st Battalion was preparing to move off into the Forest together with its sister regiment, the 8th. They met the "little gray sort of man" who was commanding the Battalion. Later Colonel Lanham told Hemingway he wasn't too happy with the officer; he might have to relieve him.

Hemingway shook his head. "Buck, you won't ever have to relieve him."

Lanham bristled. "Why?" he demanded.

"He won't make it," Hemingway answered. "He stinks of death!"

Ten minutes later, when they had just reached the 22nd Regiment's CP, the executive officer came running out. He saluted and said excitedly, "Colonel, the major [in command of the 1st Battalion] has just been killed. Who takes the First Battalion?"

Lanham looked at Papa and said, "How the hell did you know that?"[10]

Hemingway shrugged.

Now the killing started in earnest everywhere as the German machine guns rattled and their mortars began to cut great holes in the attackers. Up front, as a forward observer for the 4th's artillery, Elliott Johnson met a fellow observer running down the road after he and two companions had been hit by white phosphorus. The other two men had been burned alive before his eyes. Now his fellow observer was a broken man. "He was sobbing and falling into my arms. He kept saying, *'No more killing, no more killing, no more killing!'* "[11]

In the confused mess of the shattered trees, strange things happened as the men refused to kill each other, although they were enemies. Another forward observer with the 4th was urinating when he spotted a "German boy standing not five feet away behind a tree . . . I'm holding my organ in my hand as I turned toward him. My friends never let me forget it. I pointed my gun at him. I sat him down, took his shoes off and he handed me his gun."[12]

But there was terrible brutality in the woods, too, as the

intensity of the attack mounted, with shooting and killing going on all the time with relentless savagery. "One time," Elliott Johnson recalled after the war, "I was sent back to get a truckload of replacements, young boys. They hadn't the benefit of the long training we had in the States. I told them, 'If you hear anything coming in and if I tell you to jump, do exactly what I do.' We had to be alert for interdiction fire, artillery shells lobbed at us at an intersection. We came near this intersection and I heard one in the distance going *chok*. I told the guys, 'Get out of here!' I dove over the rail of the truck into the gutter beside the road. Out of the twenty or twenty-five boys I picked up that day, ten were dead."[13]

There was deliberate savagery in the woods too. One soldier of the 4th stood on a mine and blew off his foot. It was one of those wounds in which the arteries and veins are forced upward by the blast so that they are sealed in a way and the bleeding is not so severe.

So the wounded man lay conscious in a clearing, unable to bind his own wounds or to walk. All day the medics tried to reach him in full view of the Germans who could see the Red Cross on their helmets, but always they were fired upon. One of the aidmen was finally hit, and that stopped any further attempts till after dark.

In the meantime, the Germans had crawled out to the wounded man, stolen his combat jacket and cigarettes, and then had deliberately booby-trapped the helpless soldier. They had fixed a spring-loaded explosive charge under his back. Anyone lifting the man would kill not only him, but the rescuer.

After being out in the cold and wet for *seventy* hours, help finally came to the stricken man, who had lain conscious all the time; he had known what would happen to him and the others if he blacked out. With the charge beneath him, he quietly told the medics what to do. They cut the wires of the booby trap and carried him away. He lived.

Men went crazy in the Forest. An MP, who had been brought in with a gaping red wound where his testicles had once been, told the medics stoically, "OK, Doc, I can take it." Another man who was advancing firing a tommy gun had one of his arms blown off, but still he kept on moving and firing until he disintegrated in a direct hit from a mortar.

In the 104th Infantry Division's sector "a short gray guy with very pale gray eyes" was brought into an aid station in the woods and sat down. "His right arm had been severed below the elbow and the stump of his arm leaked blood," as one of the medics recorded later. Finally the harassed, overworked surgeon had a chance to look at the wound. Quite calmly the wounded man, a short gray guy, said, "Say, Doc, would you mind cutting this off. It's not doing me much good anymore. So I cut the two ligaments that were holding his lower arm and hand . . . One of our medics hid the hand under a rug so the others wouldn't see it."[14]

In the Hurtgen, medics, even chaplains, were ruthlessly shot by the enemy. Some reacted to the relentless terrible savagery of the battle by running wild. First Lt. Bernard Ray of the Fourth's 8th Infantry Regiment volunteered to blast a way through a line of barbed wire that was holding up the whole regiment. With slugs ripping the air just above his head, he crawled to the wire dragging a Bangalore torpedo behind him. To the surprise of the men watching, he made it, in spite of the hail of fire.

Suddenly he screamed shrilly as a mortar bomb exploded close by in a sheet of angry orange flame. His body was riddled and ripped by shell fragments so that he appeared to be bleeding everywhere.

Perhaps the young officer thought he was dying, or perhaps he just went mad. No one ever found out. For now Bernard Ray pulled a detonator cap from his pocket, attached it to the primer cord already wrapped around his poor shattered body and then fitted the primer cord to the Bangalore torpedo filled with high explosive.

Quite calmly and deliberately, he set off the detonator.

As the wire was ripped apart, his body flew into the air like that of a rag doll. Despite Ray's brave action, the 8th still couldn't get through that damned wire.

Some simply couldn't take any more. They fled the line, broken men with crazy, demented eyes, voices out of control and not making much sense. The medics, so highly regarded among the infantry, even abandoned their wounded. The incessant shelling and constant danger were just too much for them. As one doctor said, "It takes a lot of courage to be a litter-bearer and more courage to be an aid man. An infantryman has a hole and he stays in it, but when there's a casualty, the aid man has to leave what little protection he has and get out into the open. A mortar shell or 88 doesn't recognize the Red Cross on a helmet."[15]

After the same doctor had cut off the arm of the "short gray guy," he was confronted by a series of his own medics who had all been shot trying to bring in wounded men. He patched them up the best he could, promised them the nurses in the field hospitals were pretty and took a slug of gin and juice to steady his own nerves. It was just then that "a kid stumbled into the room crying, and they sat him down in a chair. He wore a Red Cross brassard. S. Sgt. John Green tried to calm him down, but it was no use for the moment. He burst out with a stream of words: "Noise, too much noise, all noise, too much noise."[16] They gave him a shot to put him out.

He was followed almost immediately by yet another one, who "lay on his belly and held his ears," as if to drown the noise of the guns, the shrieks, and moans of the wounded. Chaplain Father Quinn, the bespectacled Roman Catholic priest who had already won the Silver Star, said sorrowfully, "There is a man who *was* tough. But he's been through a lot in the last two days."[17] Then the chaplain went out to help pick up the exhausted man's buddies who still lay out there in that hell, wounded and unattended. One day later the Protestant chaplain doing the same self-imposed task was shot dead by a sniper.

But the German defenders were suffering terribly as well. In the diary taken from the body of one German medic, who had studied to be a doctor for one year, two entries were found. The one read: "It's Sunday. My God today is Sunday! With dawn the edge of our forest received a barrage. The earth trembles. The concussion takes our breath. Two wounded are brought to my hole, one with both hands shot off. I am considering whether to cut off the rest of the arm. I'll leave it on. How brave these two are. I hope to God that all this is not in vain."

Two days later there was another entry. "Last night was pretty bad. We hardly got any sleep and in the morning the artillery was worse than ever. I can hardly stand it and the planes are here again. Once more the quiet before the storm. Then suddenly tanks and then hordes of *Amis* are breaking out of the forest. Murderous fire meets him, but he doesn't take cover any more. We shoot until the barrels sizzle and finally he is stopped again.

"We are glad to think that the worst is past when suddenly he breaks through on our left. Hand grenades are bursting, but we cannot hold them any longer. There are only five of us. We have got to go back. Already we can see brown figures through the trees. As they get to within seventy paces, I turn around and walk away very calmly with my hands in my pockets. They are not even shooting at me, perhaps on account of the red cross on my back."[18]

In the German Army they applied draconian measures to those who lost their nerve and ran away. There was no such thing as "combat fatigue" in the *Wehrmacht*. Over ten thousand "cowards" and deserters were shot in the German Army during World War II. Others who offered to go back into the line were formed into special punishment battalions—the 333rd and 999th Battalions—that were basically suicide outfits and given what the Germans called cynically "Ascension Day Missions" (that is, missions going only one way—to heaven). It was rare that anyone ever returned from those two battalions.

But America, being a democracy with a powerful media back home looking after the interests of the "average Joe," could not apply such stringent measures, save in the case of Eddie Slovik. Everywhere now, the fighting grew and grew in intensity and the rear hospitals at Eupen, Liège, Verviers, etc., overflowed with wounded, and the combat exhaustion cases ran into the hundreds and thousands. The individual divisional organizations had to set up special units to deal with the latter kind of casualty.

The standard treatment for a man suffering from combat exhaustion was to knock him out with drugs. He was pumped so full of sodium amytal that he slept constantly for three days, only hauled out of his cot to be taken to the latrine. Frequently, the casualty was fed saline intravenous injections to overcome the problem of feeding him normally. During this period, as one chaplain who tried to comfort these shocked men recalled, "his subconscious condition was horrible to behold and he lived over and over again his most terrifying events of combat."[19]

When the man awoke he usually looked years older: hollow-eyed, cheeks drawn, trembling as if suffering from the DTs. The shock of combat and then the powerful drugs had been tremendous. First he was taken to the showers and allowed to soak in scalding hot water for as long as he liked. Then he would be fed good, hot, plentiful food—*if* he would eat.

"It was pitiful to observe the genuine fatigue cases in the tent wards of the rest center," one observer, Chaplain Dr. William Boice, recalled after the war. "It was time for chow and hot chow was being served. During the serving an artillery observation plane flew overhead. The effect was amazing and pitiful. One soldier poured a cup of hot coffee over his head. Another turned his mess kit of C rations over his lap. Still a third made an effort to dive in the latrine and had to be forcibly restrained . . . The wards with shattered and missing legs and arms were bad, but the hospitals with vacant and missing minds were worse."[20]

Of course, there were plenty of "goldbrickers" who knew that the medical tag on their dirty uniform reading "Combat Fatigue" meant transfer to the rear, away from the danger. Some men made the switch from line to rear hospital and rest center three and four times. The doctors had no choice unless the man was really proved mentally unstable. But in the end it never worked. The men who wouldn't fight simply wouldn't fight; they were an extra load and a danger to their comrades who would.

And those who were prepared to fight were getting fewer and fewer. In the 22nd and 8th Infantry Regiments of the 4th

Division fighting now in depths of the Hurtgen, battalion commanders and company commanders came and went, killed or wounded in a matter of days, even hours. Their soldiers fared little better. "You can't see," a T5g. George Morgan of the 22nd told a correspondent. "You can't get fields of fire. Artillery slashed the trees like a scythe. Everything is tangled. You can scarcely walk. Everybody is cold and wet and the mixture of cold rain and sleet keeps falling. Then we attack again and soon there is only a handful of the old men left."[21]

While these survivors ("old heads," even if they were barely out of their teens) were prepared to fight on whatever the conditions, they were becoming increasingly critical of the whole purpose of the operation. *Life* correspondent William Walton watched a confrontation between Col. Buck Lanham and one of his captains, a stocky young man called "Swede." The previous night Swede had apparently unwittingly given Lanham a piece of his mind over the phone about the mess the battle had become. Swede now admitted he hadn't known he had been speaking to the regimental commander.

"That's all right, Swede," Lanham said. "I know how it is when you see a lot of your friends knocked off. But you've got to treat your superior officers with more respect."

Swede was silent for a moment. Then he said, "Colonel, sir, I don't care if you break me for it. I meant what I said last night, even though I didn't know it was you on the line. That little patch of woods we're fighting for ain't any good to anybody. No good to the Germans. No good for us. It's the bloodiest damn ground in all Europe and you make me keep fighting for it. That ain't right."

Now it was Colonel Lanham's turn to be silent and pensive. Walton watched them, "The two men sitting across the table looking at one another in silence. The colonel, slight of build, keen-faced and intense. The blond captain, bulky, mud-splattered and a two-day growth of beard on his wide face, a face designed for grinning, but dead serious now and pale with fatigue."

Finally Lanham spoke. "There's nothing in the world," he said deliberately, "that I'd like to do better than tell all you boys to call it off and go home. You know that, Swede. But it can't be done. The only way we can get this thing over is by killing Krauts. To kill them you've got to get to them."

Swede grunted.

"Look here at the map," Lanham continued. "You know they're dug in all through this woods you're talking about. Once we've got those two hills then we'll be able to pour so much stuff into that patch of woods that not a Kraut will be left. Then we can push on to where the woods end and fight in daylight like little gentlemen again. Wherever there are Krauts we've got to kill 'em. I know they've killed lots of our boys in that patch but we've killed even more of them and that's what counts . . . Pour yourself a slug of good Heinie cognac," the slight colonel concluded his little lecture on the philosophy of total war.[22] Numbly Swede did so as the phone rang to announce they were attacking yet again.

9

Wherever there are Krauts, we've got to kill 'em!" seemed to be the prevailing military philosophy throughout the First Army that horrific November. The Top Brass pushed the whole length of the line, throwing in unit after unit, infantry and armor, in a frantic attempt to steamroller the stubborn Germans.

Field Marshal Model, masterminding the defense from his hunting lodge not far from the Hurtgen battlefield, was not slow to use reserve formations too. Although the *Wehrmacht* was carefully husbanding its resources for the great surprise attack in the Ardennes, which was only a month off, he somehow obtained fresh units for his own sagging front. Doggedly he launched counterattack after counterattack. With savage determination his "greenbeaks," the teenage recruits of the new *Volksgrenadier** divisions, stiffened by a few "old hares" and supported by a handful of tanks and self-propelled guns, fought back.

They made the despised *Amis* pay a bitter price for every yard of ground gained, and by the second and third day of the great offensive gains were being measured in yards. Now all hopes of making a swift and clean breakthrough to the Rhine had vanished into the mud and the thick forest. "We shall be lucky to reach the Rhine by the first of December, very lucky indeed," they were now saying dolefully at Hodges's HQ.[1] As it turns out, they would not reach the Rhine *until March 6, 1945!*

The 26th Infantry, under the command of General Huebner's 1st Division, was *inching* forward through the Forest on the

---

* People's Grenadiers.

113

second day of the great attack. More infantry was thrown in, but after two days of severe fighting the 26th had penetrated to a depth of less than one mile. As the rain and sleet set in once more and Colonel Seitz, the 26th's C.O., was preparing to commit his final battalion, the Germans counterattacked.

They struck the already weary, understrength lead battalion, commanded by Colonel Daniel, in full force. But the men of the Big Red One didn't break. The 1st (which was so proud of its reputation that other soldiers sneered, "There's the Big Red One—and ten million replacements in the U.S. Army!") slogged it out in the shattered trees. The fourth day of the battle, Daniel's battalion performed many deeds of heroism, but none braver than those of Francis McGraw, a private soldier manning a machine gun.

Under heavy artillery fire, he kept firing his machine gun at the German infantry filtering out of the shattered trees until he brought them to a puzzled, undecided halt. Then they tried to take him out with one of their own machine guns. Almost as if to show his contempt for them and carried away, too, by the crazy atavistic illogic of battle, Pfc McGraw stood upright in full view of the enemy and blasted away at them once more.

The blast of a near miss from a German *panzerfaust* bowled him off his feet and he dropped the glowing machine gun. Somehow he got it back into action and kept on firing till it stuttered to a stop. He had run out of ammunition! There, McGraw took up the one-sided battle with his carbine. He shot one German dead and then wounded another. But the odds were impossible. In the end, a burst from a German burp gun ripped his body apart. He was dead before he hit the ground, and would be awarded the Medal of Honor posthumously, one of the 21 awarded to the Big Red One in World War II, most of them also posthumous.

Not far away, its sister regiment, the 16th, was fighting and trying to capture a key height, Hill 232, which had been swamped in the fire from fifteen artillery battalions, firing five thousand shells. When it fell, it was the Germans' turn. They, too, poured a hail of fire onto the blazing summit, killing not only Americans but also their own men who had just become American prisoners.

Later, a Capt. Maxie Zera described the position after the battle in the typical "snappy" prose. "You guys should see that hill! Filled with dead. About two hundred Krauts and something like fifty of our own men . . . Later when the QM detail arrived with the burial wagons . . . a pair of Negroes lugged the *herrenvolk* out feet first. But a third darkie, unimpressed by the scene and lighthearted always, trooped behind the litter, strumming a salvaged guitar and loudly singing 'South of the Border.' "[2]

It seemed now that the battle had lost all purpose, save for that philosophy propounded by Colonel Lanham, "wherever there are Krauts we've got to kill 'em." Fighting alongside the 1st Division, the men of the 47th Infantry Regiment of the battered 9th Division also found themselves pounding away at the Krauts, gaining territory by the foot. For now these Krauts were of a different type than the relatively second-class troops that had decimated the 9th back in October. They were mostly teenagers, like the men of the *Volksgrenadier* divisions admittedly, but they wore the baggy trousers, rimless helmets, and camouflaged tunics of the German 3rd Parachute Division.

Most of them had never even seen a parachute, not to mention ever having been in a plane, but they had absorbed the traditions and fearlessness of those older paratroops who had once dropped on Eben Emael and had taken the island of Crete from the air. From now until the Anglo-Americans finally crossed the Rhine, these young *fallschirmjäger* proved to be a more determined and braver foe than the SS. Indeed, when one senior German paratroop commander and his handful of survivors finally surrendered to the British on the banks of the great river, the local British divisional commander ordered his staff to stand to attention and saluted them for their outstanding bravery.

Still, the *fallschirmjäger* could be killed and forced to surrender, but the price was high. In one case, S. Sgt. James Searles took on *fifty* enemy paras. In the end he killed two and forced forty to surrender. But the butcher's bill was still very costly.

Out of Sergeant Searles's original company of 150 men, only thirty-five men were on their feet when the paras finally surrendered.

Thanksgiving Day 1944 arrived. Still the killing continued. Graham Miller of the *New York Daily News,* who was up front in the heart of the Forest with the 1st Division's 26th Regiment, thought it "was unquestionably the dreariest Thanksgiving Day I've known."[3] It was. It rained and it sleeted. The creeks and rivers overflowed, turning yellow with the local soil. Vehicles scudded all over the place as a few *Luftwaffe* fighter-bombers ventured over the line to machine-gun American positions.

At HQ, Miller was told "Turkey dinner today . . . Turkey for every dough in the outfit."

"Ha, ha, that's a laugh. Now I'll tell one!" said Miller.

But there was, and Miller volunteered to go up with the hot turkey dinner to one of the forward companies, though as the HQ commandant, a Major Peters, said, shaking his head at such foolhardiness, "Some guys don't know enough to stay out of the rain when they can."[4]

Miller's little jaunt to the front was an eye-opener. The men at the sharp end appreciated the hot food well enough. But the Norman Rockwell vision of America with "Mom and turkey with cranberry sauce and all the trimmings" was totally alien to the kind of life they led in the heart of the Hurtgen Forest.

He noted one soldier slithering down a slope in the mud. "Blood had soaked his OD pants. He was using his M-1 for a crutch, the bayonet bent from thrusting into rocks and logs."[5] At another spot he had to stop as the trail was abruptly mortared. There he came across a lone GI bringing in a German prisoner, "wearing no helmet and scrambling through the underbrush as if herding cows in his native North Carolina. . . . He was puzzled when asked if he'd had his share of turkey. Nobody had told him it was a holiday. . . . 'I've seen nothin' but these sour Krauts,' "[6] he told the correspondent before passing miserably on his way.

Finally the correspondent arrived at the Battalion's headquarters, where he discovered the turkey dinner wasn't that important. The Battalion had just lost two companies in the woods. The colonel, who informed him of the sad news, he would next meet guarding Goering at the Nuremberg war trials exactly one year later. "But," as Miller wrote afterwards, "up at the 26th Infantry lines in the Hurtgen, the prospect of standing guard while Goering and the rest heard their fate never occurred. The object was to live until relieved. If you came out alive, you had won."[7]

This was the same thought that motivated Major Freeman that same day when he heard that the cooks were bringing up hot Thanksgiving dinners to his forward positions. He called his battalion commander and told him angrily it would be "murder, plain and simple." He pointed out that once his hungry men congregated around the cooks, the "Jerries would turn all hell loose." The battalion C.O. said there was nothing he could do about it. It was a regimental order.

Freeman persisted. He asked permission to speak to the regimental commander. The full colonel barked, it was up to Division. Somehow or other Freeman managed to get through to divisional headquarters and talked to the commanding general himself. The latter informed the major "in no uncertain terms" that the "men would be fed today."

So they were, and what Freeman feared happened. "Jerry turned all hell loose! Branded in my mind is position after position with men torn to shreds around busted up turkey containers—as many as ten in one place." The sights left an indelible impression on the major. "For many, many years after the war I would go to one of my relations for Thanksgiving dinner and before I could touch a bite, I would get up and go to the backyard and cry like a baby. I passed up a helluva lot of turkey dinners."[8]

As Major Freeman would comment some thirty-five years afterwards, "The Generals had no idea of what the men were up against . . . Someone seemed to think this was a Ft. Benning exercise instead of a penetration of a thickly mined, well fortified dense forest where you were lucky if you could see twenty feet."[9]

But right to the end the generals never understood what their soldiers were suffering and the kind of fighting they had to undertake in the Death Forest. All right, so the fighting regiments suffered appalling casualties. Well, there were always more replacements to fill the gaps in their ranks, weren't there? America was a big country. Surely it could find enough cannon fodder?

Pfc William Cox, part of that cannon fodder, remembers going up across a field littered with shot-up American tanks, "and you could smell the dead inside," past "a dead horse bloated up twice its size and three dead Germans laying in a ditch and two American soldiers laying on the road clutching their rifles." Then it was his turn to pay the butcher's bill and he was lying moaning with pain in the basement of a house with the doctors "cutting off arms and legs and the legs piling up like cordwood."[10]

In particular, the 4th's 22nd Regiment suffered tremendous casualties for advances that were no more than a couple of hundred yards. One lone firebreak, across which a man could have walked in a minute in peacetime, cost Lanham's 22nd the C.O. of the reserve battalion, plus fifty men killed and wounded. And that was just one minor action.

William Walton, the *Life* correspondent, listened in as one of the 22nd's battalion commanders, Major Goforth, talked over the replacement problem with his exec, Captain Henley, in a lantern-lit underground shelter. After a while a weary company commander stumbled in to report: "We're hunting for officers. G Company's only got two officers left. Lost three this afternoon. We can't go on like this, Major."

"Goforth shook his head sadly. 'I know, boy, but where am I going to get them? Division says we can commission any good man right here in the field. But who?' He stared around the circle of dirty, unshaven faces in the hissing white light, the features of the others drained of color like those of drowned men.

" 'There's McDermott,' said Swede.

" 'Can't spare him,' Major Goforth said. 'Practically runs G-2.'

" 'He's the last available sergeant,' Swede said. 'We've already commissioned six.'

" 'Guess we'll have to depend on replacements,' Goforth suggested.

" 'The trouble with replacements,' the Company Commander intervened, 'is that they don't last long enough. Trucks brought up thirty for me this morning. Eighteen were hit before they could get into the line. No percentage in that.'

"Just then the blanket covering the door to the dugout was pushed aside. Three young lieutenants, 'fresh-faced and grave,' entered, saluted and said they were reporting for duty.

" 'There you are, Jack,' Goforth snapped, relieved that particular problem had been solved for the time being. 'Replacements for you. Take 'em with you when you go back.' "[11]

More cannon fodder. They didn't last the day.

After four days of the great attack, Colonel Lanham asked Tubby Barton for twenty-four hours to consolidate, and Barton agreed, even though Corps Commander Gerow was breathing down his neck for results. It was one of the reasons for which he would soon be fired, though officially he was sent back to the States on medical grounds. Tubby Barton felt for his soldiers, and he knew just how badly the 22nd had been hit. Lanham had suffered more than three hundred battle casualties. (This figure doesn't take into account casualties caused by accident and sickness or combat fatigue.) All three battalion commanders, several key staff officers, about half the company commanders, and many important company officers and noncoms had been killed or wounded. Fighting in the Hurtgen was particularly rough on infantry leaders, and Lanham needed "new blood" before he could attack again.

Hurriedly Gerow called up yet another division to go into the Death Factory. This was General Stroh's 8th Infantry Division, which, like the 1st and 4th Divisions, could trace its history way back into the nineteenth century. (Indeed, the 1st's 16th Infantry Regiment was founded in 1798.) It had done well in the fighting

in Brittany and had captured the fortress of Brest, where the
paratroop general who held it, General Ramcke, had told the
assistant divisional commander, General Canham: "I am to surrender to you. Let me see your credentials." It had been a
moment for a prompt reply to the stocky German para's inso-
lence. Canham was equal to the task. He had cocked a thumb to
his riflemen, bearing the golden arrow of the 8th on their shoulders, and snapped, "Right here. Those are my credentials!"[12]

The Division was commanded by Gen. Donald Stroh, who,
like Huebner of the 1st and Allen of the 104th, had seen much
action in Africa and Southern Italy, but he had also been subjected to a traumatic experience that neither of those two generals
had suffered. At the bloody siege of Brest he had seen his own
young son—a pilot with the Air Force—shot out of the sky as he
went in on a dive-bombing attack on the port. Now, as he
ordered his leading regiment, Colonel Jeter's 121st Infantry
Regiment, into the Forest, General Stroh was almost a spent
force.

After a night drive of 172 kilometers through fog and rain, the
121st Regiment finally arrived on the outskirts of the Hurtgen.
They de-trucked in the dark and began marching 11 kilometers
through sleet and ankle-deep mud to their assembly area behind
the 4th's 12th Infantry Regiment. With no time to prepare, the
121st was ordered to be ready to attack three hours before first
light on November 21. Before the 121st lay an experience that
would have been familiar to their predecessors, the 8th Georgia,
which had fought the bloody action of the Devil's Den back at
Gettysburg.

Jeter strung his three battalions out line abreast for the assault,
telling them there were friendly troops on either side. The enemy
was to their front. So they were to go only one way—forward.

One man in Capt. Jack Melton's Company I was to do exactly
that before the enemy stopped him. John W. Minick was a
somewhat reluctant soldier who had arrived in France to join the
121st at the age of 36, a veritable granddaddy among the teenagers and twenty-year-olds of Company I. He was a swarthy,

skinny fellow, 5 feet, 8 inches tall, with a straggly moustache and a worried face. Just before his first action he cried bitterly about the prospect of being killed or having to kill someone else. It seemed to his senior officer, 1st Lt. Stanley Schwartz, that Minick wouldn't make a very good combat soldier.

But the lieutenant had been mistaken. Minick turned out to be a real fighter, winning the Distinguished Service Cross in France. But he *was* a terrible "garrison soldier," as he called it. Twice Melton busted him from sergeant to buck private for hell-raising and for his habit of addressing his C.O., who hailed from Texas, as "cowboy." All the same, as a fellow noncom said afterwards, "He was the only man I ever knew who enjoyed it when the going was the toughest."[13]

Now, as Captain Melton's company crossed the start line just after six o'clock that dark, gray morning, working their way forward through ground mist, Minick was in the lead. For two hundred yards the tense infantry advanced without a single shot being fired at them. Then they bumped into the wire. Almost immediately two machine guns opened up and their firing seemed to be the signal for an artillery and mortar barrage to begin falling on the stalled Americans.

It didn't seem to worry Sergeant Minick. He told his C.O., "Just follow old Minick, Skipper . . . and when I stop, you'd better stop because you ain't going no further."[14]

Melton nodded his understanding. Minick found a breach in the wire and started running for the machine-gun emplacements. Several others followed. They were pinned down almost immediately. Not Minick. He kept on running for the left-hand machine gun, zigzagging wildly, lead stitching up the earth at his flying feet. To the right, Lieutenant Schwartz—who had thought Minick would never make a soldier—and a private named Trusty tackled the other one.

Savagely Minick shot two Germans with his tommy gun before the remaining three of the machine-gun team surrendered. Roughly he ordered his prisoners to guide him through the minefield that was also holding up his company. They were doing so unwillingly when firing broke out. Unwittingly Minick had stumbled on the German defenders' left flank. Minick went to ground as a fierce firefight commenced, red tracer zipping through the air like flights of angry hornets. One after another, he killed twenty Germans single-handedly and took another twenty prisoner. These he ordered to the rear and moved forward yet again.

Now the lone warrior was within thirty yards of the enemy battalion's command post. There was a sudden rattle of gunfire, followed by the high-pitched, hysterical hiss of a Spandau. Sergeant Hays, who wasn't too far away, heard Minick cry wildly: "Come on out . . . Come on out and fight!" Next moment there was an ear-splitting roar. The ground erupted, spitting earth and flame. When the mushroom of sudden smoke cleared, Hays could see what was left of Minick sprawled in a bloody mess on the smoking ground. He had stepped on a mine. With an angry yell, the rest of his company surged forward past the dying Minick, who would be awarded his country's highest honor. The reluctant soldier, who had so hated "garrison soldiering," would be given the Medal of Honor. And as usual in the Hurtgen, it would be granted posthumously.

Not far away from where Staff Sergeant Minick won his Medal of Honor that terrible dawn, big, burly, ex-professional wrestler Lt. Paul Boesch was picking out sites for his mortars to support the attack of his Company G on a height. He had hardly begun when the first casualty came staggering down, a Lieutenant Zienke, whose arm had been hit. His face was "ghostly white and contorted with pain." "Is it bad?" Boesch asked.

"Not too bad," the other officer answered with a wince. "It didn't touch the bone."

"Hey looka, guys," one of Boesch's men cried to the others. "The lieutenant's went and got hisself a million dollar wound." They crowded round and "made no effort to conceal the envy in their glances or their remarks."[15]

But Lieutenant Zienke's luck didn't last long. A few months later he took a German bullet straight through the throat and died. After Zienke, another officer came staggering down the hill and had to be evacuated. He, too, would return, to be killed on Christmas Day 1944.

Now everything started to go wrong for Company G. A truck went over a mine, killing several men. A close friend of Boesch, Lt. Jack Kee, was caught by a burst from a mortar shell and was evacuated with four hundred wounds. He lived, surprisingly enough. Then Company G started to run away. A horrified Boesch spotted the C.O., a Captain Black, stumbling back with his survivors.

Black broke down when he saw the fellow officer. "Why didn't it happen to me?" he cried, dropping his head in his hands and beginning to sob. McCarthy gets both his legs blown off. Men get killed and wounded all around me. Those two sergeants were with me ever since I got here. I made them sergeant. Now they're dead. Joe loses his leg. Why doesn't it happen to me? Why, damn it, *why?*"

Boesch decided to keep the broken officer at his own CP. He didn't want to parade him before his men in such a state of shock. Therefore, he called the battalion C.O. and told him what had happened. When he hung up, Black started sobbing again and cried, "I heard you, Boesch. You're ashamed of me. You think I'm yellow. I'm not afraid of their goddamned artillery! I'm not afraid of these sonsabitching Germans! But why do all these good men get killed while I stay here and see them go? Why wasn't it me instead of them? . . . Answer me that, damn it. *Why?*"[16]

Boesch had his own philosophy to explain that overwhelming question. It was contained in a poem that ended, "I'll live and love and dine and drink. And when my number's called I think I'll say, 'Okay.' " But the big ex-wrestler knew this was not the time or place to recite his poem to a distraught Black. Instead, he told him to sleep.

In spite of their disparate actions that terrible day, Minick and Black did exemplify the nightmarish stress that the men of the 8th were under. Both had reacted to it in different ways—the one with reckless bravery, the other by breaking down and wanting to die—but in each case the reaction was an abnormal one. In the Hurtgen Forest *nothing* was normal anymore. The world had gone crazy in the Forest as for seven days the 121st Regiment (and later the 13th Infantry Regiment) tried to take the ridge that barred the way to their objective, the village of Hurtgen itself.

By the third day of the assault, the Regiment was almost completely demoralized. Under enemy artillery fire, one company simply collapsed. Impatiently Colonel Jeter relieved both the company commander and his battalion commander. Next day the new company commander was cut down by more artillery fire. In the first four days of the 121st's attack, Jeter relieved another two company commanders and a second battalion commander. In one company every officer who did not break outright under the tremendous strain was judged by his superiors to have to be relieved anyway. In the end, Colonel Jeter himself would be relieved and at the end of the month General Stroh would follow him, making him the first general officer to be relieved in the bloody, tragic battle for the Hurtgen Forest.

In desperation, General Stroh ordered a combat command of the 5th Armored Division—CCR—into the attack. Perhaps they would give a new impetus to the flagging assault of his badly hit 121st Regiment, which had now suffered six hundred battle casualties. The tanker's orders were to move up the perilous Germeter-Hurtgen highway before daylight and attack Hurtgen itself. Colonel Anderson didn't like his assignment one bit. The Germans still held the heights overlooking the highway. Once daylight came, his tanks would be under observation—and fire. But orders were orders, and he was intent on carrying them out.

The night of November 24 was cold and dark. Rain slashed down. Soon it would turn to sleet and snow. Doggedly the armored infantrymen of the 47th Infantry Battalion of the CCR slogged through the mud on both sides of the Germeter-Hurtgen highway. It was their job to protect the tanks, now rumbling up, from German suicide squads, armed with their deadly *panzerfausts*. For without infantry protection, tanks at night were easy prey for the German *Landser*.

They soon ran into trouble. During the day an enemy artillery bombardment had cut down the white tapes laid by the engineers to indicate the safe passages through the German minefields. Now the armored infantry started to blunder into deadly, unseen devices. Abruptly the night silence was broken by screams and cries for assistance. *"Medic!"* the cry went up on all sides. Captain Lewis's B Company of the 47th Infantry started to lose men rapidly.

Despite the infantry losses and a huge crater in the road ahead, the tank attack on Hurtgen began promptly at seven-thirty. In the lead Lt. Jack McAuley spotted the crater now. He called back over his radio, "I'm going to try to jump the damned thing!" His driver gunned the engine. Beneath the leather helmet, sweat stood out on his brow in opaque pearls. McAuley held his breath. Going all out, churning up a great brown wake of mud behind it, the Sherman raced full speed for the crater. At the very last moment the desperate driver gave the tank one last burst of speed and it sailed into the air.

With a great bang, the 30-ton Sherman slammed into the side of the crater and rolled over on one side, its track racing uselessly. McAuley had failed. He would, however, continue firing his 75mm cannon from this uneven position.

Hurriedly the engineers were whistled up in order to fill in or bridge the crater that was holding up the advance of a whole armored regiment. But now the Germans had spotted them from their observation points on the ridge above. Mortar and artillery shells started to rain down. Shrapnel scythed lethally through the air. The head engineer was hit and was carried away moaning. Capt. Frank Pool of the 10th Tank Battalion took over his job. A German burp gunner sneaked in and let him have a full burst as he stood in his turret directing operations. He refused to be evacuated, but staggered to the ground to continue the job, only to be wounded yet again. Things were going disastrously wrong with the armored attack intended to take the pressure off the 8th's 121st Infantry Regiment.

Lieutenant McAuley, who was doing his best to give the engineers covering fire from his wrecked tank, ordered another of his Shermans, commanded by Sgt. William Hurley, to move forward and give the column more protection. Hurley successfully guided his Sherman over the span the engineers had put up, but hardly had he rolled a few score yards when a mine erupted beneath his tank and immobilized it. The road was blocked yet again.

S. Sgt. Lawrence Summerfield tried to save the situation. Inch by inch he managed to snake his Sherman round the two other wrecked Shermans and started to roll forward. In a shower of mud, the tank turned the next corner—and ran straight into the fire of a waiting German anti-tank gun, which had been zeroed in on exactly this corner!

In horror, Summerfield in his turret watched as the solid, glowing white anti-tank shell hurtled toward him. He tensed. If the AP (armor-piercing) shell penetrated the tank, it would fly round and round inside the Sherman, ripping them to pieces. But the German gunner missed! His own gunner, Cpl. Benny Majka, didn't give the German a second chance. He pressed his firing pedal. The Sherman jerked and trembled. Hastily Summerfield peered through his periscope. There was a flash of scarlet flame, a burst of white smoke, and then the Germans were reeling back on all sides from their shattered cannon. They had done it! Benny had knocked out the Kraut with one single shot! Summerfield's triumph didn't last long. Five minutes to be exact. Not far away another German anti-tank gun cracked into action. There was the great hollow boom of steel striking steel and Summerfield's tank reeled to a stop. He had been hit too.

It was now two o'clock on a wet, gray, miserable afternoon. By this time the supporting infantry of Company B of the 47th Infantry Battalion had only eighty men left out of the original 225. Another company was brought up hastily as the Thunderbolts came zooming out of the sky to attack Hurtgen. Something had to be done to get the attack moving again.

The new plan was to sneak the fresh infantry through the woods to the left of the road where the tanks were stalled. Under the command of Captain Marcikowski the new company—

C—plunged into the shattered woods. Within minutes they ran straight into the German minefields, as machine guns firing from what was supposed to be American positions opened up a mercilessly cruel fire on them. Men started going down on all sides as the mines tore off their feet and ripped legs to gory red shreds. The infantry began to go to ground, but there was no protection for them anywhere. Every ditch and every foxhole had been cunningly booby-trapped by the enemy. Within fifteen minutes Company C had been reduced by nearly a quarter of its strength. Fifty men lay moaning and writhing in dreadful pain.

By nightfall Colonel Anderson had lost 150 men—for nothing. Sadly, he ordered the battered survivors to withdraw. The armored attack on Hurtgen had been a total failure.

Far away in his hotel headquarters in Spa, General Hodges now began to call the useless savage slaughter that was happening in the Hurtgen Forest the bloodiest battle fought in Europe!

10

On the same day that the 5th Armored Division's CCR was launched into that disastrous attack on Hurtgen, far away in London, Field Marshal Sir Alan Brooke, Chief of the Imperial General Staff, started a meeting of the Chiefs of Staff by asking the secretaries to leave the room. The clever, cold, bird-watching Chief of Staff waited till the women had left the War Office's paneled conference room before he spoke in that precise way of his. Then he told his colleagues that there was a crisis at the Supreme Commander's Headquarters in Paris. "Eisenhower, though supposed to be running the land battle, is on the golf links at Rheims—entirely detached and taking practically no part in the running of the war."[1]

According to Brooke, a bitter critic of Eisenhower, the Supreme Commander had let things slide disastrously; there was no central direction of the fierce battles being fought all along the German frontier. Indeed things had gotten so bad, Brooke alleged, that Bedell-Smith (Eisenhower's hot-tempered Chief of Staff—"Somebody has got to be a son-of-a-bitch around this HQ") and a few others had formed a deputation to Eisenhower. They had insisted that he buckle down to it and get on *running* the war.

The criticism was harsh, but not altogether unjustified. While his young soldiers fought, bled, and died in the horror of the Hurtgen Forest, Eisenhower and the rest of the Top Brass seemed strangely remote from the war. Admittedly, Eisenhower toured the front at periodic intervals, but his visits were to corps and divisional headquarters, manned by officers most of whom he had known all his life—men who had come through West Point like

128

himself and belonged to the small Regular Army clique. For them he was "Ike" and he knew them by their first names. These hearty, middle-aged gentlemen were hardly likely to disturb Ike with whatever they knew of the real horrors of the front line.

Most of the time Eisenhower lived far to the rear in his French Château, working tremendously hard admittedly, but surrounded by cronies and hangers-on who sheltered him from the harsh truths of the front. There was green-eyed Kay Summersby, now a lieutenant in the WACs, although she wasn't even an American citizen; General Hughes, his card-playing, harddrinking, womanizer crony who defined a WAC as "a doublebreasted GI with a built-in foxhole"; "Butch" (Captain Butcher, USN), his "life-of-the-party" personal public relations man; Tex, who kept his records; even a pet dog, Telek, that had the unfortunate habit of wetting the carpet in public.

In the midst of all the slaughter at the front, with two thousand casualties being air-evacuated from the First Army sector alone each day, Eisenhower and the rest seemed oddly concerned with their own personal and family matters. All of the Top Brass appeared, for instance, to have women problems. Gerow, Commander of the V Corps, which was bleeding to death in the Hurtgen Forest, was primarily concerned that November with his wife, Marie-Louise. He had married her in 1939, after his divorce from his first wife, and, like the general himself, she was of French descent. Now it had been discovered that her relatives had allegedly collaborated with the Germans during the Occupation. Indeed, they had just been sent to trial on that charge. Thus, as the battle in the Death Factory reached a horrific crescendo, Gerow himself sweated out a potential scandal in France. General Hughes, knowing a hot potato when he saw one, wrote a memo to himself stating: "Must not get involved with Gee's [Gerow's] relations—think they are collaborationists."[2]

Eisenhower had women problems too. It was not really so shocking that he kept a mistress. He wouldn't be the first great American—this future U.S. president—to keep one, or the last, for that matter.

Unlike the other generals, Eisenhower was essentially middle-class. He worried about appearances. Kay might well be a handful, if he ever decided to drop her after a romance lasting two years. Unlike Patton, Smith, and Hughes, who seemingly could take mistresses and drop them with impunity—hell, Patton had had *three* already—Ike's position in a headquarters, five thousand strong, was too public, too exposed for that. Besides there was always Mamie back in the States. He felt that she knew, through the Regular Army grapevine, that he was up to something in France. As a consequence, she was jealous and moaned all the time in her letters. On November 11, he had had enough of it. He wrote an angry letter taking Mamie to task for her constant bitching.

"You've always put your own interpretation on every act, look, or word of mine, and when you're unhappy that has, in turn, made me the same. It's true we've now been apart for two and a half years, and at a time and under conditions that make separations painful and hard to bear. Because you don't have a specific war job that absorbs your time and thoughts, I understand also that this distress is harder for you to bear. But you should not forget that I do miss you and do love you and that the load of responsibility I carry would be intolerable unless I could have the belief that there is someone who wants me to come home—for good. Don't forget I take a beating every day."[3]

Naturally Eisenhower didn't want to come home to Mamie (who was twice Kay's age), carpet slippers, and a nice comfortable old-age retirement—just yet. As it turned out, he never retired, of course. All his life he had worked for this, and he wanted to enjoy the trappings and privileges of power a little longer in this strange, isolated military coterie, cut off from the grim realities of the front.

There was a wedding reception to be arranged for his orderly Mickey, who was marrying a WAC sergeant, Pearlie Hargrave. It would be the first to be held at the chapel at Versailles since the eighteenth century, and there'd be *beaucoup* champagne. His PR man Butch wanted him to do a "little movie" that could be shown to the troops as "a kind of Christmas present." There was the problem of a headline that the correspondents wanted to use in their papers back home. It quoted Eisenhower as saying, "To get peace, you've got to fight like hell for it." Butch didn't know how to tell the correspondents that the Supreme Commander of nearly five million troops didn't wish to be quoted as saying "hell."[4]

While Eisenhower dithered at his remote headquarters, another senior soldier, who had just found himself a young secretary about the same age as Kay Summersby, was planning the blow which would shake Eisenhower rudely out of his self-induced complacency and make him realize suddenly that, as Patton would put it, "We can still lose this war." He was Col. Gen. Alfred Jodl, Hitler's Chief of Staff, a cold-eyed, extremely clever man.

Ever since the second week of September, when the Americans had first begun to cross the frontiers of the Reich in force, he had been attempting to give shape to the bold counterstroke the Fuhrer had envisaged as a war-winning plan. Then, just as it seemed there was no hope for the One Thousand Year Empire (as Hitler had proclaimed the new Germany back in the thirties), the Fuhrer had lain on his map-strewn bed, outlining his plan for destroying the Allied armies in the west.

Hitler had wanted to find a sector of the American front that was thinly held, one where the Americans would think he would never attack. By October Jodl and Hitler had decided it *had* to be the rugged, wooded Ardennes on the German-Belgian border, just south of the Hurtgen Forest. Back in 1940, the *Wehrmacht* had successfully run armor through the Ardennes, which had been declared "non-tank country" by the Anglo-French commanders of the time. Now Jodl knew, although the size of the *Wehrmacht*'s tanks had doubled from thirty to sixty tons in the intervening four years, that they could do it again.

There was also something else in the German favor in the Ardennes. By October-November it was being used for the training of new, inexperienced divisions that had just arrived in

Europe from America and as a place where the divisions shattered in the Hurtgen went to recover and refit. The 9th had already gone there, and in due course the 28th and 4th would follow. In short, the fifty long miles of the Ardennes front was defended by three or four American divisions, either understrength or unblooded. It would be an ideal place to attack.

But Jodl knew the Fuhrer's great gamble depended upon many factors. Of course, he needed tactical surprise. He needed a long period of bad weather to ground the Allied air forces—that was vital. Above all, however, he needed the Red Army to remain inactive in the east until he had destroyed the Anglo-American armies in the west.

By the last week of November, Jodl knew that the latter condition was being fulfilled. While the *Amis* bled to death in the Hurtgen Forest, Uncle Joe (as the Western Allies called the Soviet dictator fondly, misled by his pipe and avuncular air) stood by passively. Later Eisenhower would appeal to Stalin *personally* to go over to the offensive and take some of the pressure off the hard-pressed American armies. But the Russian dictator failed to act right into January 1945, while the U.S. Army staggered, reeled, and retreated under the tremendous armored blow the Germans had dealt it. "We cannot come out through Dunkirk this time," Montgomery would write sardonically to his boss Brooke, "as the Germans still hold that place."[5] Tactfully the Chief of the Imperial General Staff would excise that sentence before passing the letter on to Churchill. But at the time there would be a real danger that the Germans might well "dunkirk" the Western Allies once again.

Thus, while Eisenhower dallied and Jodl planned, the 4th and 8th Infantry Divisions, supported by the tanks of the 5th Armored Division, made their last attempt to capture their objectives in the Hurtgen Forest. The objective, for the 4th, as November started to give way to December, was the village of Grosshau. For the 8th, the objective was the village of Hurtgen, followed by another village, Kleinhau, a single street with a straggle of houses on both sides where Hemingway would state in that pseudotough manner of his, it was the place where he first saw "a Kraut dog eating a roast Kraut."*

On the night of Sunday-Monday November 26-27, one of the 22nd's patrols, led by a Lieutenant Murray, launched Company B's attack on Grosshau. They came under intense fire immediately. It was the same old sad story: American infantry out in the open running straight into the German guns. For two hours the patrol tried in vain. Only Lieutenant Murray survived. The rest of his seventeen men were all killed or wounded. The 3rd Platoon tried to advance; it was cut to pieces. The 2nd Platoon attempted to slip around the flank. Ten men got to within 20 yards of the wood containing the German gun that was slaughtering the infantry—and that was that.

It was then that Pfc Marcario Garcia, an acting squad leader, made his decisive appearance on the battlefield. Garcia, who would win America's highest honor, was not even an American. He was a despised "Mex" or "greaser," born in Villa de Castano, Mexico, who had entered the service at Sugar Land, Texas. But this particular "Tex-Mex" had plenty of guts. He went into the woods all by himself. Several grenades were heard exploding, and a little later Garcia emerged, saying in his accented English, "Goddamn, I killed three Germans and knocked out the machine gun!"

No sooner had he said this when another German machine gun burst into angry life. Garcia didn't hesitate. Although wounded, he dashed back into the wood again and assaulted the new machine-gun crew. He stormed their position, killed three of the Germans, and captured the remaining four. This time, as he came out of that wood of death, he exclaimed, "That's all of the bastards here!"[6]

Then he fought on with the survivors until the objective was finally taken. Only then would he allow himself to be evacuated. The news of his heroic action spread like wildfire in the 22nd,

---

* The half-starved dog was feasting off the flesh of a German soldier who had been roasted with white phosphorus from a shell.

but he had been evacuated so swiftly that not even his first name was known. Someone said he remembered Garcia's being granted American citizenship the year before and that was about all. Lanham swore, "That man is going to get the best medal I can give him. Somebody find out the details."[7]

But the fight for Grosshau and the last fringes of the damned woods was too hot just then for that kind of research. There were too many men still fighting and dying, some heroically and some in abject, miserable cowardice to bother about some "Tex-Mex," who was "out" of it anyway.*

On the same day that Pfc Garcia restarted the advance of the 22nd's lead battalion, ex-professional wrestler Paul Boesch was given command of G Company, not far away in another part of the Forest. After the breakdown of Captain Black, G Company had dwindled to exactly thirty men. The rest had been killed, wounded, or had deserted. Now, as night fell on November 26, Boesch's Company G and Captain Cliett's Company F were to advance toward the 8th Division's final objective: the shattered village of Hurtgen.

According to Boesch's battalion commander, Hurtgen was empty of enemy troops. There might be a few German snipers left there—that was all. Just to make sure, however, the regimental commander, Colonel Cross, who had taken over from Jeter, was going to order a heavy artillery bombardment on the outskirts of the village just before the attack went in. Cliett protested. The shells could endanger his men dug in close by. Could they pull back till the barrage was over?

"Not one inch!" Cross snapped. "We will not move that company or any other company back one single inch. We'll keep it up all night and then give them a concentrated dose in the morning just before the attack. But that company stays put!"

Cynically, Boesch reflected: "It took no genius to recognize that the solution Cliett and I offered was logical and sound. But in order to keep a map in some higher headquarters from regis-

---

* Pfc Garcia did receive the Medal of Honor, one of the few in the Hurtgen who survived to receive it personally.

tering the fact that men had taken a backward step . . . the men would have to stay where they were."[8] As always the Top Brass's virtual phobia about the American Army's giving up ground would cost men's lives.

Now, as the thunder of the barrage ceased, Boesch started to lead his handful of men across the sodden, pitted fields toward the ruins of Hurtgen. All was silent. Tense and expectant, Boesch's reluctant heroes (he had been forced to kick most of them to their feet for the assault) moved out across the field. *One hundred yards . . . one hundred and fifty . . . two hundred yards . . .* Still Hurtgen remained silent. Not a shot. Perhaps the battalion commander had been right after all? . . . *Two hundred and fifty yards . . . Three hundred!*

Suddenly, startlingly, there was the hiss of the German MG 42. Tracer zipped in a lethal morse towards them. The men went down. Boesch was not having that. He kicked and shouted at his reluctant heroes till they were on their feet again. They began to move. The fire intensified. Still they kept moving, urged on by Boesch, "shouting like a man possessed." But here and there men *were* going to ground.

Boesch came across one of his platoon leaders, a lieutenant, cowering in a hole, helmet clutched to his head with both his white-knuckled hands. "Come on, boy," Boesch pleaded, "let's get the hell into that town before we get chewed to pieces!"

"Just a minute," the terrified officer quavered, "just a minute."[9] But he didn't move. Boesch would have dearly loved to have rammed his carbine up the other man's exposed rump, but he didn't. Instead, he ran on after his men, who were moving ever closer to Hurtgen.

A soldier was shot close to him. The violence of the impact slammed the wounded man against Boesch and knocked the huge ex-wrestler to the ground. He picked himself up and staggered toward what was left of the assault force that was now digging itself in on the outskirts of the village.

Here Boesch made it his first duty to tend to his wounded. He had no drugs, no morphine, no bandages—nothing to ease their lot—and there was no hope of carrying them the half mile or so back to the shelter of the woods from whence they had come. They were cut off, with the Germans plastering the fields all around them savagely.

But one of the wounded, who had been hit in the thigh, was happy. "Oh boy," he sighed in a low, satisfied voice, his eyes staring above him at the sky, "white sheets for Christmas!"

"What did you say?" Boesch asked in disbelief.

"White sheets for Christmas," he repeated the words exultantly.

Boesch marveled at the man. He had got his "million-dollar wound." Now he thought it was all over. Boesch himself was not so sanguine. "I wondered just what he would get for Christmas—white sheets, or a white muslin mattress cover!"[10]

All that long cold day in the rain Lieutenant Boesch sweated out the long hours till darkness so that he could evacuate his wounded, perhaps even be relieved. Once he called down artillery fire to stop the Germans from overrunning his positions, but after a few rounds the artillery stopped firing and his C.O., Colonel Kunzig, came on the air. "Boesch," he told the weary officer severely, "don't knock those houses apart too badly or we won't have any place to put the C.P."[11]

Boesch slumped exhausted in the mud and cursed out loud. He felt like crying.

Finally darkness fell, and under its blessed cloak Boesch was able to evacuate the wounded, including the man who desired white sheets for Christmas. "Don't worry, Lieutenant, I'll get them," he assured Boesch. But there was no relief. Instead, the handful of exhausted survivors were reinforced by some combat engineers, transformed into instant infantry, under the command of a frightened staff sergeant.

All night he complained about the conditions. Once he said, "Isn't it time for us to go back? My men are getting cold in these holes."

"My men have been cold in the same kind of holes for about two weeks now, Sergeant," Boesch replied. "I expect to use you and your men later tonight—you'd better stand by."

But by daylight the noncom and his engineers had had enough. Again the sergeant crawled over to Boesch's foxhole. He said they were pulling out. "Gee whiz, Lieutenant," he whined. "They didn't tell me we were going on no suicide mission."

"What the hell do you think about the rest of us?" Boesch barked. "Don't you think we get a little sick of suicide missions, too?"

"But Lieutenant," the sergeant protested, "you all are *infantry*!"

Boesch's mind raced as he pondered the frightened sergeant's words. "My God," he told himself, "we were infantry. That apparently meant we were a race apart. Maybe we weren't supposed to feel, to hurt, to shiver, to be frightened, to react like other human beings." He started to tell the sergeant to get back to his hole. Then he changed his mind. He thought that these men had tasted too much warm food and slept in too many dry spots to be of any real use to them.

"You're goddamned right we're infantry," he declared proudly. "As for you, you take your men and your fancy equipment [the engineers had brought up flamethrowers] and get the hell back to the rear where you belong! We want no part of whiners. We'll get along without you. Don't worry about that."[12]

It was the authentic voice of the P.B.I. speaking—the poor bloody infantry.

Everywhere, as the Top Brass laid on the pressure, insisting that objectives had to be taken regardless of cost, the poor bloody infantry were taking a beating in those last two days of November 1944. Up at Merode, the 26th Infantry of the Big Red One had battled up the steep narrow trail through the woods to take the first houses against stiff opposition from a battalion of the German 5th Parachute Regiment. But once they were there and had commenced digging in, the trail behind them was promptly cut by the paras.

For the two companies cut off in the hilltop village an ordeal began that would end in an ignominious finale to America's premier division's fight in the Hurtgen. All through that day and the next and the next, the frantic battalion commander, Colonel Daniel, tried to fight his way through to his trapped men. Tanks were sent up, but one was hit by shellfire, overturned, and effectively blocked the trail for the rest of the action. Engineers tried to dig another route to the two companies. A sergeant tried to borrow some tanks from another battalion and was turned down. Hope started to fade for the "lost companies."

The Germans counterattacked. The batteries of the infantrymen's radios began to fade, but one last message was received at Colonel Daniel's HQ before they went altogether. "There's a Tiger tank coming down the street," the faint but plaintive voice said, "firing his gun into every house. He's three houses away now . . . still firing into every house . . . *Here he comes!*"[13]

It was the last message ever received from the trapped men. A sergeant and twelve men who had escaped previously were formed with others into a combat patrol to attempt to break through. Shellfire forced them back. Headquarters offered the 26th a fresh battalion, but Colonel Seitz, commanding the 26th, turned the offer down. "What is in town may be annihilated by now," he declared. That was that. One hundred and sixty-five men had vanished into the greedy maws of the God of War and the Big Red One had had enough. It had suffered 3,993 *battle* casualties, including 641 in the attached 47th Infantry. In particular, the 26th had lost 1,479 infantrymen, 50 percent of its strength, and this figure did not include the many hundreds of nonbattle casualties caused by weather and combat fatigue. It was time for the weary, exhausted Big Red One to be relieved.

It was time, also, for the equally exhausted 4th and 8th Infantry Divisions. Their fighting regiments had been decimated. But Tubby Barton and the new commander of the 8th, General Weaver, were not letting their men off the hook just yet. They *had* to achieve their objective! The honor of the division depended on it.

On the morning of November 29, Barton's Chief of Staff called Colonel Lanham's CP and told him that "in the name of the

The Supreme Commander, who condoned the battle, here with King George VI in Verviers, Belgium, at the start of the battle. Behind the king is General Bradley.

Into the forest. It looks deceptively peaceful.

The attackers.

The defenders.

The way they lived.

American soldiers set out to build a log shelter while another keeps watch with a light machine gun. A roof over one's head was valuable protection from the elements and deadly tree bursts.

Using sheet metal captured from the Germans, Army engineers put the finishing touches on log huts in the Hurtgen Forest.

The shot-up farmhouse – it's still there – that was prime accommodation.

Mud!

A 155mm howitzer pounds away at German positions on the Roer River front.

U.S. soldiers going up into the forest in their winter spook suits.

Men of field artillery battery attached to the 78th Infantry Division practice demolition of a German pillbox with a bazooka in the snow-covered Hurtgen Forest.

Two combat medics from the 4th Infantry Division treat a wounded GI during fighting in November 1944.

The notorious Kall Trail, where so many American dreams ended.

The forest, at the end of the battle.

Victors and vanquished.

Battle-weary Germans, who surrendered in mid-December 1944 – just a few days before the surprise German counter-attack in the Ardennes.

Forty years later: The skeleton of a German soldier is dug up, to be buried at Vossenack cemetery, where 60,000 German dead of the battle lie.

Forty years later: To take this bunker cost the lives of scores of young U.S. soldiers. How harmless it looks now.

division commander" Grosshau had to be taken that day "regardless of cost." The previous plan to surround the place and then demand its surrender was now abandoned. It would take too much time. There was to be an immediate battalion assault from the west on the shattered village.

Not far away, at the equally shattered village of Hurtgen, Boesch was told by a runner, "Lieutenant Boesch, there's a colonel in a house on the other side of the road. He wants you there immediately. He said bring your radio."

Boesch stared at the runner in amazement. "A *colonel*?" he gasped. "Up here with us? With all this action going on?" He swallowed hard. "You sure you're feeling all right?"

"I'm sick as a dog, Lieutenant," the man replied, "but honest to God, there's a chicken colonel on the other side of the road." And there was, too, a Colonel Ginder, who looked Boesch in the eye and barked: "I'm in charge of the task force attacking this town . . . Get back with your men. Keep them moving and don't stop. We're going to take this town."[14]

For the first time Boesch genuinely believed they were going to capture Hurtgen. He was right. This time they were. In their dying throes these decimated divisions were at last going to take their objectives.

It was no different at Grosshau. Lanham was putting on the final pressure to take the damned place before the 4th was relieved. He urged his men on, backing them up with tank destroyers and tanks, as they grew ever closer to their target. In the lead was his C Company, and together with *Life* correspondent William Walton, he watched as fighter-bombers came "tobogganing out of the western sky over Grosshau. Each cracking explosion fountained smoke and debris into the still air. In foxholes scooped from rotting pine needles the foot soldiers watched approvingly."[15]

"Give it to the bastards!" they cried.

"Now we're getting somewhere!"

"Lookit those houses go whammo!"

Cautiously the infantry started to advance again into the

smoke, past trees shattered into naked spears of white ugliness, over weather-stained corpses that had lain there for so long that the stench of rotting flesh was almost unbearable.

The bloody slow business of house-to-house fighting commenced as they reached the first houses in Grosshau. A series of daring spurts forward, ducked lower, body tense for the first red-hot sting of steel. A pause, chest heaving madly. A grenade into the cellar or through a shattered window. A muffled roar. A burst of black smoke. Perhaps a shrill scream, a cry of rage, a plea for mercy. Then in through the door—or better, down from the roof—machine guns blazing, bayonet stabbing, slicing, and another house would be taken with yet another patch of khaki-clad figures lying sprawled out grotesquely in the mud of the cobbled, debris-littered street. Two hundred and fifty young Americans died that day to capture a single lousy village street.

The Germans counterattacked, twice. They were not going to give up that easily. Lanham rushed up his last reserve: a couple of platoons made up of hastily armed cooks, clerks, headquarters bottle-washers. He was scraping the bottom of the barrel. "A toe-to-toe slugfest" in which no quarter was given or expected, the *Chicago Daily News* would report later in the unlovely prose of that newspaper. But the "bottle-washers" held, as did their surviving comrades inside the ruined village. At last Grosshau was American!

Hemingway went up. It would be the last time in his long career concerned with sudden, violent death that he saw the "glorious dead" of battle. He saw a dead GI flattened by a tank, "and I can remember just how he felt, lifting him, and how he had been flattened and the strangeness of his flatness." A cat eating a dead German. "It was a hungry cat, quite nice looking basically. You wouldn't think a good German cat would eat a good German soldier, would you?"[16]

Lanham went up with him to view what Hemingway called "a potato village." But he had no time for Papa's flippant, pseudo-tough approach. Normally a very rational man, he wrote later, "At this time my mental anguish was beyond description. My magnificent command had virtually ceased to exist."[17]

It had. In a mere two weeks of battle the 22nd Infantry Regiment had lost 2,678 men; five hundred of these were non-battle casualties. The 4th Division as a whole had suffered 4,053 battle casualties, plus another two thousand who had fallen victim to combat fatigue, trench foot, and respiratory complaints. Thus, the 4th now qualified for the dubious distinction of being second only to the 28th Division in casualties incurred in that dread German forest.

By now the 8th Division had captured its objective, Hurtgen, as well. It had been an equally bloody business. Colonel Ginder, the new man, had known what was to come. He had told one fearful officer in Boesch's earshot, "If you are wounded, you'll get a nice rest in the hospital. If you get killed, you won't know anything about it. If neither happens, you will have nothing to worry about. *Let's get going!*"[18]

That fatalistic philosophy worked. As the Shermans rushed by them, tracks flailing up the dirt, engines roaring all-out, the infantry came out of their holes firing as they ran, following the bold, fatalistic commander. Running with them, Boesch told himself he never could have believed that battle could be so impressive.

"It was a wild, terrible, awe-inspiring thing, this sweep through Hurtgen. Never in my wildest imagination had I conceived that battle could be incredibly impressive—awful, horrible, deadly, yet somehow thrilling, exhilarating. Now the fight for Hurtgen was at its wildest. We dashed, struggled from one building to another shooting, bayoneting, clubbing. Hand grenades roared, rifles cracked—buildings to the left and right burned with acrid smoke. Dust, smoke, and powder filled our lungs, making us cough, spit. Automatic weapons chattered hoarsely while heavier throats of mortars and artillery disgorged deafening explosions. The wounded and the dead—men in the uniforms of both sides—lay in grotesque positions at every turn. From many the blood still flowed."[19]

Then it was over. All energy spent, the infantry sagged as if some invisible tap had been opened. Legs like rubber, chests heaving as if they had just run a race, they were abruptly tired, very tired. Hurtgen—this obscure "cow village" that had given its name to the whole terrible killing ground—was theirs.

Their new divisional commander, who had now picked up the name of Wild Bill somewhere or other, would not let them rest, of course. Wild Bill Weaver, brash and aggressive, who had now replaced the broken General Stroh, wanted new victories while the 8th was still in the Forest. The Hurtgen Forest, however, would tame him as it had tamed so many other fire-eaters before.

Now the survivors tried to pick up the pieces before December came and Top Brass like Wild Bill Weaver would thrust them into new battles. Since September, twenty-three thousand men of the divisions that had fought in the Forest had been killed, wounded, or captured. Another eight thousand had fallen prey to the elements and combat fatigue. That meant there had been an average of more than five thousand casualties per division, a loss of 35 percent. This figure was naturally much higher in the rifle companies—perhaps a 60 percent loss rate on average.

Again, the depleted battalions were flooded with naive young replacements or older men unwillingly culled from the rear. Soon Eisenhower, who personally called black men "darkies," would consider "allowing" black soldiers "the privilege" of fighting alongside their white comrades in combat: a shocking suggestion in a deeply segregated U.S. Army.

Before he was knocked out for good, Lt. Paul Boesch gathered the 45 replacements sent up to his Company G in Hurtgen and gave them a pep talk. It was a strange scene. "The only light came from a crude lantern made by sticking a piece of rag in the neck of a bottle of gasoline . . . A few feet away from the lantern, it was so dark that the men's cigarettes glowed like beacons. Most of the new men wore relatively fresh uniforms and were clean shaven . . . Outside the sounds of battle continued unabated. Occasionally the cellar seemed to vibrate with the explosion of a nearby shell and dust fell from cracks in the ceiling."[20]

So everybody could see him, the burly ex-wrestler stood on a chair to give his little talk to the raw wet mouths. "To most of you," he said, "this may seem like you're looking at a Hollywood movie, only this time you yourself are in the picture. But believe me, it's not as bad as people may have told you. It couldn't be, or none of us would be here . . . There are still lots of us left here and some of us have been around a long time. We expect to be around a longer time. It isn't easy. It's tough. But if we can stand up to it, so can you."[21]

A few minutes later the exhausted officer lay down on the crowded dirty cellar floor and tried to fall asleep and escape into the world of dreams, but he couldn't. "I wanted the whole dirty war to be over so badly, I almost began to cry."[22] Finally he dozed off into an uneasy, troubled sleep as outside the guns started to thunder yet again, heralding the action of the morrow.

There were a lot of brave young combat officers and noncoms like Lieutenant Boesch in the Hurtgen, trying to inspire their hard-pressed men to continue the battle, to go into the Death Factory again, or for the first time. Most of those who fought and died there never questioned the reason for the battle, the slaughter, all that suffering and pain. They simply got on with the job, did their duty as good soldiers should. If they considered the matter at all, they felt proud of having done their duty and proud of belonging to their fighting outfits: the Golden Arrow, the Bloody Bucket, the Big Red One, the Ivy, and all the rest of those combat divisions that fought in the Forest. They would always be proud of that.

But for those who survived to grow old and white-haired, the Death Factory would always be with them. The Hurtgen Battle had stolen a part of them. Their youth and innocence had perished in those shattered, lethal woods. The chaplain of the 22nd Infantry Regiment, Dr. William Boice, wrote years after it was all over: "Hundreds of men had lost their lives for a patch of woods and the heap of rubble that was Grosshau. Perhaps in the final analysis, the sacrifice demanded in Hurtgen will be deemed worthwhile; we wouldn't know about that. We are only the men who fought the battles, who hugged the earth as our hearts dropped within us when the shells came screaming in, who lay in the slime and mud night after night, who froze our feet, who did not come out of a foxhole long enough to eat Thanksgiving dinner, for life was more precious than food, who carried our buddies back to the aid stations or turned our faces aside when we saw what was left of their broken, mangled bodies. A part of us died in the forest, and there is part of our mind and heart and soul left there. We shall never forget. We are incapable of forgetting."[23]

PART THREE

Dark December

A conqueror like a cannonball must go on. If he rebounds, his career is over.

DUKE OF WELLINGTON

11

In the whole of the vast U.S. Army there was no other unit like them, not even the Airborne. For every man who served in their ranks was a volunteer, and not even that sufficed to keep a soldier with them. If the volunteer was not absolutely in tip-top shape, he went. These men were the elite of the American Army and wore a proud flash on their shoulders. It read: *Ranger.*

Trained by the British commandos, they had first gone into action in North Africa: six companies of 65 men each, making up one battalion. After that had come Anzio, where the first two battalions of Rangers had been virtually slaughtered by the Germans. The invasion of France had followed, where the 2nd Ranger Battalion, formed in 1943, had its first taste of action at Bloody Omaha. There, at great cost, they had stormed the Ponte de Hoe and knocked out five huge 155mm guns that could have devastated the attack force.

Further fighting in Brittany had followed, but none of it was of the kind they had been trained for: swift, desperate operations in which they went in fast, did their job, and got out equally fast. Instead, they were being used as ordinary infantry, and the Rangers were desperate for some kind of special operation.

But to their intense disappointment, as they crossed the border into the Reich for the first time, they found that was exactly what the powers-that-be intended for them. On November 14, 1944, they were given the task of relieving the battered 2nd Battalion of the 28th Infantry Division's 112th Regiment at the shattered village of Vossenack, just after the 28th had been driven out of Schmidt three miles away.

What these elite soldiers saw in Vossenack shocked them.

There were dead animals and men everywhere in the shattered village. One officer recalled the dead American jeep driver just outside the church, whose hands had turned black in the bitter cold as they still grasped the wheel. "His face, too, has that bluish-black, metallic cast. His steel helmet is cocked at quite a rakish angle, and his lips are stretched tight in an awful grin. The teeth seem very white."[1]

The CPs of the regiment they were relieving were even worse. One veteran Ranger remembered forty-odd years later just how bad they were. The "CP was in a basement, jammed with men, some wounded and some combat fatigue men. The atmosphere and odor was foul, a Coleman lantern and candles were the means of illumination . . . and dead GIs were stacked around the door like cordwood!"[2]

At the command post of D and C Companies (a cellar in the middle of the shattered village) there was a headless German soldier at the door, with the gaunt rear half of a cat sticking out from his stomach, its tail twitching back and forth slowly as it ate the contents of the dead man's stomach. Corporal Lisko, who observed this terrible scene, kicked the cat and yelled, "Go eat a dead horse, you sonafabitch!"[3]

As the Germans spotted the changeover, they welcomed the "new boys" with a heavy barrage, hitting, however, not the Rangers but the departing men of the 28th Infantry. It wasn't war; it was a massacre. Hurriedly the Rangers' medics went to work to help alleviate the suffering of the wounded who were now pouring into their dressing station. Some of the wounded had to be brought in, however, and in the darkness, split by the scarlet flashes of the shells, the experience was decidedly unnerving.

One of the team, Doctor Block, was feeling around, touching the men on the ground in the pitch black, searching for the wounded to help, when he plunged his hand into something hot and wet. Hastily he pulled it back and then saw by the light of an exploding shell what he had done. His hand had slipped into the gory scarlet mess of a shattered skull. He had come up with a handful of teeth and brains! As Cpl. Lou Lisko, who was also present, recorded with horror afterwards, "He heaved right then and there. Couldn't help himself. Jeez! *Teeth and brains!*"[4]

Their spell in Vossenack did not appeal to the Rangers at all. There was little for them to do but try to survive. For five solid days they were shelled and mortared all the time. Being Rangers, however, they did not suffer the horrendous casualties their predecessors of the 28th Infantry Division had taken. During the night hours they occupied their foxholes *outside* Vossenack, knowing as experienced troops that the best way to hold a place was to do it from *outside*. Then just before daylight they would slip back into Vossenack and position themselves in the safety of the deep basements from whence they could survey the whole area without too much danger to themselves.

One of them wrote later, "Vossenack was definitely not Ranger work. Rangers attacked, killed, and withdrew to wait for another job. The Ranger theory was to hit hard—hit hard and fast—and then get out. Here at Vossenack the 2nd Battalion felt like the [man] in the carnival who has to stick his head through a hole and let people try to hit him with baseballs!"[5]

On November 19, the Rangers were relieved by men of the 28th Infantry Regiment of the 8th Division. They were exceedingly glad to go, although the rest area proved to be a tented camp in the Forest that was shelled all the time. With them they took a young replacement, who had suffered a traumatic experience in Vossenack. He had seen the head of a fellow Ranger blown off only a foot away from him. He couldn't speak. He didn't know his own name and he couldn't recognize any of his comrades. As one fellow Ranger, who had seen plenty of shell-shock cases in his time, commented: "He was in such bad shape that they sent him back to the States—and brother in those days you had to be in plenty bad shape to get home!"[6]

In spite of the dangers and the horrors of the Forest, the Rangers wanted a much more active role in the Hurtgen. They were probably the only American troops who fought there who ever did, and they would stay a record 33 days in the Green Hell of the Hurtgen! They had not been in real combat since the attack on Brest two months before (most of them didn't regard their stay in Vossenack as combat; they thought of it as some kind of rather dangerous garrison duty), and they craved a commando-type mission.

In particular, their tough C.O., Colonel Rudder, who had been with the battalion since it was established, stormed through regimental and divisional headquarters demanding a more active role. He told the regimental and divisional commanders he encountered in his travels, "Get us out of here and give us a Ranger job . . . Any kind of infantry can do what we're doing now."[7]

But for six days no one listened to him. The elite troops remained in that dangerous damp Forest, burying ever deeper into the earth as they were shelled all the time. Their day began at eight-thirty, first light, when the shivering frozen men crawled out of their holes and tried to start their fires. Here they'd cook their meager rations by throwing the cans in the embers to warm, while they tried to dry the damp blankets from the night before. That would be all the food they would get till three in the afternoon. Then the fires would be extinguished in case they were spotted by German reconnaissance planes, which were always prowling over the area looking for likely targets. If a target was spotted, they would drop butterfly bombs: small antipersonnel bombs with winglike attachments (hence the name), which were very difficult to defuse. Or they'd summon up that terrible artillery to pound the Rangers' positions yet again.

Thereafter, it was back to the foxhole with your buddy as soon as it became dark. "Sixteen hours was an eternity to spend in a hole in the ground," one remembered afterward. "Suppose you were lucky and could sleep for eight of them. That left another eight to be passed somehow. Water dripped down through the earth and logs above you, despite the shelter-half you had stretched atop them. It seeped through the sides and came up from the bottom. The blankets were wet and so were the extra layers of clothing you wore in a vain hope of keeping warm . . . Every minute seemed like an hour and you smoked innumerable cigarettes."[8]

Then, on December 6, 1944, the call for the 2nd Ranger Battalion came. *"We're moving out in fifteen minutes!"* the noncoms shouted, running up and down through the trees. *"Two blanket roll horseshoed over your pack . . . Make sure you have three rations and a full canteen . . . Moving out!"*

In Charlie Company they sat on damp ground, resting their backs with their heavy loads against the shrapnel-scarred trees. It was getting dark already, and they all wondered what their assignment was going to be. They didn't know that Colonel Rudder had finally caught the ear of the new commander of the 8th Infantry Division, Wild Bill Weaver.

A messenger came from Battalion HQ. The C.O. of Charlie Company, Captain McBride, listened to what he had to say. Then he set off for HQ *at a run*! The Rangers looked at each other in the growing darkness knowingly. It was going to be something big.

When McBride returned, he was smiling that "secret smile" of his, which, his men knew, meant only one thing. "We're going Jerry hunting." He called for the platoon leaders and the noncoms, and he pointed at the big map as best he could in the dark. "Well, it looks like the real thing this time, boys," he said. "This town here is Bergstein. That hill outside of it, Hill 400." The Rangers had their mission at last.

The 2nd Ranger Battalion was not the only outfit going in for its second taste of action in the Hurtgen Forest at the beginning of December. The 60th Infantry of the 9th Division, which had suffered so grievously back in October, was also returning to the Forest. It had absorbed thousands of replacements in the meantime, but there were a few old-timers left, like teenaged Kin Shogren, who had come up as a replacement in October, just in time for the first battle. Now, by virtue of the fact that all his former comrades had been killed or wounded, he was a staff sergeant leading a squad of green, apprehensive, complaining replacements.

The first time the 60th Infantry had gone into the Forest, they had lived well. "Steaming hot coffee and fresh-baked rolls, often with nuts and apples in them, for breakfast" and "the best steaks smothered in onions and mushroom gravy, mashed or baked potatoes for dinner," and "there was always pie for dessert, sometimes with a dollop of ice cream."[9]

This time the greenhorns were ordered to take enough canned rations for three days and as much ammunition and grenades as they could possibly carry. The war had become much, much rougher in the Hurtgen Forest since October. As it turned out, Kin Shogren recalled forty-odd years later, "We were up there a week, eating snow off the sides of trees to slacken our thirst."[10]

Despite the heavy load of food and ammunition that they were to take up with them, the squad sergeant himself had a little additional load in his pack—a sketchbook and pencils! They were highly unlikely objects to be carried around by a sergeant of infantry entering combat again, but Shogren had ambitions to become an artist. Later, as a professional painter, he would be "embarrassed by the amateur quality, and few people, not even his friends," would ever see the sketches he was soon to make right in the heart of the Hurtgen. But he would never throw them away, fortunately.

So, laden like pack animals, they slogged into the Forest to relieve the 1st Division not far from Merode, where the 28th Infantry Regiment had suffered its grievous defeats. There they dug themselves in, the enemy already beginning to shell the new boys. The forward observers of the German 3rd Parachute Division, who were sometimes only forty or fifty yards away from the American positions, had spotted the changeover and were only too eager to give the new arrivals in the Hurtgen a "taste of tinder,"* as they called it, in the form of a swift, sharp barrage.

It was December 7, 1944, the third anniversary of Pearl

---

* In German: *Zuender*.

Harbor, and as the regimental history puts it, "as defenses were improved that night, some doggies turned their thoughts to the days of peace and wondered how much longer the war would last."[11]

But for most of the men there was no time for thoughts of home and the distant future. Their concern was what was going to happen on the morrow. They knew they hadn't been brought up into the Hurtgen a second time simply to man the line. The Top Brass, they knew, had another offensive planned, and they were surely part of it.

They certainly were. General Collins, who was again in combat of this sector with his VII Corps, had a five-division attack planned for December 10. On his northern flank his 104th Division would continue attacking through Eschweiler-Weisweiler, while in the center the 9th Division, supported by a combat command of the 3rd Armored Division, would attack through the Forest to points south of Merode. Where the decimated 4th Infantry Division had been fought to a halt, opposite the hamlet of Hof Hardt and the village of Gey, the newly arrived 83rd Division (a veteran of the fighting in Normandy and Brittany) would take over. It would be supported by the tanks of the 5th Armored Division when the 83rd came to enter the Forest. It would also be the job of the tankers to maintain the link between Collins's VII Corps and Gerow's V, where it was still battling to maintain control of the Brandenberg-Bergstein ridge.

So once again the handful of veterans and the thousands of raw young replacements waited in their holes and dugouts for yet another attack in the Forest. But the enemy left them in no doubt that they were ready for an *Ami* attack. Although the Germans were vastly outnumbered (the defense amounted to the 3rd Parachute Division and the 246th Volksgrenadier Division), they did possess a formidable artillery. Now the Americans, as they waited for the order to attack, were pounded mercilessly the length of the front.

To avoid the shells, Sergeant Shogren found himself crawling about his squad position so much that his knees were damaged. Ten or twelve times a day his knee would lock and he would be unable to move. "About the only way to unlock the knee," he recalled many years later, "was by squatting and doing a deep knee bend. This put my head too high in the air and in the thick of battle I was afraid to do so. By laying on my side and wrapping both arms around the knee I was able to force it. Moments later it would lock again."[12]

But Sergeant Shogren's faith in God kept him going while the Germans stepped up their artillery attack on the waiting Americans. Once a shell exploded close to his dugout and "the concussion was so great that it seemed to have bodily lifted me a little. In the midst of such total death and destruction I had the sensation of lightness and bright light and that I was cradled in the arms of Our Lord, Jesus Christ, and that I was protected. Later on in the Hurtgen, this faith made me less protective of myself and when a German sniper shot into the bark of a tree just over my head, I said: 'I think I'll sit down,' instead of scrambling to the dirt."[13]

Not many of his men had the kind of faith that sustained Sergeant Shogren throughout the battle of the Hurtgen to come. But faith or no faith, more young men were soon going to die or be maimed in the Forest. Sergeant Shogren would be no exception. As always in the Hurtgen Forest, life was cheap, short, brutal, snuffed out as easily as the flame of a candle.

While Lightning Joe's VII Corps waited for the signal to attack once more on that same December 7, the 2nd Ranger Battalion was preparing for their battle. Their objective was Hill 400, or Castle Hill, as they came to know it later. It was of importance because any troops occupying it had a perfect observation for 15 miles around, something that Wild Bill Weaver didn't like one bit. He felt that the Germans up there could see everything his men were doing.

Now, as the guns rolled and thundered in the distance, the Rangers slogged through the mud and the abandoned wreckage of war on all sides toward their start line. Rain pelted down and they were miserable and wet, but Colonel Rudder, the perfect C.O., went up and down their line encouraging them. Almost all night he hiked with the long column, urging them on and constantly crying, "When you get there, dig and dig deep, boys!"

About midnight the Rangers contacted the 47th Armored Infantry of the 5th Armored, which was in reserve. One officer of the 47th described their arrival admiringly. "A guy came down the road, then two others, each one five yards behind the other. They were three Ranger lieutenants. They asked for enemy positions and the road to take. Said they were ready to go. We talked the situation over with the officers. They stepped out and said, 'Let's go, men.' We heard the tommy guns click, and without a word, the Rangers moved out. Our morale went up in a hurry."[14]

Others were not so pleased to see the Rangers as they got ever closer to their objective, the rain still pelting down on their bent, worn figures. One NCO who had been appointed to guide them farther up the road refused to get out of his foxhole. It was too dangerous. He hadn't reckoned with the Rangers' style of discipline. First Sgt. Ed Andrusz of B Company didn't waste any words on the cowardly noncom. He pulled him out of the foxhole by the front of his uniform, and hauling back, landed the infantryman a tremendous blow on the jaw. It is not recorded whether the infantry sergeant was in any fit state to guide the company any farther, now that his "courage" had been forced to return in such a sudden and dramatic manner.

It was two o'clock on the morning of the seventh. Three years before, on that Day of Infamy, these young men had been in high school or in college, little suspecting how the attack on Pearl Harbor that Sunday would so radically transform their lives. Now, on this wet, miserable third anniversary, tough, self-reliant, and contemptuous of the "doggies" at Bergstein (who seemed to know nothing about Castle Hill), the Rangers hastily sent out a patrol.

As one of them recalled much later: "We went on down the street, just snoopin' and poopin', and about a block from the edge of town we came to an American outpost. We asked him if there was anything between him and the church and he says that no, he's the last outpost and what's in that last block he doesn't know. So we go sneaking on and get just even with the church, right on the edge of town, and somebody hollers, 'Halt,' real low like. But we just said: 'To hell with him. These goddamn people don't even know where their own outposts are!' And we went on right by him."[15]

A little later the Ranger patrol ran into real trouble. The Germans opened fire on them with a machine gun. As one of them recorded, they took off "like striped-assed gazeeles* in full flight. When we got back to the C.P. we were so damned scared Captain Slater stuck cigarettes in our mouths and then had to light 'em for us! We were shaking too bad to do it ourselves!"[16]

But the patrol had brought back the information the Rangers needed. They were ordered to move out through the silent town, the sidewalks littered with dead Americans, a horrible, expectant air brooding over the place. A, B, and C Companies were to move into position while it was still dark and without any kind of artillery preparation. The veteran Rangers were not going to tip off the enemy by bombing them. While the right flank was secured by another unit, Companies D, E, and F would move up in the center and attack at dawn, taking the summit, while their comrades held the left flank. It was a bold, daring plan, typical of all Ranger operations, and it would pay dividends—*at first*.

Now it was almost time. They waited in the wet darkness, each man wrapped in a cocoon of his own thoughts and fears. Above them rose the hill, dark, threatening, and silent. The German observers up there weren't aware of their presence. For a week various *Ami* outfits had tried to take the place. None had succeeded. Perhaps the *Amis* had had a bellyful.

It was forty-five minutes to go. As one of the waiting Rangers

---

* The Texan pronunciation of gazelle.

recalled later, "Those few last minutes before the fight starts are always worse in some respects than the battle itself . . . You try to relax, but after the first few minutes you realize the absurdity of it . . . Your stomach has that sick empty feeling . . . You experience a strange sensation of unreality, of sick detachment; you stand aloof from yourself, as it were, and watch yourself struggle with mounting fear."[17]

At daylight Company C was spotted by the Germans. Immediately they started to mortar the Rangers, who cowered deeper in their shallow pits; the ground was too rocky to dig in well. As rock and shrapnel flew everywhere, the trees snapped off like matchwood, and the Rangers could do nothing but pray. They daren't raise their heads. If they had to answer a call of nature, they rolled onto their sides and did the best they could. It was, as the *History of the Second Ranger Battalion* states, "the most horrible barrage of artillery this Battalion had ever been subjected to."[18]

In the center, the assault companies prepared to move out. Their attack was unorthodox but simple, *deadly* simple. The men would fire one whole clip at the German positions to their front, forcing the enemy to take cover, then they would reload—and charge straight up the hill!

At the signal the companies blazed away, then they were out of their holes and pelting forward, trying not to think of the mines. A German sniper burst out of his cover, frantically crying, *"Kamerad . . . Kamerad!"* in a frenzy of fear. But the Rangers had seen too much at Vossenack. They weren't inclined to show mercy. Lt. Pat McCrone ripped a brutal burst from his tommy gun across the German's chest and he fell back into his hide, "split almost in half."

The Rangers plunge on, panting and gasping like ancient asthmatics in the last throes of an attack. Here and there a man falls wounded, but there are a mere handful of casualties. The Rangers' unorthodox tactics are paying off. Captain Massney stumbles into a German pillbox. With a swift kick from his boot, he smashes the door open. A grenade flies in. A muffled crunch. A cloud of thick black acrid smoke foams out. Next moment a dozen terrified, black-faced Germans come stumbling out, screaming for mercy.

Others aren't so fortunate. "This is a child's game," one of the attackers wrote later. "The damned Germans are running from you . . . They run or try to surrender. But you have scores to settle from Vossenack and fire fast."[19]

And then the handful of young Rangers had done it. They had taken Castle Hill within thirty minutes. At a price of exactly *four* men wounded. The attack had been a kind of vindication of their unorthodox tactics: a few bold, well-trained men catching the enemy by surprise, instead of the great khaki mass plodding forward to meet a waiting enemy, dug in and alerted by the usual softening-up barrage.

For a few minutes the Rangers enjoyed their victory as the sun came out to shine upon them. The Rangers had done it again. They had penetrated deeper into Hitler's Reich than any other Allied outfit, at a cost of four men wounded. They walked around, laughing and joking, saying the same stupid things, cracking the same old corny jokes as young men do when they are suddenly relieved from the oppressive threat of imminent, violent death, unaware that *battalions* of German guns were now being directed onto their position.

Colonel Rudder had ordered them to dig in at once and dig deep. But now, as they picked the spots for their foxholes and took out their little GI spades, they found that the summit was almost solid rock beneath a thin covering of soil, and the pine roots were thick and as tough as steel cables. Still they hacked away, faces glazed with sweat, glowing with the success of their assault and the thin December sunshine's warmth.

Abruptly the hack and scrape of shovels on rock was drowned by the first bansheelike shriek of a shell and a sound like an express rushing through an empty station at top speed. To their front, scarlet flashes ripped the whole length of the horizon. With a sudden, startling howl the first missile came plunging out of the hard blue sky to slam into the side of the hill, sending up a huge fount of whirling black earth and rock pebbles, red-hot shards of steel hissing lethally on all sides. The cruel barrage had commenced.

Thereafter, the Rangers caught out in the open heard no more individual shells coming in, for the thunder of the guns drowned out individual sounds. They all merged into one man-made terrifying cyclone of noise. As the historian of the 2nd Rangers put it: "A dozen shells are hitting the hill from three directions every time you draw a breath. The hill is in convulsions and seems to be bursting apart at its rocky seams. Trees, limbs, and rocks are mixed with the dirt and the flying steel fragments. The stench of cordite is everywhere."[20]

Captain Block, the medical officer, who had put his hand in that shattered head at Vossenack, and one of the best-liked officers in the Battalion, was killed almost immediately while severely wounded men dropped screaming all around him. Eleven men who were due for a thirty-day furlough in the States turned down the offer. They were too scared to come out of their foxholes for fear they'd be hit before they ever reached the bottom of Castle Hill. The casualties mounted rapidly. Men who had been friends and comrades since the battalion had been activated back in Camp Forrest, Tennessee, on April Fool's Day 1943; who had whored and drunk together in Bude, Cornwall, during their training in England; who had scaled those grim French heights together and had come through the hell of Vossenack, were now parted at last. The grim reaper was swinging his scythe of death with a vengeance.

But in later years the fate of none of those who died that day moved the survivors more than that of two brothers who had joined the Battalion in Tennessee. The older of the two had persuaded Colonel Rudder to allow his brother, who was in another outfit, to join the Battalion's F Company. Now under heavy artillery fire the two of them ran for cover behind a pillbox. Both were killed instantly by the same shell, but the older brother's last earthly act was to fall on the body of his kid brother, as if he were trying to shield him with his own. Thus they were found three days later, after the end of that terrible ordeal—united in death.

12

On that same September 11, 1944, that S. Sgt. Warner H. Holzinger became the first American soldier to step foot on German soil in World War II, over a thousand miles away in Occupied Norway, a 500-ton German U-boat, the *U-507*, commanded by Lieutenant Herrle, set sail from the port of Hammerfest. It was leaving on yet another secret mission in the strange, undisclosed war that had been fought in the Arctic Circle over the last four years. In its lean gray belly it contained a number of civilians who would spark off the violence and sudden death that would soon erupt on the western front.

Not that there was anything very warlike about the *U-507*'s supercargo. Although they all wore uniforms, they were all technicians, and their leader, Dr. Wilhelm Dege, a bespectacled geographer turned meteorologist, was a civilian. These men, who carried with them supplies for two years and eighteen hundred cases of equipment, were going to fight for the Fatherland, not with weapons, but with their brains.

Ever since 1915, when exact weather forecasting played a part in planning a military campaign for the first time in history, prediction had become part and parcel of all wartime operations. Each bombing raid, naval action, commando strike, paradrop throughout World War II depended upon reliable information on what the weather was going to be. And the weather in Western Europe could be accurately forecast only if the military meteorologists had prior information from the Arctic Circle.

Therefore, since early 1940 secret German weather teams had been setting out for the Arctic Circle to ensure that the *Wehrmacht* had this vital information. Over these four years, a lonely, strange, secret war had been fought all over the Arctic in wild, treacherous conditions, between the German scientists on the one side and, at varying times, Russians, Danes, Norwegians, Britons, Canadians, and Americans on the other.

It had been a cat-and-mouse campaign. Small groups of highly skilled, tough, self-reliant men hunted each other through that endless icy waste, with the Allies trying to root out each new German radio transmitter once it had been discovered. It was a secret war that was not publicized then and has not been publicized since, for although spy satellites do most of the work today, in case of war there undoubtedly will be meteorological paradrops in the same area to give instant weather reports.

Nazi Germany had sent out sixteen successful expeditions in all. In addition, it set up many robot weather stations, which continued to operate long after Berlin had been captured by the Red Army. One by one, however, the manned stations had been rounded up by the various Allied nations: the Danish Sledge Patrol and U.S. Coast Guard in East Greenland and neighboring waters; the British and Norwegians who kept guard on Jan Mayen Land and the Svalbard Archipelago; and the Russians who controlled Franz Josef Land. Now Dr. Dege was being sent out to set up a new station to allow the experts to predict the right weather for the Führer's bold new plan of attack.

Dege picked as his site "the island of Nordostland off Spitzbergen, nearly fifteen thousand square kilometers in size and regarded as one of the toughest areas in the whole of the Arctic."[1] Dege had to reach the landing place before September 15, when the bad weather would set in. Unfortunately, Lieutenant Herrle, commanding the U-boat, had learned that six or seven British destroyers, which knew the *U-507* had left Hammerfest, were waiting for them off the west coast of Spitzbergen. So the scientist and the "Lords," as the U-boat men were known throughout the German Navy, decided to make a run for it along the island's tough east coast.

Almost at once the U-boat bumped into a huge Allied convoy off the notorious Bear Island, where since 1941 more than ten thousand Allied seamen had lost their lives to U-boats while trying to run supplies in for the hard-pressed Russians at Murmansk. Somehow *U-507* dodged the enemy destroyers and corvettes to arrive safely at its destination only to find, as Dege recorded later, "a situation that had not occurred for over a hundred years—the area was completely free of ice."[2]

Dege had the use of the supply U-boat for exactly two weeks. Now he put his own men and the Lords to work building the weather station (they even built a sauna), while he set off on a rowing trip around the island. When he came back, the *U-507* was ready to sail back to Norway. As he recorded laconically in his diary, "Now we are alone."

They were. In mid-October the sun dipped below the horizon and bade good-bye until the following March, leaving the little camp, some six hundred miles below the North Pole, in the gray gloom of the polar winter. But Dege and his men had enough to do recording, assessing, testing. For 127 days before their transmitter was picked up by the Allies, they sent to Berlin the vital weather information on which German operations were based.

Here the *Wehrmacht*'s chief meteorologist, Dr. Karl Recknagel, was in charge of the team that assessed and predicted on the basis of the Dege reports. Recknagel was a self-assured pompous kind of a man who was fond of displaying his gold watch and remarking that it had been "given to me by the Fuhrer in person for my hundred percent accurate weather forecasts before the Norwegian campaign."[3] Indeed, he had been personally forecasting the weather for Hitler for four long years now, and he had rarely made a mistake.

Colonel Steinhoff, the German fighter ace, was in the same hospital as Recknagel at the end of the war and found him insufferably pompous and full of pride still. When the scientist told the blinded fighter ace* that he had predicted the weather for the Ardennes attack, Steinhoff rounded on him angrily, yelling: "Did you, *Herr Doktor*, seek to persuade him [Hitler] of the

---

* Steinhoff recovered his sight—though he was terribly mutilated—and later became head of the new German Air Force within NATO.

wrongness of making the success of the Ardennes offensive almost exclusively dependent on two weeks bad weather—the most undependable factor of all?"[4] In the summer of 1945 Recknagel had no answer to that overwhelming question.

But in the last week of November 1944, Recknagel had no such inhibitions. He confidently predicted that the weather in the last two weeks of December would be "Führer Weather." This came in two sorts: brilliant sunshine and warm for ceremonial parades, or rainy and misty for an operation when the *Wehrmacht* was faced by a superior enemy air force. For the period December 16–30, Recknagel estimated that there would be rain, damp fog, and probably heavy snow in the Eifel-Ardennes area on the German-Belgian border. It was the kind of weather Hitler would need to conceal his final preparations for the great new counterattack. It would also be the type of weather that would protect his advancing troops against *Ami* air force attack. Now, as Lightning Joe Collins prepared to launch his next attack through the Hurtgen toward the River Roer, Hitler could finally fix a binding date for the start of his great counteroffensive. It would commence on the morning of December 16, 1944. That Saturday would see the start of what was to be known soon as America's European Pearl Harbor.

When the Boy Marshal, Model, had first heard of Hitler's proposed new offensive from Colonel-General Jodl, he had barked angrily at the Chief of Staff, "You can tell *your* Führer from me, that Model won't have any part in it!"[5] On November 4, he and General von Manteuffel, who would lead the Fifth Panzer Army in the attack, set down in writing their objections to the plan. They felt that Hitler's plan to drive to the great Allied supply port of Antwerp, capture it, and thus split the British Monty's from the American armies (plus cutting them off from their supplies) was too ambitious. Model and his subordinate preferred a smaller solution.

This was an attack to the north and south of Aachen into Belgium with Liège as its objective. It would mean, if it was successful, that Eisenhower would lose most of the U.S. First Army currently fighting in the Hurtgen—some ten to fifteen sorely needed divisions, or 25 percent of the Americans' strength. Jodl gave them Hitler's reply the very next day. He snapped, "The Fuhrer has decided that the operation is unalterable in every detail."[6]

It was about this time that Model made his last will and testament, setting his house in order and providing for his wife and son (who would be a general in the postwar German Army one day). Had he some dark inkling of the debacle to come? Although he still held to the smaller solution—at least he paid lip service to it—he began to accept the Führer's grandiose counterattack, throwing all caution to the wind.

Caution—Collins's, Hodges's, and Gerow's—caution had been the cause of the long nightmare of the Hurtgen. The overriding motivation for sustaining the month-long battle in the Forest had been the First Army's concern about the safety of Collins's right flank. If the Top Brass had been more aggressive, they would have bottled up the Hurtgen and driven for the Rhine, leaving the German defenders to wither on the vine. After all, the First Army had all the resources needed for a bold armored offensive; Model hadn't. But Model began to *act* as if Hitler's Germany still possessed the air power, the armor, the resources of manpower and matériel to carry out such a daring, major counterstroke.

When the German 5th Parachute Division arrived at the front from Holland, for instance, only one of its three regiments was fit for combat. Most of its personnel were parachutists in name only. Mainly they were culls from the *Luftwaffe* who had never been trained for ground combat, including two of the regimental colonels. Its artillery was manned by former antiaircraft gunners who did not know how to engage ground targets, and it was virtually without heavy transport. A report on the unit on December 1 stated that, "It was fit for defensive operations under certain conditions."[7] This was the unit that was going to *lead* the infantry drive of the German Seventh Army. Yet Model told its commander, General Heilmann, a hero of the Monte Cassino fighting in Italy earlier in the year, "The parachute troops will find their way forward. I am confident of their courage!"[8]

Just as previously the American commanders had ascribed poor morale and poor quality to the German troops defending the Hurtgen, Model now did the same thing with the Americans. The rear was defended solely by bank clerks dressed up as soldiers. Once the thin crust of the front had been cracked, the *Amis* would "take their heels into their hands," as the Germans phrased it, and run for their lives.

Although Model knew well by now just how hard the Americans could fight in the Hurtgen, he issued reports to his troops to show the poor quality of the *Amis*. The Americans, they were told, avoided hand-to-hand combat at all costs. They did not fight at night and they didn't know how to look after themselves in rain and snow. American armor was overly cautious and had a Tiger phobia; American tanks would not venture off the roads into cross-country attacks. The tankers kept up a constant chatter over their radios that gave their positions and intentions away (which was indeed true). Progressively, as the days in December passed and it was ever closer to the start of the great counter-offensive, he built up the morale of his men by exaggerated accounts of the American fighting man. With considerable help from the Minister of Propaganda and People's Enlightenment, Dr. Josef Goebbels (known popularly as the Poison Dwarf, because of his size and vitriolic tongue,) he managed to convince most of his soldiers that the average American infantryman would not fight unless he was supported by his colossal supply system and masses of aircraft and armor. It would be a fiction that passed into the popular German mythology of the second half of the twentieth century. The *Ami* won, in the end, only because of his massive superiority in men and machines against the poor old *Landser*, who had been forced to rely solely on his own two feet for transport and his antiquated "08" carbine for defense.

As the dates for both attacks—Collins's of December 10 and Model's of December 16—grew closer and closer, the Top Brass on both sides seemed to have lost contact with reality. Despite what he knew of the resources at his disposal and the quality of the American opposition, Model still felt he could achieve at least the smaller solution, the destruction of Hodges's First Army. For their part, Collins, Hodges, and Gerow thought victory was just around the corner—despite the terrible casualties they had incurred in November and early December without achieving any results of significance.

Overall, the U.S. Army fighting the frontier battles was now losing three thousand men a day, 90,000 per month. Reinforcements were amounting to only 53,000 each month. The divisions in the line were at only 78 percent of their normal strength. Twice, on December 6 and 13, in General Patton's Third Army, for example, 5 percent of the manpower in the rear was transferred to the line. But this levee produced only 6,500 men. In Washington, Marshall concluded on December 7 that the only way to make up for the losses on the western front was to starve the Pacific of troops. For the time being, all new reinforcements from the States would go to Europe, but they would arrive too late to play any role in the battle to come.

Yet in spite of their losses, the American generals continued with their battle in the Hurtgen. Their preoccupation with that battle seemed to blind them, too, to the sudden changes in the German order of battle during November and the first week of December. Manteuffel's Fifth Panzer Army had disappeared from Intelligence's map. So had the SS Panzer divisions, reportedly grouped together in a new army, Dietrich's 6th SS Panzer. Where had they gone? What was the reason for their disappearance? Where were they going to be employed when they reappeared? No one seemed to concern themselves with these major changes, save for a few obscure intelligence officers. Hodges, Collins, Gerow, and the rest of the Top Brass didn't.

The old euphoria of October-November had admittedly disappeared. The battle in the Hurtgen had become a desperate slugging match. There was little hope of a decisive breakthrough. Even Lightning Joe Collins, impatient and aggressive as he was, realized that. All the same, the thought that his opponent would come roaring and slugging out of his corner never appears to have entered his head. The German was reeling on the ropes, virtually all strength spent, in no way capable of fighting back. General Collins and all the rest of them, safe and warm in their grand manors and châteaux to the rear, had not reckoned with that evil genius, Adolf Hitler. They thought that the German High Command would share their own caution about protecting the flanks and all the rest of it before attacking. But Field Marshals von Rundstedt and Model were only in nominal command. The man who really dictated German military policy was Hitler, and caution was anathema to the Fuhrer. He was unpredictable and reckless. The Leader of Greater Germany didn't give a damn about the flanks.

Up front, the troops in the Hurtgen continued to suffer—purposelessly. Just before the 8th Infantry Division was withdrawn, one battalion commander stated: "The men of this battalion are physically exhausted. The spirit and the will to fight are there; the physical ability to continue is gone . . . These men are shivering with cold and their hands are so numb that they have to help one another on with their equipment. I firmly believe every man up there should be evacuated through medical channels."[9]

In that first week of December, Robert Barr of the BBC vividly described the scene at Grosshau as the infantry waited to attack again. "An infantry platoon was approaching the village, crouching watchfully in the ditches then moving forward to the next turn in the road and crouching again. Three riflemen lay flat in the thick mud on the road itself, rifles to their shoulders . . . A German with his leg swathed in bandages came limping . . . with his hands up. Three of his comrades lay dead and mud-splashed behind a garden wall. Behind the garden wall the debris had been pushed aside to clear a coal chute which led down to the cellar. One of the soldiers pulled back from his peep-hole and pointing his thumb at the coal chute said, 'Go down there and mind your feet.' "

Barr went down carefully and in the poor light could make out "some forty soldiers lying in groups of threes and fours around fires made from the grease-soaked cardboard of their ration boxes. Over the flames they were heating water to make coffee. One Joe began to fidget with an over-heated can of pork loaf . . . An officer was crouched over a table talking into a field telephone. He was covered in mud, his cheeks were gray and hollowed and his eyes sunken and red-rimmed. Somebody said, 'They're mortaring the road again.' "[10]

Even as they waited to attack, the riflemen suffered. The Germans shelled them all the time. It rained and sleeted constantly with freezing temperatures. Trench foot and frozen feet became endemic. The cases of respiratory complaints rose into the thousands. All day long they slogged about in the mud and rain, and soldiers broke down and sobbed openly with the sheer physical strain of moving themselves and their supplies through these conditions. At night it froze, and when they came staggering out of their foxholes and dugouts in the morning, all was crisp and startlingly white with hoarfrost.

Sergeant Shogren was one of the hundreds who finally succumbed to frostbite. Like the rest of his squad he had gone into the line without any winter clothing, not even gloves. Veteran as he now was, he took some galoshes off a dead GI, but it didn't help. He developed frozen feet and a frozen right hand. "Crossing running streams, always wet, cold at night, not active on a stationary front, our feet were becoming numb. You couldn't massage them for the skin would just rub off. I assigned my men by twos on imaginary patrols just to keep them walking and hopefully the blood circulating. Too much activity might just have drawn the attention of the enemy."[11]

But all his precautions didn't help Shogren. He was taken to an aid station, where a "thick needle was thrust into my toes and then into the ball of my foot. No feeling! A general came by all the wounded and frozen, lined up on the bare floor like firewood, and thanked each one of us."[12] And that was the end of Sergeant Shogren's combat career.

Cases of self-inflicted wounds started to mount again. Men

would shoot off their little fingers or big toes in order to avoid combat and end the misery. These would be their million-dollar wounds. But the authorities were getting wise to the tricks of these reluctant heroes. They had come to the conclusion that anyone shot through the left hand or foot had done it himself (most soldiers are right-handed). As it was almost impossible to convict a man for a self-inflicted wound, the authorities convicted for carelessness, which rated a six-month sentence.

Even that didn't stop those who wanted to get out of the fighting. They convinced their friends to shoot them (in the right hand or foot, of course), firing through a loaf of bread so as not to leave a telltale black powder burn. Others would shoot themselves in the foot in full view of their comrades and noncoms, maintaining the weapon had accidentally discharged itself, or they would shoot each other in a kind of mutual mutilation pact. General Patton remarked cynically of these pacts in his own Third Army: "However since friends were frequently inaccurate and took off too many toes, the practice was never highly developed."[13]

Desertions from the front line rose once more too, as enemy resistance stiffened and conditions became tougher. One infantry sergeant managed to buy and fake leave passes so successfully that he finally reached Chicago after leaving his line outfit in the Hurtgen. Here he remained undetected until he surrendered after the war was safely over.

Most deserters, however, went over the hill to the big cities immediately behind the line—Paris, Brussels, Louvain, and the like, where they lived off the black market, whores, and their wits. A few simply left their companies and went to the rear, where they led a nomadic life hiding in caves and cellars and little dens made of logs and camouflaged with pine branches, eking out a miserable existence on the cans of food which were to be found everywhere.* Their lives were probably not very different from those deserters from Grant's infantry who fled the appalling bloodshed of Wilderness back in 1864.

---

* Even today you can come across these aging cans in the Forest everywhere. Where dumps of cans were buried by the clean-up squads, the floor of the Forest squeaks under one's feet.

* * *

Perhaps because he had begun to hear through the stockade's grapevine that the authorities were having to get tougher with deserters to stop the flow of men going over the hill, Eddie Slovik addressed a plea for mercy to the Supreme Commander one day before the start of the Collins's attack. Misspelling the theater commander's name—"Dear General *Eisenhowser*"—he explained a little of his life and history and how he had only wanted "a transfer from the line."

Slovik ended his appeal with: "How can I tell you how humbley [*sic*] sorry I am for the sins I've committed. I didn't realize at the time what I was doing or what the word desertion meant. What it is like to be condemned to die. I beg of you deeply and sincerely for the sake of my dear wife and mother back home to have mercy on me. To my knowledge I have a good record since my marriage and as a soldier I'd like to continue to be a good soldier.

"Anxiously awaiting your reply, which I earnestly pray is favorable. God bless you and in your Work for Victory: I Remain Yours for Victory, Pvt. Eddie D. Slovik."[14]

Of course, Eisenhower never read the condemned man's pathetic letter. It would not have made an iota of difference to Slovik's fate even if he had. The whirlwind on the western front was about to burst loose. By the time Eddie Slovik's problem was brought to Eisenhower's attention, his confidence in his ability to conduct the war in Europe had been dealt a severe blow. His front had been shattered. Hundreds, perhaps thousands, of American soldiers were throwing away their weapons and bugging out. Someone—it mattered not who—would have to serve as an example and a warning to the rest of what their fate would be if they deserted on the western front.

The undersized, petty ex-con, who had grown up in poverty at the height of the Great Depression and who had shown himself incapable of adapting to the short, brutish, frightening life of a combat soldier in the Hurtgen, had to pay the price of that desertion. The powers-that-be thought a well-publicized execution would stop the rot.

On December 23, with his world falling in pieces all about him, Eisenhower made his decision. Not since Lincoln had an American commander in chief ordered one of his soldiers executed. For the first time since 1865 Eisenhower did that; Eddie Slovik was to be the first soldier shot for desertion in nearly a hundred years. The pitiless necessity of making an example of Slovik was proof of Eisenhower's anxiety about the crisis in morale at the front.

This December of 1944, with the old crooner belting out "White Christmas" from every loudspeaker and radio behind the line, was going to be one of the darkest Decembers in the entire 180-year history of the United States Army. White Christmas it certainly would be, but any dreams that America's generals might have had for it would be shattered—totally, irrevocably, terrifyingly. They had failed to learn the lessons of the *Hurtgenwald* in September, October, November. In December they would pay the bitter price of that failure.

13

They brought the Rangers down after dark on December 8, 1944—what was left of them. The Germans had attacked five times. One hundred to two hundred men, waving, shrieking, firing as they came. By midday of the first morning on Castle Hill, the 2nd Rangers' D Company had seventeen men left out of its original sixty-five. Company F had only fifteen.

Attack followed attack. In the breaks between the attacks, as the surviving Germans fled the way they had come, leaving the shattered earth littered with the gray-clad corpses of their dead, a hellish barrage would descend upon the Rangers, who were getting fewer and fewer by the minute. By four o'clock that afternoon, with darkness already beginning to descend upon that lunar landscape, only twenty-five out of the original 130 were left on the hill, but as one of them wrote afterward, "You stay in your hole only because you are a Ranger." Their pride in themselves and in their outfit kept them there on that terrible hillside. There were no Sloviks in the 2nd Rangers.

Night fell. It brought no relief for the handful of weary survivors. As the historian of the 2nd Rangers wrote afterwards: "That was the longest night we ever spent: fifteen hours of weird, black nightmare; of flares streaming their hellish glow on the tortured hillside; of mortar shells crumping in a few yards away, beating the breath from our lungs, leaving us gasping and dazed; fifteen tense hours of tense straining to detect the approach of the Hun, who did not come often, for to move on the hill that night meant death, swift and violent. Then the red dawn came again for us; but we were tired and dulled with sleeplessness and shock. We were so few . . . so very few . . ."[1]

They were. But there was a respite for them that dawn. Out of the sky came the flashing silver metal birds of the TAC Air Force, wheeling and screaming overhead at treetop height, blasting the German positions. Meanwhile one platoon of E Company plodded up the cratered height to fill out the tragic gaps in D and F Companies.

Clouds rolled in from the east and the fighter-bombers screeched back to their bases in Belgium and Holland, unable to help anymore. At midday the Germans, urged on by their officers and noncoms, charged the Rangers' position in force, coming in from three sides, determined this time to wipe them out. Although they had been reinforced, the Rangers looked as if they were going to be overrun, so determined was the German attack. Then, at a crucial moment, when all seemed lost, Sergeant Secor, his own weapon useless, seized two captured German machine pistols. Holding one under each arm, he stood up in full view of the field-greys only yards away, and like a western marshal in a movie shootout, blasted them from left to right. Germans went down everywhere, screaming and writhing, crying piteously for *"Sanitäter,"* who were already dead or wounded themselves. It was too much for them. They broke and ran, streaming down the way they had come, stepping on the bodies of their own dead, pushing and jostling each other in a desperate attempt to get away from the murderous firing.

Just before dusk they tried one last time. This time they came in even greater strength. Somehow the battered, infinitely weary survivors held them, and the Germans fled once more. They never came again. Angrily the German artillery and mortars poured a hail of vindictive fire at the Ranger positions as though acknowledging defeat. But as the night wore on, the German fire slackened until in the end it was "no more than one or two exploding each second," as one survivor recorded.

Shortly after midnight the relief came. What were left of the Rangers were brought out, their places taken over by fresh infantry. Their losses had been high. They had lost a quarter of their original strength in battle. In Dog Company, stumbling blindly to the rear, there were only fifteen men left out of the original fifty who had gone up Castle Hill on December 7.

The figures were typical. The 8th Infantry and the 5th Armored Divisions, under whose command they had come, had lost four thousand men, of whom twelve hundred had been felled by exposure and combat fatigue.

The survivors huddled in their crude shelters in the Forest, from which they had been summoned with such high hopes in what now seemed another age. "The wind sighed heavily through the snow-blanketed pine branches, pushed its way in through the cracks in the rude shelters and jostled the smoky flames of the crude gasoline lamps," as the historian of D Company recorded. "Flickering shadows played over the drawn dirty faces of the Company's fifteen men. They slept and when outgoing shells rustled overhead, tired bodies jerked and twitched in automatic nervous reaction."[2]

Outside in the Forest it had begun to snow again as the guns thundered and rolled. This was the barrage heralding the new offensive. Yet again they were softening up the new German positions. Once more they were going to attack into that damned Forest.

December 10, 1944, dawned one of those days that the weathermen call "partly cloudy." As the artillery rumbled and the gray sky here and there was split by the sudden pink flash of shells exploding short, the stiff anxious men waited for the word to move, puffing nervously at their cigarettes, urinating in the ditches and against the trees far too often—a sure sign of nerves. It wouldn't be long now.

In the center there was the 9th Infantry Division, supported by a combat command of the 3rd Armored Division. To the right of the 9th, also attacking into the fringes of the Forest, was the 83rd Infantry Division, having its first taste of the Hurtgen. It would be supported by the 5th Armored Division. It was going to be a four-division thrust, some thirty thousand men, against a mixed bunch of defenders, paras, and the grandly named "people's grenadiers," perhaps five to six thousand of them.

But as always the Germans were well dug in, had strong artillery support, and were prepared to fight fanatically hard to defend the holy soil of the Reich. For all of them knew now, even the humblest stubble-hopper, that something was going on here on the frontier; that the tide was about to change. "Of course, we didn't know exactly what was going to happen," ex-people's grenadier Heinz Luetgens recalled many years later. "The big shots kept everything pretty well secret that December. But suddenly there were great piles of ammo and gas to the rear and the very roads were covered with straw to keep down the noise of the supply trains which moved at night. In fact, every single road had a special officer allotted to it to check and see everything moved swiftly and securely. And from a pal who had just come from Wittlich,* I heard that the place was full of fresh troops and daily more were arriving at the station there . . . There was something in the wind, we all knew that, and it gave us a shot in the arm. After three weeks in the Hurtgen we all needed cheering up, I can tell you."[3]

The attackers needed cheering up too, as they gazed apprehensively at what lay in front of them: a lunar landscape of cratered fields, grotesquely shot-down trees, ruined and already rusting tanks—and bodies everywhere, bloated, stinking bodies, some with their stomachs ripped open, the prey of marauding foxes, savage dogs, even cats. It was an ever-present reminder that death waited for them all.

At 7:30 A.M. the attack commenced. The 9th Infantry Division advanced swiftly against light opposition. Still there were casualties, and some were incurred in a minefield. The medics hesitated as the wounded cried out for help. Not Capt. (Father) Anthony DeLaura. He went into the uncharted field of sudden death and voluntarily evacuated ten casualties. Then he was wounded himself, but he continued his work of mercy, evacuating more wounded. In the Hurtgen even the dog collar of a man of God was not proof against enemy weapons.

---

* A German town, not far from the Moselle, which was one of the main railheads for the Ardennes Offensive.

By midday the advance was progressing nicely when a German counterattack hit the advance in force. Aided by tanks and artillery, the men of the 9th managed to ward it off, but that was the end of their advance for that day.

The 9th's 60th Regiment was thrown into the attack, supported by Task Force Hogan. Colonel Hogan, a cleft-chin veteran who had been in the thick of the border fighting ever since September, cracked into action with his usual aggressive energy. The combined tank-infantry team rolled up the opposition swiftly, moving toward the wrecked township of Echtz, their objective. For a while they paused, the infantry crouching in the muddy ditches, the Shermans tightly buttoned up, as the artillery battered the place. Then they attacked against scattered resistance. By nightfall Echtz was American, but to their horror, the victors discovered something that even the veterans of the 9th and 3rd had never seen before—*the retreating Germans had booby-trapped their own dead!*

That afternoon Lightning Joe Collins came up to see General Craig, commanding general of the 9th. As usual he was his vital, aggressive self. Roughly he asked Craig why he was still holding on to his 39th Infantry Regiment. Why hadn't he thrown it into the great attack already?

Craig knew trouble when he saw it. General Stroh had already been sacked for having been too slow, in the opinion of the Top Brass. Tubby Barton of the 4th would soon follow. Craig didn't intend to be the third general officer to lose his command in the damned Hurtgen. He ordered the 39th Infantry into the attack in what the divisional history called later "one of the finest examples of maneuvering in military history."[4]

The 39th's objective was Merode, in particular its castle, where two weeks before the Big Red One had failed so lamentably. Merode Castle, a typical eighteenth-century structure of the area with slate-covered, onion-shaped towers, dominated the township. From its elevated position it commanded excellent observation over the whole area and could control the advance of anyone attempting to leave the confines of the Forest.

So the men of the 39th were now faced with an operation that smacked of the Middle Ages. For Merode Castle was surrounded by a moat, twenty feet wide and six feet deep, and there was only one way across—the bridge, a narrow stone structure that could be easily defended by a handful of brave men. In this case, the defenders were really brave; they were the young fanatical paras of the 3rd Parachute Division.

Craig went up personally to look the situation over. He knew the pressure was on, and in the age-old Army fashion he applied the squeeze to the next in line, Colonel van Bond, commanding the 39th Infantry Regiment. Bond didn't let him down. Boldly he proclaimed he would set up his command post in Merode Castle before nightfall and that he would be delighted to entertain the commanding general to drink there this very night. It was the sort of thing that senior officers always said to each other on such occasions: the kind of remark that went into the history books. The remarks of the men who were going to carry out that promise—the poor bloody infantry—went unrecorded. After all, afterward a lot of them weren't around anymore to make remarks, boastful or otherwise.

With no less a person than Lightning Joe Collins himself observing, the attack of the 39th Infantry got under way. Supported by tanks and the buzz boys of the TAC Air Force, a two-battalion assault went in. Steadily the Americans advanced, exerting a tremendous pressure on the couple of hundred enemy paratroopers defending the place in a last-ditch stand by the 3rd Parachute Division. Unknown to the Americans, the 3rd Para was being pulled out of the line that day. In six days it would spearhead the German drive on General Hodges's HQ at Spa, together with the tankers of *Obersturmbannfuhrer* Peiper's Battle Group of the 1st SS Panzer Division—the Adolf Hitler Bodyguard.

The paras counterattacked. The Americans threw them back. One after another they reduced the enemy bunkers and pillboxes, which were everywhere. A barrage was brought down on the eighteenth-century castle itself. Shells gouged great holes in its walls so that they looked as if they were suffering from the symptoms of some loathsome skin disease. The men of the 39th's 1st Battalion peppered it with short arms and bazooka fire at close range. The air was full of flying shot and shell. The first of the paras surrendered, faces gray with dust, eyes wild and unseeing with shock. The Americans rushed forward over the debris-littered bridge, and then it was all over. They had captured Merode Castle. As the divisional history put it grandiloquently: "Colonel Bond awaited visitors that night . . . his command post was Merode Castle if anyone wanted to know!"[5] Nobody mentioned the dead.

The objective of the new boys to the Hurtgen, General Macon's 83rd Infantry Division, was the two villages of Gey and Strass, northeast of Grosshau. After the 4th had finally captured Grosshau, it had been too exhausted to advance any farther. Now it was the 83rd's task to capture the twin villages. To do so, Macon assigned a whole regiment, some three thousand strong, to each place. The 330th Infantry went to Strass on the right, and the 331st went to Gey on the left. It was massive overkill, but Macon was not going to repeat the mistakes of his predecessors. To back the infantry up there was a whole combat command of the 5th Division.

With so much force at his disposal, General Macon anticipated capturing the two villages in one bold fast stroke. He was mistaken. Always in the Hurtgen, things didn't work out as the generals anticipated. On this second Sunday of December, Adventsonntag, where before the war every household in the twin villages would be lighting the second candle on the advent-wreath* and there'd be coffee and cakes, a murderous house-to-house battle broke out now.

Strass surrendered, but not for long. The Germans threw in a vicious counterattack, supported by tanks. The Americans retreated, while in Gey the struggle from house to house continued

---

* In Germany the run-up to Christmas is celebrated by lighting a candle set in a wreath of fir twigs each Sunday of advent.

with bitter, cruel doggedness. The Americans were making progress, but their losses were high and Macon knew he needed tanks up in the beleaguered villages—*and soon!*

The 744th Tank Battalion of the 5th Division was whistled up. The Shermans didn't get far. They followed the tracks over which the infantry had passed safely, but no one had checked them for anti-tank mines, the big round German Teller mines that could lift a 33-ton Sherman right into the air. One after another three of the steel monsters ran over mines and came to a sudden halt, hulls smoking, tracks spread out behind them like severed limbs.

Then the German artillery observers spotted them. Instantly shells began to fall, as the engineers, desperate and hard-pressed, attempted to find a way through for the rest of the battalion. But the shrapnel lying on the earth was too thick. The steel fragments made it impossible for the engineers to use their mine detectors.

The German defenders in Gey were strengthened by more infantry reinforcements. Colonel York, commanding the 231st, did the same. The result was a stalemate, and without tanks, Colonel York could not advance any farther.

Meanwhile, casualties were flooding the 5th's advanced aid station where the two MO's, Captain Holbert and Captain Tempel, worked all-out, red-eyed with fatigue. They treated casualties from all the units involved in the battle for the two villages. That first day they attended to one hundred grievously wounded men. On the morrow it would be twice that number and climbing all the time. Jeep after jeep came rolling in with its pitiful cargo of shocked, wounded soldiers, their bandages bloody, as they moaned with the agony of it all.

The twelve aidmen up in the rifle platoon, of whom only two would not become casualties themselves, worked flat out trying to patch up those who could not be evacuated. For now, as the Germans started to fire at the jeeps (the Americans did the same at their half-tracked ambulances), only tanks could get the wounded through safely.

One aidman had had enough. After making three attempts to

crawl into an open field to evacuate a casualty and each time being driven back by sniper fire, Sgt. Leon Kraskin stood up and *walked* to the wounded man. The sniper fired again. A slug grazed the back of the brave noncom's head, driving a piece of his steel helmet into his scalp. Kraskin disregarded his own wound, tended to the casualty, and then dragged him to safety.

The Division's chaplains were up front, working with the medics too. One, Chaplain Palmer, was spotted by a GI in his foxhole. The latter expressed his surprise. "I looked up from my foxhole and there was ol' Chaplain Palmer. 'You'd better get down in here,' I said to him. 'You do the shooting and leave the praying to me,' he said, and I'm damned if he didn't crouch right there in the open and say one. It made me feel a hell of a lot better."[6]

On the night of December 10, that terrible second advent Sunday, Strass was secure. But the Germans had already begun their old tricks of the Hurtgen. They infiltrated under cover of darkness and cut the road to Strass with anti-tank guns. At the same time there was a half-mile stretch between Strass and Gey where they controlled the road linking the two places. In effect, both battalions holding the two villages were cut off.

Nevertheless, Macon insisted to General Oliver, commanding the 5th Division, that armor must be moved along the road to Strass on the morrow. "The road is about as open as we can get it," Macon snapped with an air of finality. "We can't keep out the snipers."[7]

Oliver had been in the Hurtgen much longer than Macon. He knew what happened to unguarded tanks in the Forest. He wasn't convinced. He took the matter up with Lightning Joe. The latter checked with Macon and then ordered, "Go on ahead."[8]

Violence came with the dawn. As always the Germans reacted more quickly than the Americans. While the American generals had been *discussing* what to do next, they *acted*. Just before dawn they came out of the trees around Strass in force. Almost immediately a ding-dong battle commenced that continued all day.

Macon began to worry. He stated, "We may have more to do than we anticipated."[9]

Another battalion was flung in. Oliver decided he would send in armored infantry in front of his precious Shermans. They bumped into Germans after going only a few hundred yards down the vital road. Hurriedly they flung themselves from their half-tracks and went into action. Again casualties mounted, but the Germans could not be budged. With heavy losses, especially in company and platoon commanders, the 5th's armored infantrymen of the 15th Infantry became hesitant and disorganized. Brave officers and noncoms twice rallied the armored infantry and led them into another attack to get the vital supply link opened, but by nightfall every single company commander had been killed or wounded and the attack bogged down.

In Strass as darkness fell at last, the trapped infantry battalion was in a bad way. They had just beaten off the third German counterattack of the day. They had suffered sixty casualties and were in need of medical supplies. They were out of food and water. Ammunition was running low and they had only seven tanks left. In the first two days of the new offensive in the Hurtgen, the infantry battalion had run through *four* commanders—one killed, one missing, and two wounded. Strass was a death trap.

That same evening the intelligence staff at Hodges's HQ in Spa issued its estimate of what the Germans would do next: "It is plain that the enemy's strategy in defense of the Reich is based on the exhaustion of our offensive to be followed by an all-out counterattack with armor between the Roer and Erft supported by every weapon he can bring up."[10]

Still the Top Brass was suffering from tunnel vision. Their eyes were fixed exclusively on the battle for the Hurtgen. What was happening just south of the Forest seemingly did not enter into their deliberations. Of course they were right about an all-out counterattack with armor. On that very December evening, between Monschau and Trier, a front of sixty miles, *eighteen* German divisions were massing, a quarter of a million men. Right they were, only they'd gotten the place of the German counter-attack utterly, totally, completely *wrong!*

In the American Army of World War II you stood a better chance of being assigned to the infantry, after being drafted, if you were a clerk, teacher, or piano tuner than you did if you were a boilerworker or vice-squad cop. Boilermakers, bricklayers, riveters, and the like went into the Corps of Engineers. Vice-squad patrolmen were assigned to the Military Police, while detectives were thought especially suitable for the Provost Corps. The great majority of those of draft age who volunteered opted for the Army Air Corps.

As a result, drafted bookkeepers, piano tuners, shipping clerks, teachers, a whole range of white-collar occupations, were usually recommended for any arm or service. As it turns out, they were mostly shipped to the infantry, and unlike the British and German Armies, which had several categories of physical fitness according to muscular strength, endurance, agility, etc., the U.S. Army recognized only two: "fit for general service" and "fit for limited service." Whereas in the British Army, for example, an infantryman going overseas for active service had to belong to the top category of physical fitness (A-I,) his American counter-part needed only to be "fit for general service."

Little thought was given by the powers-that-be to the question of whether the infantryman would be able to fight in hand-to-hand combat, march long distances with a heavy pack on his back, endure on little food the kind of conditions pertaining in the winter of 1944 in the Hurtgen Forest. It was thought in Washington that regardless of previous occupation and physical and mental health, anyone who was "fit for general service" was suitable to become a "SSN 745," that is, a *rifleman!**

In 1943, when the mobilization of American manpower for combat had reached its final state, twelve thousand infantrymen, fit for general service as replacements, were examined at Fort

---

* An enlisted man's classification system, "specification serial number."

Meade. The results were not very good. They were found to be inferior in height, weight, and education to the average for the Army as a whole. In that same year, the Fifth Army in Italy reported that "squad leaders and patrol leaders with initiative were scarce."[11] It was discovered that there was a direct link between panic in combat and resultant combat fatigue and poor junior leadership, particularly in the infantry. As one medical officer at the front reported: "I saw one whole platoon of an infantry company go out because the platoon sergeant went 'wacky.' "[12] During the 70th Infantry Division's first week of combat in France, another observer saw a whole squad keel over, one after another like a set of dominoes, when one of their members, an NCO, fainted during action.

Yet, despite the knowledge that there was something wrong with the general quality of the infantrymen they were sending overseas (Brigadier General Marshall would report after the war that *half* the infantrymen he interviewed just after combat reported they had not even fired their rifles), the authorities clung to the old system.* Teenage replacements were sent into combat after only thirteen weeks of basic training, led (more often than not) by "sixty-day wonders" straight from college and without any combat experience whatsoever.

The situation was little different in infantry divisions that went overseas as a complete unit. Those divisions, which had been established in 1942 and 1943 and had remained in the States till after the invasion of Europe, had been constantly drained of trained, experienced men to form new cadres or to provide replacements for outfits already overseas. The gaps in their ranks had been filled with mostly unwilling culls from the coastal artillery, the military police, and Army Air Corps ground staffs. As the time to go overseas came ever closer, these men would be pushed swiftly through an infantry training course and reclassified as SSN 745s.

In the case of the 78th and 106th Infantry Divisions now

---

* In January 1945, when the war was almost over, there was unanimous agreement in the War Department that better use must be made of soldiers according to physical capacity.

going into the line in Western Europe, the former had lost 4,698 men between February and September 1944, while the latter had lost a staggering 12,462 men from its activation in 1943 until its departure for Europe in November 1944. "Trained" divisions like these were coming into the line now completely green, commanded by senior officers who had perhaps never been in combat at all, or whose last taste of action had been as young lieutenants and captains back in 1918.

In the case of the 106th Division, for example, which started taking up its sector of the front just below the Hurtgen Forest on December 13, its commander, Major General Jones, at 53 had spent twenty-eight years in the Army without ever having heard a single shot fired in anger. Of his three regimental commanders, only one had been in action before—as a GI in World War I. None of his battalion commanders had ever fought before. In the light of what was soon to come, it was a recipe for disaster.*

While the ill-fated 106th Infantry Division waited unwittingly and passively for the great blow that was going to annihilate it in the Ardennes, the 78th Division went straight into action. On an icy, snowbound December 13, the completely green division went into its first attack, one of many formations that were marched off the boats bringing them from the States and were thrown recklessly into battle by the Top Brass. After two and a half years of training, its moment of truth had come. The 78th Division was to attack into the Hurtgen and take the toughest objective of them all—*Schmidt!*

Schmidt had been won, lost, recaptured, and lost again at the cost of so many young American lives this terrible fall and winter. How would the greenhorns fare?

---

* Within seven days of entering combat, the 106th Division was virtually destroyed, ten thousand of its men surrendering to the enemy—the second greatest surrender of U.S. troops since the Civil War. See C. Whiting: *Death of a Division* (Stein & Day) for further details.

14

The men of the Lightning Division, as the 78th called itself, advanced silently through the dawn mist, creeping, like gray, predatory timber wolves, ever nearer to the German pillbox line. The going was slow and icy and the temperature was subzero. But as the divisional history records: "the biting cold which had made the night miserable was forgotten as the fear of battle clutched at their hearts."[1]

There was no sound save that of their own heavy, apprehensive breathing and the boom of the 155mm guns in the distance. The new boys had learned something from their predecessors in the Forest. This time there was no preliminary barrage to soften up the enemy; this time they hoped to catch the Germans off guard.

The lead battalion of the Division's 310th Regiment climbed and panted up the steep cliff that was its line of departure. Then, sliding and plunging in the ice and snow, they came down the other side, still covered by the gray mist, and deployed on the ice-and-snow-covered field to attack the first objective, the village of Rollesbroich. Everything was going exactly according to plan.

Suddenly, startlingly, there was a blinding flash followed by a mushroom of black smoke. Someone yelled in agony. The greenhorns came to a halt. Tense faces, which had been illuminated momentarily, turned to where a dark shape lay writhing on the snow. A soldier had stepped on a mine. The 76th Infantry Division had suffered its first casualty in battle.

"Move on, men . . . Let's go, men." The reassuring voices of the officers and noncoms got the shocked greenhorns going once more. Now, as they advanced up a slope, it was beginning to

grow light. The advancing soldiers started to show up in shadowy groups, young men going into their first battle on a cold December morning in the middle of nowhere.

Abruptly, the ridge line in front of them erupted into fire. The Germans had spotted them! The greenhorns did what most inexperienced troops do when they come under fire for the first time; they dropped to the snow to figure out the next move. But not all of them. One squad leader kept his head as the German defenders blazed away furiously. He waited until the German fire seemed to be weakening. Next moment he was rushing in, followed by his wildly cheering men. The Germans surrendered tamely, caught just as they were beginning to run out of ammunition. A few minutes later the hill was in American hands, and below lay the dim outlines of Rollesbroich. After two long years of training, as the divisional history records proudly, "they had taken their first hill"[2] on the way to Schmidt. There would be many more hills to be taken before they reached Schmidt. By that time, over two months away, a lot of the young men so proud of their first conquest would be long dead.

Now the real resistance commenced. From a machine-gun nest on a hill to the right of the village a machine gun started to chatter hysterically. One of the greenhorns fell into the snow. The lead men wriggled back to cover. A mortar bomb came hurtling out of the sky. Suddenly there was a great steaming brown hole in the middle of the snowfield. Another followed, and another. The battle was on.

Now their own 105mm howitzers started to return the German fire. Shells shrieked over the heads of the Lightning men as their harassed, red-faced officers tried to get them moving again because they were on the exposed, reverse slope of a hill. To advance would be suicidal, but that was what their commander, General Parker, wanted them to do.

His junior officers thought differently. Hastily they revised the plan of attack. As *fifteen* battalions of American artillery started to plaster the German positions, the leading companies slipped to the southwestern edge of Rollesbroich. Now the American commanders knew it would be too dangerous to keep the artillery firing; the shells might kill their own men. They were ordered to cease firing. In a loud echoing silence, they advanced on the first half-timbered, white-painted house.

A rifle cracked like the sound of a twig being snapped underfoot in a dry summer. *"Sniper!"* someone yelled urgently. A soldier darted forward, zigzagging expertly like one of those Hollywood heroes in a war epic. He ran to a clump of bushes and heaved a grenade at the nearest house. It bounced off the wall and exploded harmlessly in the garden. Undeterred, the unknown soldier tried again, tossing two grenades through the windows of the lower floor. A muffled crump. A burst of black smoke through the suddenly shattered door. A shrill scream of agony. A smoking figure in tattered field-gray. And the culls, the unfit, the ill-trained—the reluctant heroes of the 78th Infantry Division, fighting their first battle, had killed their first Krauts.

As the hardened, middle-aged officers, who bore the stars of generals, liked to call it, they had been "blooded."

Meanwhile, in the section held by the 83rd Infantry and 5th Armored Division, each gray new day was the same. The morning started with the same merciless killing attack against stubborn, obstinate German resistance. The infantry would stumble forward, firing and dying as they advanced across the frozen fields. *Twenty yards . . . fifty yards . . . one hundred . . .* and that would be about it. They would take no more for a while. Sweating like pigs, breath harsh and hectic, they would hack away at the unyielding earth to scrape out a foxhole before the Kraut mortar or artillery barrage descended upon them. They knew it would come. It always did. The Germans were a very methodical people and had gotten the business of killing people down to a fine art by now; after all, they had been working at it for nearly six years.

They had a respite of a kind: a couple of hours at the bottom of a shaking hole rocked by artillery shells. Then the whistles would shrill again and there'd be that old, old cry, *"Let's go, men!"* Off they'd go for another hundred yards and another damned foxhole. And all the while they were losing more and more men, leaving them on the snow—a carpet of still khaki.

In the Hurtgen that second week of December, heroism was accepted as nothing less than duty. Wounded during the first day of the attack, S. Sgt. William Carter of the 5th Division's armored infantry was evacuated to the aid station. Next day he returned to the fight, and wounded once more, was returned to the aid station again. Both times he was told to wait for an ambulance, which would take him to the rear; both times he slipped off and returned to his company. When he turned up at the aid station a third time, the surgeon knew that this time he couldn't slip away. He had been shot in the foot and couldn't even walk!

On the same day that the 78th Division went into its first attack to the south of the 5th Division, one single battalion of the 5th reported that its three line companies were down to four officers and 170 enlisted. At full strength the battalion in question—the 15th Infantry—had 18 officers and 735 enlisted men. As always the Hurtgen was demanding its bloody toll.

Still the tankers and infantry continued to fight on in this slow, agonizing manner, gradually working themselves out of the Forest to where 1,200 yards of open ground covered by a dozen German guns lay to their front. All the battalion staff came up to encourage the weary survivors. Everyone knew that an attack across that open space was going to be suicidal. But everyone also knew that the Top Brass was yelling for results. Why? What was the value of a piece of sodden, snowbound German real estate? No one could ever explain later.

On the morning of Thursday, December 14, 1944, the 5th's CCB launched its attack. Its objective was a quarry that lay in some other woods directly across the exposed ground. Three companies of the 15th Battalion were to carry out the assault with each company being supported by a platoon of Sherman tanks.

As always the guns thundered, pouring fire on the German defenses. Then the first cautious files began to creep out of the shattered woods, rifles at the high port, bodies held tense and apprehensive, waiting for that first red-hot poker burn of steel. They came to a draw. There was the obscene howl and thump of massed mortars as the Germans turned the fire of every available piece on the crouching infantry.

Men started to go down on all sides, dropping their weapons and crumpling silently to the snow, as if they were very tired and wished only to sleep. Some, dying violently, writhed and twisted in their final throes, flinging up their arms, faces upturned in savage fury, appealing to God Himself, it seemed, for mercy. But there was no mercy on high this terrible Thursday. The Germans savaged the stalled infantry.

Sgt. Robert Rufiange gasped with horror as he saw ten of his platoon drop, seriously wounded. With fingers that felt like clumsy sausages, he patched up his moaning, groaning men the best he could until the bandages were exhausted. Then he hurriedly ran to the rear while under fire to fetch aidmen.

Shermans rumbled forward in an attempt to shield the stalled infantry, showering mud everywhere. Three were hit and staggered to a halt, rearing up on their bogies as they were struck, gleaming silver holes suddenly skewered in their steel sides. Others couldn't even start. The Germans had learned long ago in Russia what America's planners back in Washington had not, that tanks needed broader tracks in mud and snow. The Shermans bogged down on all sides. Then the tanks' commander, Capt. Robert McNab, was wounded—and that ended the tank attack.

As the divisional history of the 5th Armored recorded after the war: "Artillery, mortars and machine guns blasted and pounded the open ground over which the men were trying to advance. To advance was impossible. Nothing could live in that open field more than a few seconds. The men slowly pulled back from the exposed ground into the woods, carrying their wounded with them."[3]

The Hurtgen had beaten the Americans again.

On that same morning of December 14, a terrified Luxembourg woman in her early forties, Madame Elise Dele from the abandoned village of Bivels, crouched shivering on the wet, eastern bank of the border stream the Our and waited. Four days before, she had been going about her business when she had run into two German soldiers who had questioned her about the *Amis* holding the town of Vianden before they had sent her to the nearest German *Kreisstadt,** Bitburg. There she had noticed the bomb-shattered country town was filled with troops, especially infantry of the SS.

Madame Dele, who had relatives serving in the *Wehrmacht* and spoke German (at least a dialect of it called *Letzeburgisch*) as her native tongue, realized that something was afoot. She still remembered 1940 when German troops coming from Bitburg had landed all over her native country in two-man planes spearheading the main attack. Madame Dele decided she wanted to get back to Luxembourg before the trouble started.

Now at last she was almost safe, because she could already hear the muffled chink of oars as a little boat set off in the morning mist heading across the fast-running Our toward her. She had contacted the Resistance. Two young men were risking their lives to take her home. However, since 1940 Luxembourg had been incorporated in the Reich and all Luxembourg citizens had become *Reichsdeutsche,* so her two rescuers were therefore traitors. If they were caught they faced the death penalty.

Greetings were exchanged in that slow, ponderous dialect of theirs, which the average German from the north might well have thought a foreign language, and then the three of them were off. The two young men pulling against the current were well aware that from the heights behind them the Germans would be able to see everything once the morning mist had lifted. While they rowed, Madame Dele told them what she had seen in Bitburg. A naive village woman of no great education, she had

---

* County seat.

seen enough of soldiers these last four years to know the "Prussians," as they still called the Germans in their native dialect, were coming back.

In Vianden, dominated by its ruined castle, once the family home of the "Delanoys," distant ancestors of the American President Franklin Delano Roosevelt, she told the Americans what she had seen. They seemed to be impressed, and they gave her food and coffee—real bean coffee. Then she was bundled into a jeep and driven across the next ridge line into the next-largest town, Diekirch, known locally up to now only because of its brewery, but soon to hit the headlines all over the world.

Here she told her tale once again to a senior intelligence officer of the battered 28th Infantry Division, which was trying to recover from the ordeal of the Hurtgen in this pretty, rural area, known as Luxembourg's Switzerland. Again she was given coffee, as excited discussion broke out all around her in English, which she didn't understand, and then it was into the cab of a truck and she was on her way to Wilitz. On this Thursday, December 14, 1944, Madame Elise Dele from the Luxembourg hamlet of Bivels had abruptly become a very important person.

The information that she had brought with her now started to make the wires buzz as it went up the chain of command from the headquarters of the 28th Division in Luxembourg to those of General Middleton's VIII Corps (which held the Ardennes) in a red-brick barracks in the Belgian town of Bastogne, known hitherto only for its annual nut market.* From there it passed on, being coded and decoded three or four times en route, until it finally reached Spa, the HQ of the U.S. First Army. There, at exactly fifteen minutes to midnight, a G-2 clerk entered it into Intelligence section's files.

Col. Benjamin Monk Dickson, G-2 of Hodges's First Army, was the intelligence officer whose task it was now to assess the

---

* Interestingly enough, the local citizens first thought McAuliffe's celebrated reply of "Nuts" (in actual fact it was something much cruder, but the PR people cleaned it up later) to the German demand for the surrender of Bastogne had something to do with their celebrated nuts and their market.

value of the information that the Luxembourg peasant woman had brought with her from Bitburg in the heart of the enemy camp. Dickson had been to West Point and had gone to Siberia with one of America's abortive expeditionary forces against the Bolsheviks in 1919. But after World War I he had not seen much future in the Army and had resigned his commission to become a mechanical engineer. However, he had stayed in the Army Reserve, and, as he was proficient in French and German it was not surprising that when he was recalled in 1942 it was to military intelligence.

Thereafter Dickson saw service in North Africa and Sicily before moving to England with Bradley. There, in the rank of colonel, he was handed on to the new arrival, General Hodges, as his chief of intelligence. By this time, although very extroverted, with a good fund of stories, he was regarded in staff circles as something of a nervous Nellie. He had experienced the debacle of the Kasserine Pass* in 1943 in North Africa and was inclined to pessimistic assessments of German intentions.

Now, on this quiet Thursday night, one day before he was due to go on leave to Paris, Dickson pondered the woman's information—*"she observed many horse-drawn vehicles . . . pontons, small boats . . . many troops in light gray with black collars (SS troops) . . . river-crossing material"*—and wondered what it could all add up to.

Four days before, he had guessed that the Germans were preparing a counterattack. He already possessed information about German commando and sabotage raids behind American lines. He had noted, too, that freshly captured German troops were full of high spirits and that their morale had achieved a new peak. "This has been expressed by attempts to escape," he had written on the tenth, "and avowed eagerness on the part of the prisoners to return and rejoin the battle for Germany."[4]

Then his attention, like that of most of the Top Brass, had been concentrated on the Hurtgen Forest and the Roer dams

---

* See C. Whiting, *Kasserine* (Stein & Day), for further details.

beyond. He had anticipated that the counterattack, when it came, would come in that area. But what was he now to make of the buildup in the Bitburg sector, well to the south of the Hurtgen?

There were other factors to be taken into consideration. He had learned that same Thursday that many PWs had told their interrogators that an offensive was to be launched by the *Wehrmacht* between the seventeenth and twenty-fifth of December. Other prisoners had spoken of the recapture of the Imperial city of Aachen, the first one in the Reich to be taken by the Americans. It would be a Christmas present for the Führer.* There were also reports of massive reinforcements for the front arriving at railheads in the Eifel from Dueren to the Moselle town of Wittlich. The whole of the U.S. First Army's front was being flooded with new German troops. *Why?*

Suddenly Monk startled the other staff officers by slapping his hand against the big wall map, his fist resting on the area between Monschau, Germany, and Echternach in Luxembourg. *"It's the Ardennes, gentlemen!"* he exclaimed excitedly.

His staff was not impressed—they knew just how impetuous and volatile their boss was. Nor were his other listeners impressed, most of them Regular Army officers who were set in their ways, unlike this Johnny-come-lately. They remembered how, back in September, Monk had actually dared to wake the Commanding General, Hodges, to inform him excitedly that a monitored German radio broadcast had just reported the Army was disarming the SS at Field Marshal von Rundstedt's orders. Germany was throwing in the sponge. She was ready to sue for peace. It turned out that Dickson had been very badly duped. Intelligence had intercepted one of its own "black" propaganda broadcasts beamed from Radio Luxembourg and aimed at destabilizing the German civilian population.

In the end, Dickson's completely accurate guess was dis-

---

* The PWs had got the time and the place wrong, but SS Chief Himmler had indeed promised Hitler a present in the coming offensive. It was another Imperial city, Strasbourg, that was to be captured for him as a New Year's present.

counted. His next intelligence report would state merely that the Germans were resorting to "attack propaganda" to bolster the morale of their troops, though a "limited counterattack" might be launched around Christmas to give the German home front some sort of victory. With that done, Monk Dickson went to bed. On the morrow he would be setting off for a well-earned four-day leave in Paris with the full approval of his chief, General Hodges, who was suffering from a bad cold and had gone to bed early. The last chance to save the nearly 80,000 young American soldiers who would soon be killed and wounded in the battle of the Ardennes had vanished. It was midnight, December 15, 1944. There were now exactly 30 hours before the tragedy occurred.

By now the 78th had suffered twelve hundred casualties, more than 20 percent of its strength, but the greenhorns were learning fast. When they ran into minefields, they didn't panic. They tested every hump in the snow with their bayonets, every point in the snow-covered ground that looked "different." They were learning other things, too. Not to eat snow, for instance, since it gave them the runs. Alcohol was also shunned. The instant burn they got from a stiff drink of scotch or rum vanished quickly. It was followed by a lowering of the body temperature that set them off shivering almost uncontrollably. They were learning, too, to change their socks as often as possible to prevent trench foot; to keep the morphine syringes for the wounded underneath their armpits to keep them from freezing; to dump their overcoats, the skirts of which soon became clogged with mud and ice. Instead they wore two shirts, changing them at regular intervals so that the one that was damp with sweat was transferred to the outer layer. Again, this stopped the body's temperature from falling. They learned to stuff their uniforms with copies of the *Stars and Stripes* as the hoboes had done in the hungry thirties, and how to heat a can in a porridgelike mix of earth and gasoline. They were also learning how to kill.

When snipers (everyone's pet hate) didn't surrender quickly

enough, they were shot, the cry of *"Kamerad"* dying on their lips as they came out to surrender. If a hamlet or a village resisted too long, the infantry backed off and let the buzz boys of the TAC Air Force and the artillery take care of it for them. The result would be a heap of smoking ruins littered with dead bodies of Germans who—courtesy of the U.S. 78th Infantry Division—had now finally achieved their aim of dying for *Volk, Vaterland und Führer.* It was overkill, admittedly, but they reasoned that the U.S. artillery had plenty of shells, and after all, the only good Kraut was a dead one.

But there were moments of humanity, too, among all that destruction and death in the Hurtgen. Just after Rollesbroich had been captured, a group of seriously wounded GIs from the 310th's L company were found by a German patrol, abandoned at a crossroads. The Germans were dirty and tired, but not hostile, as infantrymen often are in that condition. Instead, they carried the wounded into their own bunker and dressed the Americans' wounds in the warm interior.

A little later the Germans brought in three unwounded men from the same company. Now a mixed group of Germans and Americans sat around the glowing, potbellied stove that heated the place, talking in a mixture of German and English with frequent recourse to sign language. All night long the Americans tried to persuade the Germans to surrender, while the lone officer sat by himself, brooding moodily.

However, just before dawn the German officer snapped that there would be no surrender. He ordered some of his men to take the three unwounded men back to a prison cage. The mixed group set off unhappily into the freezing darkness. They didn't get far. From some bushes to their front, one of the prisoners saw an arm raise as if in signal. The prisoner reacted correctly. He whispered something to his buddies. The three of them dropped as one. Next moment a BAR burst into life angrily, spraying their captors. At that range the ambushers couldn't miss. Two dropped dead instantly as the rest flung down their weapons, crying *"Kamerad"* madly.

Two grinning L Company men rose from their bushes. They had been waiting all night for "a break like this," as they phrased it happily. The former prisoners who were now captors were nonplussed. They had spent hours with the men who were now dead or captive, smoking their cigarettes, warming themselves at their stove, talking, talking, talking. Now two of them were dead, sprawled out on the cold ground in the extravagant postures of those done to death violently. It all seemed so purposeless.

Nothing seemed to make sense anymore. Nothing was what it seemed. In newly captured Rollesbroich, the weary men of the 78th could take nothing for granted. To enter houses and pillboxes and find fires burning in the stoves and bunks with mattresses was like coming home to them, after three days in the cold and snow. But they had already learned not to trust even these modest homey comforts.

Those cans of food so neatly stacked in the corner sometimes had a stick of TNT planted behind them. To sprawl out luxuriously on that fat, comfortable-looking mattress might well blow up the whole place. Nothing was what it seemed; anything might be booby-trapped. Even the booby traps might be booby-trapped. For the Germans who had held and then fled the first settlement captured by the new boys had been experts at the double booby trap: a device that made a booby trap easy to discover—the so-obvious abandoned pistol or pair of binoculars that set off a larger booby trap when the decoy was removed.

But while some of the new boys rested in a booby-trapped Rollesbroich, their comrades of the 2nd Battalions of the 309th and 310th Regiments attacked toward their next objective, the village of Kesternich. Supported by the tanks of the 709th Tank Battalion, the two infantry battalions fought up and down the wooded hills and through knee-deep snow, while German mortars made their life hell, picking them off all day long.

The artillery was whistled up. Eight whole battalions of heavy, medium, and light guns started to shell the draws in which those terrible mortars were hiding. When they had finished, as the divisional history records, "the screams of wounded men could be heard. The enemy was suffering, too."[5]

By the end of the day the steam ran out of this first attack on Kesternich, now clearly silhouetted on the hill to the weary infantrymen's front. The officers gave in. They ordered their men to dig in for the night. Grimly, the cold, hungry, unshaven infantrymen started to hack away at the frozen earth. As the divisional history details their mood that night of December 15, "there was no hope here, just death lurking in every shadow, every hollow, every house. Another night for men who were too tired to notice the cold, too cold to sleep—a night spent in foxholes flooded with water, a night of mortar shells exploding all around and men dying quietly by themselves. Word came down from headquarters: "We're going to try again in the morning."[6]

But on the morning of Saturday, December 16, 1944, it would be the Germans who would be doing the attacking—a quarter of a million of them.

15

Saturday, December 16, 1944.

Later, the Top Brass claimed that they *had* known to some degree what was to come that dawn. Reports were fudged, files disappeared, and conversations were doctored to show that the generals really had taken the threat of a German counterattack on the western front that December very seriously.* None of them ever admitted in their various memoirs that they had been taken completely, totally by surprise.

In fact, on that gray gloomy morning when their world fell apart over forty years ago now, the Top Brass played. While hundreds, perhaps thousands, of British, French, Canadian, and American soldiers fought and died that Saturday, the generals amused themselves. After all it was Saturday, wasn't it, and rank hath its privileges, of course.

The day before, Hodges at Spa had received some visiting firemen, professional baseball players such as Bucky Walters, Dutch Leonard, Mel Ott, and the like. This morning, still heavy with a cold, he received yet more visitors, fellow generals Bradley and Pete Quesada of the Army Air Corps. They were fitted there for shotguns to be custom-made by the Belgian gunmaker Monsieur Francotte from nearby Liège. (But it would be many weeks before Francotte could deliver his prized wares, and by that time General Hodges would have long fled Spa for a much safer HQ farther to the rear.)

That done, General Bradley, who couldn't fly to Paris because

---

* In a letter to the author Gen. Sir Kenneth Strong, Eisenhower's Chief of Intelligence, admitted that he hadn't known until the mid-sixties that the key intelligence file on the run-up to the Ardennes had been "accidentally" shredded just after the war.

of the bad weather, set off in his sedan for the French capital, where he would see Eisenhower in the afternoon. First he'd have lunch at the Ritz, where the champagne always flowed and there were *beaucoup* celebrities. It was rich living for a man who had been an obscure light colonel back in 1941.

As for the Supreme Commander that fatal morning, he was throwing a champagne reception for two of his staff. About ten o'clock Eisenhower and most of his immediate staff went across to the Louis XIV Chapel at Versailles to see the first marriage solemnized there in nearly two hundred years.

The happy couple consisted of his valet and ex-bellhop, Mickey McKeogh, and a diminutive, bespectacled WAC sergeant, Pearlie Hargrave. Ike was convinced McKeogh brought him good luck, and the man also wrote a weekly report back to Mamie on his boss's activities (well, most of them at least).

Ike genuinely liked the two of them. It was the democratic thing to do, as well—the important man who commanded the destinies of millions of men and women attending the wedding of these two humble NCOs. Besides, it made for good public relations.

Later at the reception, with the drinks provided by the Supreme Commander, the champagne flowed. Ike kissed the bride and heartily shook the hand of his good-luck charm, and the champagne flowed even more. Indeed, as Kay Summersby would record one day later when her lover's divisions were reeling back in scared confusion all along the front, "half the headquarters was soggy with the silence of plain, unadulterated, ordinary hangovers!"[1]

At the reception Eisenhower was buttonholed by an old crony—hard-drinking, skirt-chasing Gen. Everett Hughes. Hughes wasn't there for Pearlie and Mickey. He was there to congratulate Ike. He told the latter happily, "I couldn't bear the idea of having gotten drunk when you received the fourth star and not having a drink with you on your fifth."[2]

The Supreme Commander gave him the benefit of that ear-to-ear smile, which had become familiar to cinema audiences all over the Western world in those last few years, and invited Hughes over for dinner that night. Brad (Bradley) was coming this afternoon to have a chat about the shortage of riflemen at the front. That night they'd have a comfy, all-male dinner party and shoot the breeze just like in the good old days before the war.

Hughes said he'd be there. He'd bring a bottle of Highland Piper scotch, and in Hughes's reddened eyes there could be no deeper mark of respect than that. In a headquarters awash with French champagne, captured German schnapps, and *Kognak* there was always a chronic shortage of good scotch whiskey.

Ike told Hughes that someone had presented him with a bushel of oysters, which he adored (people were always giving the Supreme Commander gifts of food). His "darkies," as he called his black mess servants, were already preparing oysters on the half shell, to be followed by oyster stew, with fried oysters concluding the festive pre-Christmas meal. Hughes said he wouldn't miss it for the world. It would be a swell way to celebrate Ike's fifth star. There was only one problem, however. The Supreme Commander wondered how he was going to fit those five stars on his jacket. Perhaps he could find someone to embroider them on it for him? The party continued.

Earlier that morning the forward observer of the 903rd Field Artillery Battalion, supporting the infantry of the 78th Division, had spotted a flicker of movement in the predawn darkness. Instantly he whispered into the field telephone, "Counterattack! Counterattack forming . . . Coordinates 005278 . . ." Within minutes, as the fevered staff worked out the position, the cannoneers were at work on their howitzers, sighting and loading, trundling up more shells, sweating in spite of the freezing cold. The order went out to all the divisional artillery, whole battalions of guns. All battalions were to fire at exactly the same time, and not one volley, but *five* in rapid succession.

The battery executives stood by, ready for the word. Then it came over the phone—*"Fire!"*

Scores of lanyards were pulled. The earth shook. The guns

thundered into action with an ear-splitting roar. Night turned to day. In violent bursts of scarlet a furious barrage descended upon the advancing Germans. The very ground seemed to erupt all about them as if there had been a sudden earthquake. Once, twice, three times. In the forward positions the shocked infantry clutched for support as the Germans screamed with terror and pain. Minutes later they broke, running back the way they had come in disorganized, terrified twos and threes. Behind them they left the snow littered with their dead.

That had been half an hour before dawn. By midmorning the Germans were attacking in full strength. Backed up with self-propelled guns, the 10th Panzer Division, which had once been commanded by the legendary Desert Fox, Rommel himself, swept all before it, heading straight for newly captured Kesternich. The C.O. of the 2nd Battalion and what was left of his shattered battalion surrendered and was whipped off into the bag. Kesternich was recaptured and the surviving defenders, a captain and 56 men, were taken prisoner.

Hurriedly the 3rd Battalion of the 309th Regiment and a task force of the 310th's 2nd Battalion were flung into a counter-attack at Kesternich. Clerks, drivers who had lost their vehicles, cooks, heavy-weapons men—anyone who could hold an M-I—were formed into the "task force" that drove into Kesternich that grim Saturday, before the Germans, in overwhelming strength, flung them out again. The Germans seemed to be attacking everywhere. *What was going on?*

A few miles away, what was left of the 2nd Ranger Battalion had been resting for six days now. Nerves were still taut from the terrible beating that the battalion had taken on Castle Hill, and the survivors were hoping desperately that they would be sent home, just as the survivors of the shattered 1st and 3rd Battalions had been after the slaughter at bloody Anzio.

But that wasn't to be. At midmorning on that Saturday, the 2nd Rangers were alerted for an immediate move. The green-horns of the 78th were crying out for help. As the battalion history of the 2nd Rangers records it: "Every available soldier had to be thrown into the battle. The Germans had to be stopped, if it took every rifleman, cook, and clerk . . . in the theater."[3]

So once again the handful of Rangers were loaded into the freezing, open trucks and sent off for the front as flares sailed into the sky, the guns rumbled, and overhead V-1s—"buzz bombs," the Rangers called them—putted and putted, sounding like two-stroke motorbikes, carrying their one-ton loads of high explosives toward Liège and Antwerp.

As the convoy rolled toward the grim sounds of battle, the Rangers prayed that it wasn't going to be another Castle Hill. They couldn't take that kind of slaughter again—not yet, anyway. But as the battalion history recalls, "It started out, though, the same way that Bergstein and Hill 400 had started: the interminable delays; the wind and the cold; the lying along the side of the road; the waiting for they knew not what."[4]

Finally they reached their destination, the outskirts of the village of Simmerath, next in the line of the German counterattack. Here they were met by an obviously very frightened officer from the 78th, who actually *whispered* their instructions to them, as if the Germans were just around the next corner. "Be careful. Challenge everybody. Jerry paratroopers have been dropping like flies in this area. Don't make any noise. The front line is just three hundred yards from town. And they're on three sides of us already."[5]

"The Germans only three hundred yards away . . . Jerry paratroopers dropping like flies . . . challenge everybody. . . ." As the harassed, confused Rangers took up their positions in the cellars of Simmerath, where they would remain till January 2, 1945, and prepared to fight to the death, they too asked themselves that puzzled question—*what the hell was going on?*

Farther north, the men of the 9th and 83rd Infantry Divisions were also posing the same question as they were struck by the "most unremitting and concentrated artillery barrage of the whole campaign,"[6] followed just after dawn by a battalion-size German attack, supported by tanks and assault guns. In Strass, on the fringe of the Hurtgen Forest, the 83rd's trapped battalion (what was left of it) fought for its very existence. Where in God's name had the Krauts gotten all this strength from? Back in the States the pundits of the press were predicting the war would be over by Christmas. Here, with one week or so to go, the Germans were counterattacking all out. *What was going on?*

It was no different at Heartbreak Crossroads. Just south of where the 78th was battling, the 2nd U.S. Infantry Division had been attacking through the green 99th Infantry, attempting to take the crossroads at Wahlerscheid. There the 2nd had launched their attack on the 13th, the men burdened with enough rations, ammunition, and anti-tank mines to last for twenty-four hours without resupply. For the commander of the 2nd, General Robertson, had made sure that his division wouldn't suffer the fate of the 28th Division in the Hurtgen, which had had to depend upon one supply road for its disastrous attack on Schmidt.

Drenched, exhausted from the approach march, and frozen, the 2nd Division's 9th Infantry Regiment had assaulted what turned out to be a small fortress at the crossroads. Grouped around the road junction were ten bunkers protected by rows of barbed wire, minefields, and a kind of moat formed by the deep ravines around the position.

That first day the road junction earned the bitter nickname which would stay with it until it was finally captured in 1945. Despite repeated attacks, the 9th Infantry had been totally unable to make even a dent in the defenses. In despair their CO, Colonel Hirschfelder, pulled his battalions back a few hundred yards and ordered a massive bombardment on the crossroads. At the same time, huge 155mm cannon ("Long Toms") were called up to blast away at the pilboxes at point-blank range, while brave men volunteered to destroy the rows of barbed wire with bangalore torpedoes.

Things started to move in the Americans' favor. A patrol found a gap in the wire. Immediately Colonel Higgins, commanding the 2nd Battalion, set off personally, leading his battalion successfully through the gap. Before the Germans knew what was happening, the infantry were assaulting their pillboxes, running from one to the other in a line, blasting their way inside and killing the occupants. By daylight Heartbreak Crossroads was American—*for a while!*

For now on this Saturday, December 16, terrible things started to happen to the green 99th Infantry Division through which the 2nd was attacking. Capt. Charles MacDonald, the future military historian, then a 22-year-old company commander with the 2nd Infantry, later recalled watching as the battered remnants of a battalion from the 99th, two hundred men out of the original nine hundred, came streaming through his own lines. Two of them volunteered to stay and fight with his company, but the rest kept on going through the trees to the rear. Their fear was overwhelming. Now MacDonald and his men waited tensely for the next troops to come over the ridge to their front, for they would be German.

"I lay flat on my back," MacDonald recollected afterward, "in the slit trench, the platoon phone to one ear, the receiver of the battalion radio to the other. The chill from the frozen earth seeped through my clothes and I shivered but I was surprised at my own calmness . . . Surely this was the most serious situation in which I had ever found myself."[7]

And then they were there, "wave after wave of fanatically screaming German infantry," storming the slight tree-covered rise held by his three platoons. Somehow MacDonald's men held them although they were hopelessly outnumbered, while the captain called battalion HQ frantically for help. But there was no help forthcoming. He was ordered to hold until every last man was killed or wounded. MacDonald wondered "and what is to be gained? *Nothing but time. Time born of the bodies of dead men. Time!*"[8]

Half an hour later, what was left of MacDonald's company were running for their lives, as an enormous 60-ton Tiger tank bore down upon them, its long, overhanging gun swinging from side to side like the snout of some monster seeking out its prey. MacDonald ran with them, slipping and falling in his slick overshoes. "I rose and fell again. I found myself not caring if the Germans did fire. Snow had gotten inside my shoes and my feet were soaked. My clothes were drenched. Perspiration covered my body and my mouth was dry. I wanted a cigarette.

"I felt like we were helpless little bugs scurrying blindly about now that some man monster had lifted the log under which we had been hiding. I wondered if it would not be better to be killed and perhaps that would be an end to eveything."[9]

A lot of young Americans must have felt a little like that on Saturday, December 16, 1944. Abruptly, after they had been thinking for months that Allied victory was in sight, that the end of the war was just around the corner, the Germans were launching a massive counterattack. Soon they would have 600,000 men in the field, sweeping all before them, shattering whole American divisions. After the terrible blood-slogging match in the Hurtgen Forest, four long months of it, all that pain and sacrifice, the tremendous losses, how could the Germans still execute an attack of such magnitude?

The feelings of the ordinary American civilian soldier, caught up in the vast impersonal war machine that had dumped him in this remote border country just in time for the great German counterattack, telling him the war was virtually won, are perhaps expressed best in the words of Mel Brooks. The Jewish comic, actor, and moviemaker expressed his own brief experience of the fighting in this way: "Then one day they put us all in trucks, drove us to the railroad station, put us in a locked train with the windows blacked out. We get off the train, we get on a boat. We get off the boat, we get into trucks. We get out of the trucks, we start walking. Suddenly all around us *Waauhwaahwaauh!* Sirens! Tiger tanks! We're surrounded by the Germans. It's the Battle of the Bulge. 'Hands up!' 'Wait,' I say. 'We just left Oklahoma. We're Americans. We're supposed to win!' *Very* scary, but we've escaped . . . And then *they* start shooting. Incoming mail! Bullshit . . . Only Burt Lancaster says that. We said: 'Oh God, oh Christ! Who knows, he might help. He was Jewish, too. *Mother*!' "[10]

The horror of the front in the Hurtgen and now the Ardennes meant little, it seemed, to the generals. The farther back the generals were, the more complacent they appeared. The disjointed, panicked accounts that were filtering through now were discounted. Hodges still stuck to that tunnel vision of his. He felt that the new counter-offensive was "a spoiling attack," designed to disrupt his own attack through the Hurtgen against the Roer dams. In the First Army office diary it is recorded: "The General (i.e., Hodges) was neither optimistic nor pessimistic during the day . . . It was unfortunate that during this busy evening the General had to entertain Lieutenant General A. E. Grasett, G-5 of SHAEF." With one of his divisions virtually surrounded (the 106th) and another crumbling (the 99th), Hodges was concerned with entertaining an obscure staff officer!

It was no different at the next-higher headquarters, Bradley's Twelfth Army Group HQ in Luxembourg City. Here Bradley's chief of intelligence, General Sibert, saw the offensive as a "diversionary attack." Just like Hodges, he thought it was meant to disrupt American attacks to the north (through the Hurtgen) and the south (into the German Saar) of the Ardennes. Sibert reasoned that "the day's events cannot be regarded as a major long term threat."[11] How woefully wrong he was!

The picture was similar at Eisenhower's HQ in Versailles. *After* the war much was made of Eisenhower's reaction to the news that the Germans were attacking in the Ardennes. Every student of the Battle of the Bulge knows the scene at that fateful conference with Bradley on the question of replacements, which was Eisenhower's explanation *later* for Brad's trip to Paris (Kay Summersby in her diary maintains quite simply the latter came "just to spend the night").

At four in the afternoon, with a gray leaden sky outside indicating that snow would soon fall, General Betts, "normally a calm, phlegmatic man," suddenly appears at the door of the conference room, looking shaken. He asks for his boss, General Strong. There's a hurried whispered conversation. A moment later Strong announces in his thick Scottish accent: "Gentlemen, this morning the enemy counterattacked at five separate points across the First Army sector."[12]

Instant consternation! Bedell-Smith, Eisenhower's Chief of Staff, rounds on Bradley angrily for having failed to spot the Ardennes as a weak spot. Hadn't he sent Strong to Bradley's HQ only the week before to warn him about Ardennes? What had he, Bradley, done? *Why, he'd laughed in the Scot's ugly face!*

Bradley blusters. "The other fellow knows that he must lighten the pressure Patton has built up against him. If by coming through the Ardennes he can force us to pull Patton's troops out of the Saar and throw them against his counteroffensive, he'll get what he's after. And that's just a little more time!"[13]

In the midst of the accusations and counteraccusations, only the Supreme Commander keeps his head. Naturally, *he* has seized upon the essentials straightaway. "This is not a local attack, Brad," he snaps incisively. "It's not logical for the Germans to launch a local attack at our *weakest* point." Of course not!

Weakly Bradley persists, "If it's not a local attack, what kind of an attack is it?"

Sagely Eisenhower reserves his judgment. "That remains to be seen," he announces. "But I don't think we can afford to sit on our hands until we've found out."

Eisenhower, the man who has been so often accused of not being able to make a decision without a committee to help him, is snapping right into action, mind racing electrically, as he reacts instantly to the new threat. Well, that's the way the military historians and the generals' biographies portrayed it *after* the war.

"What do you think we should do, then?" Bradley asks weakly, his ego suddenly deflated. Abruptly, he's no longer so popular at Supreme Headquarters. He's got them into trouble—and just before Christmas, too!

Eisenhower knows the answer to that plaintive question immediately. "Send Middleton* some help. About two armored divisions."

"I suppose that would be safer," Bradley agrees. Then he

---

* Gen. Troy Middleton, commanding the VIII Corps in the Ardennes.

remembers his *bête noire*, George Patton, commander of his Third Army. "Of course, you know that one of those divisions will have to come from Patton?"

Eisenhower is masterful. *"So?"* he demands coldly, his famous grin vanished now, his face like thunder.

"So," Bradley says lamely. "Georgie won't like losing a division a few days before his big attack on the Saar." What a fool Bradley is. Can't he read the storm warning?

Complete master of the situation now, Eisenhower is not going to tolerate any moods from the prima donna Patton. "You tell him," he snaps, *"that Ike is running this war. . . ."*[14]

Thus, the received picture of that conference so long ago. It shows Bradley chastened, even embarrassed by his failure to recognize the danger spot in the Ardennes, although he had been warned of the potential danger there by Eisenhower's highly competent staff. Justly chastened, for he has let the side down. For his part, Eisenhower is masterful, instantly aware of the full extent of the problem at the front, taking control without a moment's hesitation.

But the generals' subsequent behavior that evening belies the apparent urgency of the matter. It seems to show that the massive German counterattack in the Ardennes didn't worry them very much, as if they didn't take it that seriously at all. Of course, senior commanders are supposed to display a certain degree of sangfroid in the face of adversity. It stops panic. It is good for the morale of the troops.

The behavior of the American Top Brass that night, however, smacked more of complacency than sangfroid. Their oyster dinner was duly served and enjoyed by all present, save Bradley, who hated the things. Hastily the kitchen staff scrambled some eggs for his benefit. Afterward, they cracked a bottle of champagne to celebrate Eisenhower's promotion to five-star general.

For the celebration of Eisenhower's promotion was the *real* high point of the evening and the reason that Bradley was there in the first place, *not* the surprise counterattack. After all, Eisenhower had been stuck in the rank of major for sixteen long years and he had often cautioned Mamie he'd never wear the eagles of a colonel. Now, in three years, three months, and sixteen days, being promoted every six months, he had risen from colonel to the U.S. Army's highest rank—five-star general! In the eyes of his old friends from before the war, this really was something to celebrate. The misery, the slaughter, the panic of the new battle paled into insignificance in comparison.

After the feast of oysters the generals played five rubbers of bridge and undoubtedly attacked that treasured bottle of Highland Piper brought by Hughes, who spent much of his time and pay looking for scotch in Paris. The front seemed to have been forgotten. There was no attempt made to reach Hodges to find out what was the true situation in the First Army. No one thought of sending out liaison officers of the kind used by Montgomery to keep him in touch with the front, just in case the Germans had cut the land lines* to Versailles. Even as the intelligence picture hardened shortly before midnight and more and more new German divisions were identified, no urgent decisions were made. Bradley felt no constraint to hurry back to Luxembourg and take command of his army group. Instead, he stayed in Paris and gossiped with Hughes, who wrote in his diary later: "Brad says Germans have started a big counterattack toward Hodges. Very calm about it. Seemed routine from his lack of emphasis."[15]

Up front the two corps commanders concerned with the Hurtgen fighting acted. Lightning Joe put the 1st Infantry Division, just withdrawn from the Forest, on a six-hour alert. Gerow swore, "What are these damned bastards of Huns up to?", and then in desperation called his chief, Hodges. This was at one o'clock, while Eisenhower was still at the wedding reception and Bradley was eating at the Ritz. He asked Hodges for permission to call off his attack in the Hurtgen and to reinforce his hard-pressed 2nd and 99th Divisions. Hodges refused. He said, "No,

---

* Soon the enemy would indeed cut the land lines between Hodges's and Bradley's headquarters.

proceed with the offensive in the north and hold where you are in the south."[16]

All that day Hodges in Spa could hear the thunder of the German guns coming closer and closer. Still he refused to act, while at the front his hopelessly outnumbered divisions crumbled. The next day, when he finally did act, he was unable to contact his superior, General Bradley, until early evening, although he had called the latter's HQ several times. The reason was simple—Bradley, after a leisurely breakfast (after all, it *was* Sunday, the day of rest), was still in his sedan, driving through the back roads on his way to Luxembourg city.

Two days later Hodges was fleeing Spa in panic, leaving hot food on the tables and secret maps on the walls, as two officers of the 7th Armored Division noticed when they happened to wander into the now deserted Hotel Britannique. For the point of *Obersturmbannfuhrer*, Peiper's armored column, was less than a dozen miles away from Spa.

When the last of his truck convoy left the health resort, the frightened mayor went personally to the local jail and released twenty suspected collaborators. Hurriedly the American flags, which had lined the broad main boulevard between the rows of hotels for the last three months, were torn down, as were the pictures of Churchill and Roosevelt, which adorned every window.

The Germans were coming back!

PART FOUR

The Race for the Dams

I may lose a battle, but I will never lose a minute.

NAPOLEON

16

On December 26, 1944, at the height of the Battle of the Bulge (as Churchill had named the battle now going on in the Ardennes), Lt. Gen. John C. H. Lee, Com Z Commander, made perhaps the most famous announcement in the whole course of his long career with the U.S. Army.

Lee, a religious fanatic who would become a lay brother in a monastic order after the war and was always invoking the Lord's name whenever it seemed to his advantage: "We thanked the dear Lord every day for having learned to put our faith in Him and to start each morning at His altar whereon we laid our problems."[1] Lee was the most hated man in Supreme Headquarters. He was fake, pretentious, and a bully, ruling his rear area command, which spread all over Western Europe and Britain, with a rod of iron. But he had powerful backers in Washington, and although Eisenhower disliked him with a passion (Lee issued orders often without consulting the Supreme Commander), Lee could afford his grandiose, bullying manner.

Lee and his religious mania, unusual in a red-blooded U.S. general, have been long forgotten, but on that gray Tuesday in December, with the snow falling and Paris in the grip of an unprecedented spy scare,* General Lee made history. With the front crying out for infantry replacements, the portly supply general made a spirited appeal to his mainly black troops. He asked black soldiers, who had had some previous infantry training, to volunteer now for the front to be assigned to *mixed* companies of black and white infantrymen!

---

* German commandos were supposed to be in Paris already, preparing to kill the Supreme Commander and other military notables.

"It is planned to assign you without regard to color or race to the units where assistance is most needed," he declared in his special appeal that day. "Your comrades at the front are anxious to share the glory of victory with you. Your relatives and friends everywhere have been urging that you be granted this privilege. The Supreme Commander, your Commanding General, and other veteran officers who have served with you, are confident that many of you will take advantage of this opportunity and carry on in keeping with the glorious record of our colored troops in our former wars."[2]

In a U.S. Army that had been deeply segregated since the turn of the century the announcement came like a bombshell. Lee was offering *integrated* combat companies, not black outfits led by white officers, as hitherto!

Black Americans had served as fighting men in the U.S. Army since the days of Washington. After the Medal of Honor was introduced in the Civil War, twenty blacks won their country's highest award. In the Indian campaigns of the next quarter of a century, another twenty black soldiers gained the Congressional Medal, followed by eight more who won it during the Spanish-American War of 1898. Thereafter, the black American disappeared from the lists of award winners for fifty-two years (till the Korean War).

For under the command of "Black Jack" Pershing (his nickname gained by commanding black soldiers, the 10th Cavalry), the U.S. Army in World War I became strictly segregated, with blacks becoming basically labor and service troops—cooks, clerks, drivers, and the like—remote from the scene of action.

Naturally, prior to Lee's startling announcements there had been a few black combat outfits. There was the "Spookwaffe" in Italy.* There were several black artillery units in combat at the front in Germany and two black tank battalions, attached to Patton's 3rd Army. Despite the fact that "Ole Blood and Guts" seemed to hate every race under the sun, he welcomed them

---

* A bitter pun on the fact that they were the invisible soldiers (spooks), fighting the *Luftwaffe* in their own black air force.

effusively, telling the 761st Tank Battalion, "Men, you are the first Negro tankers ever to fight in the American Army . . . I don't care what color you are as long as you go up there and kill those Kraut sons-of-bitches!"[3] Another black tank outfit was told by Patton, "When your grandkid sits on your knee and asks what did you do in the war, granddaddy, you'll be able to say, *"Well, I wasn't shovelling shit in Louisiana!"*[4]

But these few black combat units were still strictly segregated, invisible soldiers in the great khaki mass of their fellow white Americans at the front. Therefore, it was understandable that Lee's appeal, made under pressure that December 26, caused an immediate outcry in the States. The War Department in Washington was embarrassed by this abrupt departure from official policy. There was also an immediate outcry in the black press and among black organizations and pressure groups, who believed the attempt was being made to integrate black soldiers into white combat outfits only because of the parlous situation at the front. Otherwise the black soldier would have remained where he had always been in the U.S. Army in the twentieth century—"shovelling shit in Louisiana."

Hastily Lee's original announcement was reworded, and now, as the Army newspaper the *Stars and Stripes* recorded enthusiastically, "thousands of applications were received from men in port companies . . . In one company of one Negro Engineer GS regiment, 171 men out of 186 volunteered to fight. Four first sergeants in the unit accepted reductions to privates to qualify for the training plan. In another Com Z unit, a QM Laundry Co, 100 men out of 260 wanted to fight, but only 36 were 'allowed' to go."[5]

A white squad leader in the Hurtgen was interviewed about the latest recruits for the infantry. Pvt. Harold Cothran from Greenwood, South Carolina, stated (so the *Stars and Stripes* reported, at least): "I don't give a damn what color a man is as long as he's up here helping to win this war."

One of his squad, a black man, said: "I came into the Army to fight, not to labor. That's why I volunteered for this." Another,

Pfc Leroy Kemp, a BAR man and proud of it, maintained stoutly with suitable patriotic vigor: "We're all in this thing together now, White and Negro Americans in the same companies. And that's how it should be. That's why I volunteered. Most Negro troops are inservice outfits. We've been giving a lot of sweat. Now, I think we'll mix some blood with it."[6]

Back in Washington, the U.S. Army's most senior soldier, General Marshall, who had once been Black Jack Pershing's Chief of Staff in the old war, was not impressed. He thought the experiment was not very promising. That February, a black division—the 92nd Infantry—had turned and run before the Germans in Italy. Marshall felt that black soldiers were no good unless they were led by white officers and noncoms. The blacks, it was reported, would not stand fire or stay out at night, whether they were under fire or not. As Marshall remarked unkindly to Henry Stimson, secretary of war, "The only place they can be counted on is in Iceland in summertime—*where there's daylight for twenty-four hours!*"[7]

Marshall's comment reflected the prejudices of the Regular Army officers. It was recognized by those older and more cynical black soldiers, who had been longer in the service and had been at the receiving end of white prejudice during training south of the Mason-Dixon Line. They had been treated as third-class citizens, threatened with lynching, been refused food in snack bars where their supposed enemies, the Germans (now prisoners of war), were fed. As some of them observed bitterly after the war: "We were fighting the *wrong* war against the *wrong* enemy in the *wrong* country."

One black noncom, S. Sgt. Chester Jones, later recalled, "combat officers coming around asking the truckers" (he was with the Red Ball Express) "to volunteer for infantry duty at the Bulge. My opinion was: they said I didn't have sense for combat soldiering stateside—well if I didn't have it then, then I damned sure didn't have it in *their* emergency."[8]

Another black artilleryman got drunk with a couple of buddies "and under the influence got carried away and volunteered for the infantry." They went to their officer, who was black too. "He told us to go to hell. He wanted to know if we were out of our minds . . . Afterwards when sobriety returned I knew I must have been out of my tree for such a brilliant idea."[9]

In the end, some 2,500 of these invisible soldiers did go.

The Battle of the Hurtgen Forest, followed by the Battle of the Bulge, resulted in so many thousands of casualties in the rifle battalions that it brought with it a fundamental change in the attitude of the old segregated U.S. Army, which had maintained that blacks had no staying power as infantrymen. Strictly from necessity—having nothing to do with a radical change of heart on the part of the Top Brass—blacks were now needed at the front to fight within the sadly depleted ranks of white outfits.

As January 1945 slowly gave way to February and the Bulge in the Ardennes was finally nipped off by the First and Third Armies, the planners prepared to regain lost ground. The U.S. Army would attack into the Reich once more. In the Hurtgen Forest the battered outfits that had stuck it out there on the defensive ever since December 16 readied for one final effort too. They had suffered severe casualties as well as the men who had fought in the Ardennes. They badly needed reinforcements. White or black—they needed bodies, *urgently!*

By now General Gerow, the longtime commander of the V Corps, had been kicked upstairs. He had been given command of an army, the Fifteenth, which existed solely on paper. We do not know why. Perhaps his performance in the Hurtgen had not been good enough. Perhaps the scandal of his French in-laws had made him too hot for Western Europe, where they were busy shooting collaborators by the hundred every week that fall and winter.

In his place, the V Corps was commanded by General Huebner, a martinet of the old school. Since 1943 he had commanded the Big Red One, an outfit which hadn't taken kindly to discipline from outside. Indeed, the Big Red One had booed Patton in Sicily after the slapping scandal. A soldier since 1910, Huebner had held every rank in the 1st Division from private to commanding general, and soon licked the men of the Big Red One into shape. They hadn't liked him, but they had respected him, as he led the Division into the Hurtgen, after they had captured Aachen, the first city taken by the Americans in Germany.

Now Huebner was going into the Hurtgen for the second time, commanding a corps of several divisions, instead of a single one, and he was not going to make the same mistakes his predecessor, Gerow, had made. For this time, the objective had been clearly defined at last. It was not to be merely a masking operation to protect the flank of another corps to the north. This time V Corps's mission was vital. As he told General Parker, who was commanding the 78th Division, which was now filling up with some of those black volunteers, Schmidt had to be taken first and then the Schwammenauel Dam.

At long last the planners had realized the vital importance of the Roer dams. As Huebner spelled it out to Parker, the attack soon to be launched was the most vital on the entire western front. Until the Schwammenauel Dam was taken, the U.S. 9th Army to the north dare not cross the Roer. If the dam remained in German hands, they could use its waters to flood the whole area and make the 9th's attack very dangerous.

Parker didn't like his assignment. His division was still green, although it was now up to full strength again, having absorbed 1,500 replacements, including several hundred black soldiers. Both the original men of the division and the replacements had heard of Schmidt, that awful killing ground, which had been figuring in American dispatches and newspaper reports ever since the previous October. Now his inexperienced division was to be given a prestige assignment that entailed first capturing Schmidt, "a name," as the U.S. official history puts it, "that had become a kind of bugaboo among American soldiers after the beating another division had taken there in November."[10]

Parker also knew he faced the same kind of problems that had confronted Cota back in 1944. The Germans still dominated the high ground, and, apart from one narrow trail through the woods, there was one lone approach road running along the crest of the Schmidt ridge. It was the same old recipe for disaster, he must have told himself: the Germans able to observe his every movement from the heights, with all his supplies running up one single road that could easily be cut just like the Kall Trail.

Huebner, noting his subordinate's jitters, hastily assured Parker that he would have the support of a combat command of the 7th Armored Division, the fire of the whole of the corps artillery, and that of the planes of the XIX TAC Air Force. It was a formidable display of air and artillery power to assist a *single* division; indeed it was more than the entire prewar U.S. Regular Army would have been able to muster in one spot. Parker still seemed nervous, and Huebner told himself he would have to keep his eye on General Parker's "Lightning" Division.

While Parker pondered the tough job ahead of him unhappily, another general who would attack into the Hurtgen to his right, two days before Parker, decided he'd have a look at the terrain personally. Gen. Slim Jim Gavin, the 38-year-old commander of the 82nd Airborne Division, was a veteran too, who had worked his way up from private to commanding general over the twenty years he had spent in the service. He had fought in Sicily, Italy, France, Holland, Belgium, and now he was going to conduct his first battle against the Germans on their home territory.

But first he wanted to see the ground over which his men were to fight. For Gavin believed that, although lip service is paid to the view that the general belongs as close to the scene of action as circumstances will allow, the fact is that not many generals behave this way. Not Gavin. He thought that "the place for the general in battle is where he can see the battle and get the odor of it in his nostrils."[11] The odor of the coming battle in the heart of the Hurtgen was not going to please the handsome, tall, young 82nd Airborne commander one bit.

Like so many nameless infantrymen who had gone to the slaughter never to return, Gavin now left his jeep and started down along the Kall Trail, last used by the Americans the previous November. It was an eye-opener, "a shambles of wrecked vehicles and abandoned tanks," he wrote later. "The first tanks that had attempted to go down the trail had evidently slid off and thrown their tracks. In some cases the tanks had been pushed off the track, and in the bottom of the canyon there were four abandoned tank destroyers and five disabled and abandoned tanks."[12]

But the ruined, rusting metal monsters of the previous year's fighting were not the real horrors that now confronted Gavin. It was the dead. "All along the sides of the trail just emerged from the winter snow, there were many, many dead bodies . . . Their gangrenous, broken and torn bodies were rigid and grotesque, some of them with arms skywards, seemingly in supplication. They were wearing the red keystone of the 28th Infantry Division, The Bloody Bucket."[13]

Gavin and his orderly pushed on down this trail of horror, past an abandoned litter station where the aidmen had fled, leaving their charges trapped on the stretchers to die a lonely, frightened death—dozens of them, the bodies long dead, and past the minefields, where American and German dead sprawled within yards of each other—a dramatic example of what the fighting must have been like in the Hurtgen . . . savage, bitter, and at close quarters.[14]

Now the general, who was hardened to the horrors of the battle and not a very impressionable man, had had enough. "The sun was setting and I was anxious to get back to the other side of the valley before darkness. As darkness descended over the canyon, it was an eerie scene like something from the lower levels of Dante's *Inferno*. To add to the horrors a plaintive human voice could be heard calling from the woods some distance away."[15]

Slim Jim was not the only one affected by the horrors of the Hurtgen that day. Just before daylight the general, good soldier that he was, went up to visit his lead battalion, getting in position for the attack soon to come. There he came upon a young soldier, a replacement, who was looking at the dead everywhere. "He began to turn pale, then green and he was obviously about to vomit." Gavin talked with him soothingly, trying to calm him. The general "assured him that we never abandoned our dead, that we always cared for them and buried them. I knew his state of mind. Every young soldier first entering combat is horrified by the sight of dead bodies that have been abandoned for some time. They always equate themselves with the dead they see and think that it could happen to them."[16]

Gavin, the good soldier, managed to reassure the frightened replacement and sent him on his way to meet his destiny, whatever it may have been. But there were not many good commanders, like Gavin, who could motivate their men to enter the Death Factory, where so many other, similar young men had perished miserably—anonymously—before them. The very Forest itself had a frightening effect.

One old soldier, Staff Sergeant Giles, whose engineer battalion was supporting Gavin's 82nd Airborne Division, was not an emotional man. Yet he felt the oppressive, frightening atmosphere of the Forest too. In his diary he recorded, "We are in the middle of the Hurtgen Forest. For a long time today we came through the battlefield—nothing but stumps of pine trees, limbs all blown off, upper halves splintered. You could sure tell that there had been one hell of a battle. It was weird & spooky & gave you the creeps. I don't see how men ever fought in this mess. No wonder the 4th Inf took 7,000 casualties."[17]

But even Sergeant Giles, unimaginative as he was, knew it went deeper than that. Like so many others now entering the Death Factory for the first time, it wasn't only the sight of the dead and the mass destruction that affected them, it was also the knowledge of what was soon to come. As Giles noted, "This is the part of the war I have dreaded most—being in Germany. I even dreaded crossing the border and knowing I was in Germany. But I don't remember now any special feeling when we did cross. I have always thought the Krauts would fight like devils for every inch of German soil—and in a way, they are. I dreaded this Siegfried Line. I still dread the Rhine. It stands to reason they have their backs to the wall & that lunatic Hitler will fight till the last German is dead before he gives up."[18]

As it began to snow once more in that remote border coun-
tryside, with the stark black, shattered boughs of the trees heavy
with new snow, the wrecked hamlets and villages filled up with
the attackers waiting for the order they dreaded: "OK, guys, let's
move . . . let's move out!" Everywhere there was the controlled
confusion of Sherman tanks, White half-tracks, great lumbering
8-inch cannon, self propelled guns, boxlike ambulances, bridging equipment, the great mass of olive-drab machinery clogging
every track, every field, every tumbledown hamlet of the Hurtgen and all indicating the new offensive soon to come.

There is a picture still extant of men of the 78th Infantry
Division waiting for the attack that last week of January. It is
obviously posed for propaganda reasons. A group of white and
black soldiers, carbines slung, some of them wearing white-
painted helmets and smoking pipes as if they were confident
combat veterans.* But there is no mistaking the apprehension on
the young unlined faces beneath the heavy helmets. Even the
skill of the Signal Corps photographer could not hide that.
Standing there in a circle in the dirty snow, apparently enjoying
a chat before action as good comrades should, their strained faces
show all too clearly that they know what is soon to come in the
Death Factory.

Again, as combat medic Pvt. Lester Atwell noted that week,
"a wave of self-inflicted wounds broke out. Time after time men
were carried into the aid station from nearby houses wincing with
pain, shot through the foot. Each swore it had been an accident.
'I was cleaning my rifle,' sometimes the wounded man would say,
pointing to a friend. 'He can tell you. He was in the room with
me.' And often on the face of the friend there would be a look of
duplicity, as he backed up the story."[19]

But there were genuine casualties too, the envy of those who
were going to stay and fight. A friend of Atwell's was brought in
one morning, grinning all over his face and shouting good-bye.

---

* All the same, Corps Commander Huebner must have liked the performance of his black
infantrymen. For immediately after the war he forced through the integration of all units,
black and white, in the Army of Occupation in Germany.

"Where are you going?" Atwell asked his old buddy.

"Home, I hope," the other man replied. "I have a pair of winners here. Two frozen feet." He asked if he could see the MO. Twenty minutes later he was out, the coveted medical evacuation ticket pinned to his greatcoat.

"He's a lucky bastard," the men of C Company commented enviously. One of them moaned. "And there I was, leavin' my feet out, stickin' them in ice water, trying everything." In disgust he snorted, *"They wouldn't freeze!"*[20]

Again men started "to vote with their feet" and desert. A company commander would go around his positions in the morning and find that a dozen or so men had sneaked away during the night. Where they went to was anyone's guess, for now the authorities were wise to the ways of the reluctant infantry. They had placed stop lines all along the rear areas, and now on the frontier with Belgium, new signs had been erected to replace those which had once said, *Warning, you are now entering an enemy country*. These read: *No one will leave this area without official permission!* Now Belgium, the refuge from combat, had become the Promised Land, almost.

Although the new battle in the Hurtgen had not yet started, there were already cases of combat fatigue, those symptoms of cowardice which General Cota hated so much. There were the "goldbrickers" too, actively working on themselves so as to qualify for that sought after combat evacuation tag.

Atwell came across one whom the medics finally nicknamed the "Noise" in disgusted cynicism. Atwell had first met him one evening, with shells exploding in the distance. "Stars came out and in the bitter, cold dusk a soldier approached me uncertainly. When he was close, I saw that his eyes, pale in a dark-complexioned face, were fixed and dilated. He was talking in French, as if in a daze, then half whispering, half aloud, drawing the word out, he said, 'Noi-i-se! The no-i-se!' "[21]

Atwell took him to the aid station, gave him a hot drink, and sent him on his way, after he had been given twenty-four hours of KP to soothe his nerves. But that wasn't the last of the

"Noise." A few days later he was back at the aid station, escorted by two worried buddies, still staring and crying "the noi-i-se" before relapsing into French. This time his performance was so good that the MO decided the "Noise" could stay in the line no longer.

Afterward Atwell met him in the icy vestibule of the aid station. There he heard him whisper to one of his buddies, "Hey, I *made* it. I'm going back to Regiment. Isn't it *wonderful*?"

Angered at this so blatant goldbricking, Atwell snapped, "I wouldn't be so loud about it. You're not back yet."

"Thanks," Noise said, startled, and allowed himself to be led to the waiting ambulance, filled with really sick and wounded soldiers, still moaning *"the noi-i-se"* and muttering darkly to himself in French. He had made it. He was *"out"* . . .[22]

But as zero hour for the attack in the Hurtgen grew ever closer, the Top Brass decided to act to put a stop to the rot at long last. Infantry replacements in Europe were running out. The radical solution that had brought in 2,500 black infantrymen had been a drop in the ocean. Now they were sending young men up the line who had exactly *eight* weeks of infantry training. The barrel was about scraped clean. The men at the front had to be shown dramatically, publicly, that there was no escape; that it didn't pay to run away. For the road to escape led only to death.

17

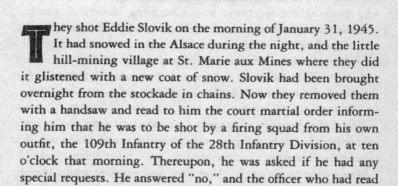

They shot Eddie Slovik on the morning of January 31, 1945. It had snowed in the Alsace during the night, and the little hill-mining village at St. Marie aux Mines where they did it glistened with a new coat of snow. Slovik had been brought overnight from the stockade in chains. Now they removed them with a handsaw and read to him the court martial order informing him that he was to be shot by a firing squad from his own outfit, the 109th Infantry of the 28th Infantry Division, at ten o'clock that morning. Thereupon, he was asked if he had any special requests. He answered "no," and the officer who had read the charges out to him noted that Slovik was "exceptionally calm and resigned" throughout.

A little while later he was confessed and handed over to the priest, Father Cummings, a bundle of letters from his crippled wife. With tears in his eyes for the first time, he told the priest, "The only break I ever had in life, Father, was this girl. But I've lost her now. Everything we had will be gone. They wouldn't let her be happy."[1]

Outside they waited for Eddie in the walled courtyard of No. 86 Rue de General Dourgeois,* protected from the curious eyes of the locals: the brass from Corps and Division, the firing squad (twelve combat-experienced infantrymen), several chaplains, a colonel carrying the black hood they would slip over Eddie's head before they shot him—and Gen. Dutch Cota. He carried a black

---

* For those interested in such things, the house where they shot Slovik no longer exists. It has disappeared in the foundations of an apartment house. The locals found out what had happened in their remote village only when they saw the U.S. television documentary on Slovik on their local TV.

swagger stick with a brass handle and casually asked one of the men of God present when he was going to get him more chaplains. He had lost a third of his in the recent Battle of the Bulge. The chaplain, who was a little surprised at the seeming irrelevancy, said he was doing his best.

Now the execution procession moved into the courtyard. There was something tragically beautiful about the scene. The snow-covered Vosges all around; the knowledge that these men who made up the spectators would be going into battle on the morrow; and the little man, bareheaded, in a field jacket with no insignia, who was going to die—*violently*—at the hands of his fellow countrymen soon, his wrists bound behind his back.

General Cota slapped the swagger stick smartly beneath his right arm. He opened his mouth and shouted, his breath fogging on the keen air, *"Attention!"*

The hollow square of spectators snapped to attention as the procession halted, Slovik now with a blanket wrapped around his skinny shoulders for warmth.

Again the charges against him were read out to him by a Major Fellman, who asked him, "Private Slovik, do you have a statement to make before the order directing your execution is carried out?"

"No," Eddie mumbled.

Now it was the turn of the Catholic chaplain. "Private Slovik, do you have a last statement to make to me, as a chaplain, before your death?"

Again Eddie said, "No."

Fellman barked, "Prepare the prisoner for execution!"[2] The spectators tensed. This was it!

Swiftly the execution party tied Eddie, calm and unprotesting, to the waiting pole, strapping him around the knees, ankles, and shoulders so that he couldn't fall when hit. Then came the hood. Eddie's face disappeared. He would be no longer of this world when they saw it again; they all knew that.

Lieutenant Koziak, in charge of the twelve-man firing squad, barked an order. There was the crunch of marching feet on the snow as the men came out trailing their M-1s. With eyes set on some distant horizon, the spectators unseen, they filed into the path specially dug for them in the snow and faced the hooded man: twelve young men who were going to kill a fellow American for cowardice this cold January.

Major Fellman didn't give them a chance to develop sudden nerves, though most of them were convinced that Slovik rightly deserved to die. He had run away. He was yellow. He had let down his comrades who had stayed in the Forest and had fought, perhaps died there. All of them were going to aim to kill. "*Squad!*" Fellman yelled. "*Ready.*" Up flashed the rifles as one, the experienced infantrymen socking the butts into their right shoulders, squinting down the length of the barrels through the sight at the blinded man strapped to the pole. "*Aim!*" They caught their breaths, white-knuckled finger curling around each trigger, taking first pressure. "*FIRE!*"

The M-1s blasted into noisy life as one. Some of the spectators jumped, startled. The birds in the skeletal trees rose in angry protest. Someone gasped. One of the firing squad spun around halfway. His rifle had been dirty. The blast had nearly broken his collarbone.

At the pole, Slovik's hooded head fell forward, sudden, scarlet patches on the khaki OD. But he wasn't dead—yet. Slowly the doctor crunched over the frozen snow toward him. The spectators could hear the steady, somber crunch-crunch of his boots on the surface as he fingered his stethoscope.

The MO applied the instrument, noting that Slovik had been hit by all eleven bullets. As was required by tradition, one of the firing squad had been given a blank. The heartbeat was still there, faint but very rapid. He guessed Slovik wouldn't need a second volley, so he played for time.

Behind him Fellman gave the order to reload. The chaplain snapped angrily, "Give him another volley if you like it so much!"

But Fellman was impatient to have the damned thing over and

done with. He called to the MO to pronounce Slovik dead or stand aside for a second volley.

The MO shook his head as he straightened up, folding his stethoscope. "The second volley won't be necessary, Major," he said quietly. "Private Slovik is dead."

Later General Cota would recall: "That was the roughest fifteen minutes of my life."[3]

Slovik had served his purpose. Later, one of the firing squad, a Private Morrison, recalled: "I think General Eisenhower's plan worked. It helped to stiffen a few backbones. When the report of the execution was read to my company formation, the effect was good. It made a lot of guys think about what it means to be an American. I'm just sorry the general didn't follow through and shoot the rest of the deserters instead of turning them loose on their community. I want my children to be raised to believe that this country is worth dying for . . . and that if they won't fight for it, they don't deserve to live."[4]

Noble and fitting sentiments, no doubt. Yet that winter there seemed to be one law for the poor and one for the rich. Five days after General Cota, acting for the Supreme Commander, had Eddie Slovik shot, he, too, was responsible for a grave misdemeanor. On the night of February 5, 1945, one of Cota's signals officers left a truck containing top secret cryptography (of a kind the existence of which was not revealed to the general public till thirty years later*) unguarded. The truck and all its top secret gear was stolen, probably by French black marketeers. A massive search was launched throughout the European Theater on the direct order of an enraged Eisenhower. All over Western Europe trucks were stopped and searched while Eisenhower agonized; a secret was potentially compromised that was known only to a handful of men at the top in the Allied camp.

For, if the Germans *had* stolen the equipment, the whole of the Ultra secrets systems, upon which the Allies relied for virtually all their intelligence, would be hopelessly compromised.

---

* In 1973 Group Commander F. Winterbotham published his *Ultra Secret*, the first account of this tremendous secret, which had been kept since 1940.

Just as the Ultra system, by which the Allies could read Germany's top secret messages almost as soon as they were sent, was the greatest intelligence coup of World War II (perhaps of all time), its discovery by the Germans would be the war's greatest intelligence failure.

It was weeks before the truck with the missing secrets was found abandoned in a French wood with two of its three safes intact (the third was never discovered). In the meantime, however, Washington and London demanded that heads should roll. The senior investigating officer recommended that Cota, his Chief of Staff, and four signals officers should be relieved of their commands, and the latter four court-martialed. Eisenhower intervened. After all, he had been at the "Point" with Dutch, and General Devers, commanding the Sixth Army Group to which Cota's 28th Infantry Division now belonged, readily obliged. The investigating officer's recommendation was quashed. Instead, Cota's punishment was reduced to an official reprimand. Despite his long combat experience, Cota would never get a corps, as did so many of his contemporaries, but he did continue to command the 28th Division until the end of the war.

Cota's crime, which *potentially* could have caused the deaths of many thousands of Allied soldiers if the Germans had been able to lay their hands on the great secret, remained secret. Even when after the war Kay Summersby and Bradley told the story of the missing truck, the reason for the massive search for it was not given. Cota went to his grave bearing his secret crime with him. Eddie Slovik's was publicized throughout the Army.

As Colonel Rudder, the thrice-wounded former commander of the 2nd Rangers, now head of the 109th Infantry Regiment, laid it on the line in a personal message to his men: "Today I had the most regrettable experience I have had since the war began. I saw a former soldier of the 109th Infantry, Pvt. Eddie D. Slovik, shot to death by musketry by soldiers of this regiment. I pray that this man's death will be a lesson to each of us who have any doubt at any time about the price that we must pay to win this war. The person that is not willing to fight and die, if need be, for his country *has no right to life.*

"According to record, this is the first time in eighty years of American history that any United States soldier has been shot to death by musketry for deserting his unit and his fellow men. There is only one reason for our being here and that is to eliminate the enemy that has brought the war about. There is only one way to eliminate the enemy and that is to close with him. Let's all get on with the job we were sent here to do in order that we may return home at the earliest possible moment."[5]

Eddie Slovik had served his purpose.

Now the guns recommenced their old song of death in the Hurtgen. The sky over the shattered woods lit up a startling orange as the barrage descended upon the handful of Germans holding the line, where—in what now seemed another age—the 28th had attacked back in November when everyone at the top had been so confident that it would all be over by Christmas.

It was a fantastic pattern of myriad stabs and flashes of orange flame taking shape abruptly and dying just as abruptly. As the bitter February rain beat down, the tracer zipped back and forth in a lethal morse. Rockets hissed into the night sky like man-made forked lightning. Here and there a maverick shell exploded short and tossed up a ball of sudden fire like a Roman candle. Awed and gaping like village yokels, the blast slapping their astonished faces like a blow from a flabby damp fist, the waiting infantry of the 78th watched and waited.

The real backbone of the German defense, Colonel Liebach's young paras of the 8th Parachute Regiment, also waited for what was to come. By now even they were beginning to lose heart. But Colonel Liebach was a cynical martinet who brooked no weakness. His motto was, as he had expressed it often enough to his teenage soldiers: *Strong and true for Führer and Reich!*

Just before the battle commenced, he had told his men: "We know that we parachutists always draw the toughest assignments. The proud tradition of our branch makes us think back to the men of Crete, the many battles in the east, west, and south which have added . . . more glory to our banner."[6] Liebach's paras would be a tough nut to crack.

At three o'clock on the morning of February 5, 1945, the 78th Infantry Division began its attack. The rain pelted down, the guns thundered, and the infantry—black and white—started to slog through the mud. Their task was to attack through the woods above the River Kall and seize the road leading into Schmidt. Although Corps Commander Huebner had tried desperately not to make the same mistakes that Cota had done back in November, the attack plan worked out by General Parker commanding the 78th was little different from that which had proved so disastrous for the 28th Infantry.

At first, however, all went unexpectedly well. The lead infantry of the 3rd Battalion, commanded by Col. Floyd Call, slipped by the German defenses—a pillbox line held by 135 Germans—without a single shot being fired. They pressed on, slipping through successive German checkpoints, the night and the pelting rain covering their progress ever nearer to Schmidt. At regular intervals they whispered back their position by radio telephone to a tense, anxious regimental commander and then they were off again passing through the Germans like gray ghosts. *"No enemy contact!"* they reported time and time again. *"No enemy contact!"*

At headquarters they were jubilant. Engineers were ordered to follow up Call's Battalion. The combat team of the 7th Armored was alerted for action—an armored thrust toward the dam. The 78th's second regiment of infantry, the 310th, was ordered to be ready for an immediate move through the 309th. Everything was going perfectly. General Parker was overjoyed, as was Corps Commander Huebner, conducting his first battle in that position.

Dawn came, wet and gray. Colonel Call reported he was advancing toward the final objective and meeting only scattered small-arms fire. Shortly thereafter his happy doughs overran a German barracks, surprising the *Landsers* at their breakfast of "nigger sweat" and "old man."* All was going splendidly and now the 310th was moving up to take over from the 309th when the time came.

But now the Germans were becoming aware of the imminent threat to the dam and the presence of a whole *Ami* regiment so close to Schmidt. The attackers grew nervous. A platoon-size attack on the right flank was reliably reported to be an attack by a whole German company. Uncontrolled small-arms firing broke out in the woods from which the supposed counterattack was coming.

Parker started to worry. At noon he ordered the 309th to go on beyond its original objective, the barracks, while at the same time the 310th was to attack straight through the 309th. Parker was overruled fifteen minutes later by Huebner. He insisted that the 309th should keep on going as far as it could, heading straight for Schmidt. He knew the two roads available were not yet open and no heavy weapons or tanks could be brought up. But that didn't matter. The infantry could do the job by themselves.

Confusion ensued. While the two regiments jockeyed for position and some of their units were occupied trying to mop up the pillboxes to their rear, darkness overtook them. Abruptly, for no apparent reason, Huebner revoked his noontime order. The two regiments were to resume their original missions. The 309th would halt and the 310th would pass through it at three o'clock on the following morning.

Naturally, as the official U.S. history puts it, "both regiments were in low spirits, thoroughly confused by the day of changing orders. Men of at least one battalion of the 309th learned that both division and corps commanders were displeased with their performance."[7]

They were not the only ones. Slim Jim Gavin, commander of the 82nd Airborne Division, was unhappy, too, with the role

* German Army slang for ersatz coffee made out of acorns, and tinned meat from Italy that bore the letters AM—German for "old man"—on the can, which the soldiers joked was made of old men from Berlin's workhouses.

allotted to his division, which Huebner had ordered to attack on February 7. One of his regiments was to cross the Kall and, moving cross-country, cut the enemy's escape route from Schmidt, the 78th's objective. Unlike Parker and Huebner, Slim Jim had been up front, as we have seen, and had viewed the terrain. "It seemed obvious to me," he wrote later, "that the regiment could not be supplied across the Kall River canyon, certainly not if the enemy interfered or if artillery fire covered the trail. In addition, the trail was impassable for vehicles. A catastrophe must have occurred there in the fall of 1944. I could not understand why the bodies had not been removed and buried. Neither Corps nor Army headquarters must have been aware of the conditions in the canyon. Otherwise the bodies would have been buried and the disabled tanks removed."[8]

Now Gavin went to Huebner's headquarters to make his point of view clear to V Corps' Chief of Staff. He stated there was an alternate supply route for his regiment—the road from Lammersdorf to Schmidt. The Chief of Staff laughed in his face. He said, "Have you tried pack mules?"

Gavin was furious. There is nothing that angers a combat soldier more than a higher headquarters staff officer belittling the problems of the combat infantryman.[9] While he was speaking he noted Huebner and Parker bent over the map. Huebner was drawing short lines on it with a blue grease pencil. Each line represented a battalion, and an angry Gavin heard him suggesting to Parker tactical schemes for moving these battalions about.

Gavin was overcome by a strange feeling. He "realized how remote they were from the realities, from what it was like up there where the battalions were. The thought crossed my mind that the disaster that had befallen the 28th Division in the Kall River Valley might have had some relationship to the lack of understanding in higher headquarters of what was the actual situation on the ground. It turned out to be true, as I learned later."[10]

Indeed, the whole month-long battle for the Hurtgen Forest had been conducted at several levels. At the Supreme Headquarters some one hundred fifty miles behind the front, where filing cabinets were dusted in the morning, where all was order and quiet, where the "soldiers" had never heard a gun fired in anger, they knew *they* had always done all that was humanly possible. They had read all the books, studied all the maps, felt they knew the thinking and reactions of the German enemy—the other fellow, as Bradley called the Germans quite aptly—and had made plans for every conceivable contingency and emergency. It was in the lap of the gods.

Closer to the front at army and corps headquarters, they could indeed hear the rumble of the guns at the front, watch the boxlike ambulance trundle by with their broken bodies, hear the urgent appeals and demands from the line—*by telephone!* Why, sometimes they even went up to the front . . . well, as far as regimental headquarters at least! But they were clean, well-shaven, and ate their three squares a day. They had time to pursue office intrigues, have love affairs, and if they did go up to the front, well, they came home each night to sleep in a proper bed with sheets.

But the man on the spot saw things at a vastly different level. He knew nothing about the correct way to isolate a battlefield. No one had consulted him about the length of the softening-up barrage. The meteorologists had not informed him about the state of the weather to come. All he knew was noise, misery, confusion—and sudden, violent death. There were no filing cabinets in the front line, no pretty secretaries with whom to flirt, no official historians toting up the figures of the dead and wounded on both sides and trying to make sense of the whole bloody, purposeless business.

Watching these elegant staff officers playing their little games at the cost of other men's lives, Gavin felt his anger mounting. The vast gulf between the bitter reality of the front and the seemingly deliberate lack of understanding at V Corps HQ sickened him. For the very first time since the Battle of the Hurtgen Forest had started back in September 1944, a general officer posed the overwhelming question that the generals should have asked months before.

"I asked why in the world they had attacked through the Hurtgen Forest in the first place?"[11]

The enraged general received no reply. For as he wrote bitterly, perhaps even cynically, many years later, "that was a 'no-no' question."[12]

18

On the same day that Gen. Slim Jim Gavin posed his overwhelming question at V Corps Headquarters, another American general officer to the north, no less than an army commander, waited impatiently, too, for Clarence Huebner to make a success of his battle in the Hurtgen Forest.

In the Regular Army he had always been nicknamed "Big Simp" by his friends from the Point, to distinguish him from another regular officer who bore the same surname. The latter was nicknamed—predictably—on account of his diminutive stature, "Little Simp." Regular Army officers have never been noted for showing flights of imagination.

He was Gen. William Simpson, the commander of the U.S. Ninth Army, a tall rangy officer with a craggy face and a completely bald and shaven head. Indeed, to some he looked like a fierce, scalp-hunting Indian chief of a Hollywood B-Western. In fact, he was softly spoken and rarely lost his temper. He was, indeed, much respected by his staff, and Eisenhower thought very highly of him. After the war, the Supreme Commander stated that to the best of his knowledge Big Simp had never made a wrong move throughout the campaign in Europe.

Nor was Gen. William Simpson about to make a wrong move in this first week of February when his Ninth Army prepared to launch its first real offensive. All throughout the recent Battle of the Bulge, the Ninth—the newest U.S. Army in Europe—had held the line, fighting what was basically a defensive battle under the command of Field Marshal Montgomery. Now the ten divisions at Simpson's command were readying for the assault.

Lined up along the west bank of the River Roer, Simpson had

303,243 men (twice the size of the prewar U.S. Regular Army in which Simpson had been an obscure major) who were going to attack across the river into the heart of the Reich. Constantly a worried Big Simp warned his subordinate commanders, who were not used to directing such enormous numbers, not to mix their units. "Keep your battlefield orderly," he admonished them, taking a leaf out of the book of the overall commander, Montgomery, who always loved a "tidy battlefield." "Keep your units intact."[1]

Simpson knew that his assault was only part of a much larger attack in which everything depended upon order and split-second timing if it were to be a success. On his left flank a huge British-Canadian army of half a million men was scheduled to jump off three days before his own attack. This assault was calculated to draw off the Germans to the point of Montgomery's Anglo-Canadian attack. As soon as the Germans were committed in an attempt to stop Montgomery, Simpson would be faced solely by one single weak German division out of the ten German divisions currently holding the line against Montgomery's armies.

But no matter how much Simpson emphasized and planned, the ultimate success of the Ninth Army's attack depended upon the state of the River Roer and General Hodges. If Huebner's V Corps of Hodges's First Army failed to capture the dams beyond the Hurtgen and the Germans managed to destroy them, all hell would be let loose. Millions of tons of water would flood the flat plain on both sides of the Roer.

Normally the Roer was a placid, slow-running stream some 90 feet wide. But Simpson's engineers had calculated that, if the Germans flooded it from the dams, it would turn into a lake *a mile and a half wide!* Then it would be a tremendous engineering feat to cross it. Even after the floodwaters receded, it was thought that the Roer Valley would be soft and marshy. As a result, the only way to move vehicles, even if they were tracked, such as tanks, would be along the roads. Simpson's trump card, his massed armor, would be lost to him.

There was something else, too. If the Ninth Army failed to jump off in time, that is, three days after the main assault of Montgomery's First Canadian Army, the Germans might well fling in their total reserves to attempt to stop the "little fart" (as an angry Patton always called the self-opinionated Britisher) while an impotent Simpson marked time on the *wrong* side of the Roer.

Now, seemingly, the whole huge operation up north involving a million men—British, Canadian, American—depended upon one single green U.S. division—the 78th Infantry—capturing the dam at Schwammenauel before the Germans blew it up.

On Simpson's left flank, Montgomery's concentrations were complete. By now he had half a million men hidden behind the Anglo-Canadian front. Everywhere trucks, tanks, guns, and soldiers were packed into houses, fields, lanes, and the few roads. As Brigadier Essame of the British 43rd Infantry Division later described it, "The tension could be felt—the kind of feeling which runs through the crowd before the Derby."[2] As always the British seemed to think of war in terms of horse racing and cricket!

Up front on that February 7, 1945, Gen. Brian Horrocks, who commanded Montgomery's XXX Corps, felt he had done all he could. Without being detected by the enemy he had brought up two hundred thousand men of the initial assault wave and thirty-five thousand vehicles. Now they were in place, though the skinny ascetic British general, who had seen much of war as an infantryman, felt that if "Jerry" dropped as much as a pea in the area of his Corps, it was bound to hit something—the men were so tightly packed. Now, as dusk started to fall, Horrocks surveyed the gray dripping horizon for any sign of German activity. There was none. No unusual German activity whatsoever. The enemy would be caught completely off guard.

Night fell. The only sound was the drone of many heavy bombers. The anxious, waiting infantry were told they were

Bomber Harris's boys. RAF Bomber Command was out in full force, bombing the many enemy targets behind the front to prevent men and matériel being brought up when the real attack commenced.

The seventh gave way to the eighth of February. At one minute to five that morning all was silent, tense, and gray; the only sound was the steady dripping of the raindrops from the stripped, dreary firs. Five o'clock! The greatest bombardment of World War II thundered into tumultuous, crazy life.

"It was a fantastic scene, never to be forgotten," the historian of the British 4/7th Dragoon Guards wrote later. "One moment silence and the next moment, a terrible, ear-splitting din, with every pitch of noise imaginable. Little bangs, big bangs, sharp cracks, the rattle of machine guns, and the ripple of Bofors intermingled with the periodic swoosh of a rocket battery. The night was lit by flashes of every color and the tracer of the Bofors guns weaving fairy patterns in the sky as it streamed off toward the target."[3]

Up front, General Horrocks squatted in his forward command post—a ladder propped against a tree—and watched the initial bombardment, the curtain of shells from a thousand guns falling to his front. Horrocks had fought in France, and Russia in the First World War, and then in France, North Africa, and North West Europe in the Second; he had seen much of what the British call the sharp end of the stick. But even he was impressed as that tremendous barrage smashed down on the German lines, moving forward a hundred yards every four minutes while a protective white smokescreen blanketed the British assault battalions of four infantry divisions from the enemy's view.

As the infantry started to move out in their kangaroos, cut-down Shermans with their turrets removed in order to carry the foot-sloggers in relative safety, nature first took a hand in the great battle. It started to rain, huge cold drops that beat down on the helmeted heads of the infantry. Everywhere, the massed tracked vehicles started to bog down. Watching the progress of his troops, Horrocks's original jubilant mood started to vanish.

The reports that now began to be brought to him by harassed young staff officers were bad.

His 3rd Canadian Division was already marooned in the villages they had taken. The 51st Highland Division was cut off from supplies to the rear. So far only one lone Weasel had managed to get through to them, bearing five hundred cans of self-heating soup normally intended for the commandos. Horrocks didn't know it at that time, but those five hundred cans of oxtail soup would be the only warm food the whole of his two-hundred-thousand-strong XXX Corps would receive that long cold February day. *Mud* was thwarting the whole damned, so carefully planned attack, the worried corps commander told himself.

"*Mud!*" he wrote bitterly after the war, "and still more mud. It was so bad that after the first hour every tank going across country was bogged down, and the infantry had to struggle forward on their own."[4] Now Horrocks wondered, with a growing feeling of apprehension, what would happen if the Yanks didn't succeed in capturing the Roer dams in time. If the Germans flooded the River Roer now, with his troops already beginning to bog down in the mud caused by the heavy rains, he would be in trouble, serious trouble.

Clarence Huebner, the V Corps Commander, was not only worried, he was also furious. His first mission as a corps commander, after thirty-five hard years of trying to get to the top in the U.S. Army, was not going well at all. After its initial successes, the 78th Infantry Division was now making lamentably slow progress. General Parker's men had had three damned months to get to know the Hurtgen terrain over which they were fighting; they were tremendously well supported, yet they were not even within sight of the vital dam on the Roer. What in Sam Hill's name was holding them up?

What was holding them up was the dogged, last-ditch German defenders, every bit as tough and tenacious as their fathers, who had stalled a similar offensive in World War I in which Huebner as an infantry battalion commander had been twice wounded. The handful of Germans, paras and ordinary infantry, turned every cottage and barn into a strongpoint that had to be reduced by a formal, planned attack. They fought to the last, often holding up whole companies and battalions!

The little hamlet of Kesternich, for instance, which barred the 78th's progress to the key town of Schmidt, held up the Americans for two long bloody days. Here, as usual, the defenders turned every humble stone cottage into a fortified stronghold and the Americans had to pay dearly for each one they captured. Probably the capture of the shattered village would have taken longer if it had not been for one Sgt. Jonah Kelley. (All his life he had taken some ribbing on account of that given name.)

Time and time again Kelley was first in when they attacked a house, kicking open the door as his squad covered him, spraying the inside with wildfire and then charging in to finish off the surviving defenders. Twice Kelley was wounded during his self-imposed mission at Kesternich and twice he refused evacuation. The sergeant's Irish blood was roused. But by the evening of the first day of the attack on the village, Kelley's left arm was useless and he was constrained to fire his M-1 by resting the weapon on his forearm.

But even the luck of the Irish does not last forever. On the second day of the assault, wounded as he was and weak from the loss of blood, he led yet another attack on a German fortified position. Not for long. A cruel burst of machine-gun fire ripped his chest apart. He staggered and fell mortally wounded, blood dripping from his wounds. Still, as he lay dying, he pumped off his last three shots, killing the crew of the enemy machine gun that was holding up the advance of his battalion.

A few hours later, Kesternich was in American hands at the cost of 224 men, one third of the strength of the battalion involved. The advance to the Roer could continue, thanks to all those nameless young men—and Sgt. Jonah Kelley. Once again an American soldier won his country's highest honor—the Congressional Medal of Honor—in the Hurtgen, and yet again it would be awarded posthumously.

But the bravery of individual soldiers meant little to Huebner, isolated from the action and bloodshed in his remote headquarters. The Top Brass was breathing down his neck to capture those dams before it was too late. Hodges had told him he was holding up the operations of three armies to the north. He, Hodges, was coming to visit personally with General Parker, commanding the 78th Infantry. Huebner knew what that meant. If he didn't succeed in capturing Schmidt and the dams on the morrow, heads would roll, starting with his own.

Huebner quickly alerted the 2nd Ranger Battalion to assist the 78th. They were rushed to the banks of the Roer, which they found a mysterious and oppressive spot. The veterans of D-Day and Brest and the new boys were told they were going to cross the Roer at night and capture one of the dams by a *coup de main*. They were not pleased with the assignment, although the enemy on the opposite bank was completely inactive; not a single shot was fired at them on their arrival.

But they knew that would all change once they started to cross. As the *History of the Second Ranger Battalion* records: "The situation was serious and the prospects were enough to fill even old Rangers with dread. If ever the Battalion had drawn a suicide mission, this was going to be it!"[5]

Nobody in the Battalion liked their new assignment. "This undoubtedly was the most depressing place we ever were in," John Riley said later. "The other bank was steep and it was wooded to boot. And that damned mist that kept rising off the river made the place seemed haunted kind of."[6]

One of Riley's men, George Schneller, thought the same: "Definitely Wagnerian" was his verdict. "There's no doubt about it, the place did have a rather sinister brooding quality that worked on you."[7]

Fortunately, however, the Rangers were reprieved. Orders came down from Huebner's HQ that the river crossing was to be postponed for another twenty-four hours. The doughs of the infantry had not yet captured Schmidt and there would be no attack on the Roer until that key township was in American hands. The Rangers would never make the dreaded assault over the Roer to capture the dam. In the end, as we shall see, the infantry failed to take their objectives in time.

Meanwhile, Huebner had ordered all three regiments of Parker's 78th Division to attack toward Schmidt. To precede the attack there was to be a short, sharp artillery barrage. Unfortunately this fell on the German rear guard and not on the main positions of the enemy 272nd Volksgrenadier Division, which defended the area. Naturally the Germans, who had been totally unscathed by the heavy fire, took their toll as the Americans came advancing over the wet fields at dawn. Here and there battalions faltered and tended to go to ground. Huebner, however, brooked no hesitation. He threw in yet another battalion of tanks to support the reluctant heroes of the 78th. Hurriedly the tankers of the 744th Tank Battalion went to the aid of the hard-pressed infantry. Momentum picked up again and the Americans started to crawl forward once more toward that elusive hilltop town of Schmidt, which had been just within grasping distance, and yet as remote as the moon for all those weary, bloody months.

Field Marshal Model realized the danger. It was taking all his strained resources to hold the massive Anglo-Canadian thrust farther north. But he daren't commit his last reserves just in case Simpson's Ninth attacked across his sector of the Roer. Instead, he attempted to stop Huebner with whatever he could lay his hands on: veteran paras, culls from the Navy and Air Force, youngsters—barely seventeen—just called to the colors, old men whose last taste of action had been in the trenches during World War I.

One such member of what were called alarm companies, 17-year-old Kurt Kaares, recalled many years later going up to the front in the Hurtgen in a train smelling of Oriental tobacco, leather equipment, malt coffee, and human sweat. They were the usual mixed bunch of recently drafted teenagers and culls from the *Luftwaffe* and *Kriegsmarine*. In the fetid darkness of the blacked-out coach Kurt could hear the noise of a silk-stockinged leg belonging to a blonde in her mid-thirties being rubbed against the boot of their NCO, a former pilot now transferred to the infantry, "at first gently and then more and more hectically."

The NCO finally moved up to the blonde, put his greatcoat over her and his lap, and they got down to business in the darkness. "Hands, then fingers sought and found their targets. Men had become rare in the Homeland. Those men who stayed behind had good chances with the women and girls," he noted long afterwards.[8]

But there was nothing romantic or sexy about the front itself, that was for certain. The paras, in particular, had now become completely brutalized by the hardships and the bitterness of the battle in the Forest. Another young recruit was horrified to see one old hare, as the veterans were called, calmly sitting on the body of a dead comrade eating meat out of a can with his knife. Angrily he protested against this cold-blooded abuse of a fellow German soldier. The veteran wasn't moved. "I'll get a cold ass if I sit on the ground, it's soaked," he said. "The stiff's nice and warm. Besides, he's snuffed it, ain't he? He won't feel nothing."[9]

Like their opposite number, these green replacements didn't last very long in the Hurtgen. One of them recalls being taken back wounded to a makeshift hospital in a school basement to the rear. There, packed in with other wounded, he howled like a baby, as the hard-pressed doctor, his apron soaked in blood, probed for a mortar splinter in his knee. In the end the doctor lost patience with him and bellowed, "Stop that goddamn bawling! What are you, man—*a soldier or a pants-shitter?*"[10]

The wounded soldier stopped his moaning, shamed into silence. But he was the only one. The other wounded men being treated without the benefit of drugs, their wounds covered with bandages made of crepe paper, continued to howl like demented and tortured animals, which, in reality, they were.[11]

Another wounded youngster on the Hurtgen front recalls being stripped naked in the company of half a hundred other injured, then placed on muddy and bloodstained wooden duckboards to be showered in ice-cold water in a school gym. Thereafter an orderly and a great hulking female nurse came round smelling the open wounds of the naked men lying on the soaked floor. They were seeking the telltale odor of gas gangrene. In his case they found it. Later, in a semiconscious haze, he could hear the woman and the male orderly wagering five marks whether or not he would survive the night. He did, and the gleeful nurse collected the money from the disgruntled, sour-faced orderly, who normally never lost his bets, for "I've got a nose for them who're gonna croak it."[12]

But even with this ragbag of veterans and raw recruits, hastily shipped to the crumbling front in the Hurtgen, Model, the Boy Marshal, couldn't stop the *Amis*. There were just too many for him. Besides, Huebner was running out of time—*fast*. The pressure was on. Parker simply *had* to capture Schmidt now and advance on the dams. In exactly forty-eight hours Simpson was scheduled to kick off his attack across the Roer, and he didn't dare do that if there was any prospect that Model might flood the river. Simpson and his third of a million soldiers couldn't hang on much longer. Either the dams were captured or Simpson would have to postpone his assault!

By midmorning of February 7, Parker's 311th Infantry Regiment, supported by tanks of the 744th Tank Battalion, captured a commanding height barring their way into Schmidt, Hill 493. It was a gain that its sister regiment, coming through the woods, had been waiting for. Hastily the commander of the 311th Infantry pushed forward down the main road to Schmidt. Supported by a company of the 744th's tanks, they reached the woods on the edge of the shattered township.

Hurriedly they grouped with the infantry mounting the Shermans. Before them lay a mile of soaked, open fields. It was a potential death trap. But Parker was demanding results. Casualties didn't matter. He wanted Schmidt—*now!* So the combined forces' leaders decided on a bold, almost suicidal dash across the fields. Once the infantry were close enough, they would dismount and tackle the last-ditch German defenders.

Whistles shrilled. Noncoms bellowed orders. Drivers gunned their engines. The damp afternoon air stank of fumes. Hastily the infantry grabbed for support as the drivers rammed home first gear and the Shermans lurched off, splattering mud in a huge wake behind them. They were on their way. The recapture of Schmidt was in sight at last.

In low gear the tanks and their loads of tense, expectant infantry rumbled up the hill to their front. There was no enemy reaction. Not even a single rifle shot. Hardly daring to believe it, the infantrymen began to tell each other that the Krauts had perhaps finally abandoned Schmidt after all the long bitter months they had held it. They had fled, leaving Schmidt open for the taking.

The Shermans began to spread out. Soon they would breast the rise. Then they would be in full view of whatever Germans may have remained behind. On the shaking steel decks and grouped around the turrets hung with bits and pieces of tank equipment, the infantrymen pressed themselves closer to the metal instinctively. Here and there the more anxious of them tried to squeeze themselves into tight balls, helmeted heads clutched between their hands.

Suddenly the first Sherman was in the clear, plainly exposed on the crest of the hill. It was now or never! Abruptly there was that familiar rushing, tearing sound, like a huge piece of canvas being ripped apart. *"Eighty-eight millimeter!"* someone screamed in a frenzy of fear as the great shell slammed into the side of the lead tank, rocking it back onto its sprockets, scattering the infantry on its bucking deck like chaff.

With a groan it came to an abrupt halt. Thick white smoke started to pour from its ruptured engine, as the last of the defenders at Schmidt opened up a vicious hail of fire and that deadly cannon cracked into action again. Next instant the Sherman burst into flames.

That one burning tank sufficed. The drivers of the 744th turned tail immediately. Some swung around in great, mud-splattering arcs; others slammed into reverse and charged backwards, scattering other Shermans to their rear. Within a matter of moments the attack had fizzled out, the tankers refusing to go any farther until the infantry had cleared away the opposition. As always, in the final analysis, it was left to the poor bloody infantry—the P.B.I.—to do the dirty work. Wearily, shoulders hunched like those of men resigned to their fate, the infantry formed up. They would attack Schmidt without the aid of the Shermans.

There was no time for fancy tactics; Parker was screaming for results. The harassed infantry commanders decided they would not attack Schmidt frontally, but assault from the flanks. Covered by fire from light machine guns dug in on the height, the thin khaki lines moved out, carrying their rifles at the high port, their young bodies tensed for the first hot, hard blow of steel, which had to come.

Like all those thousands of nameless young men who had ventured into the Death Factory before them to end their short lives in violent anonymity, they were going in alone, unaided by tanks, planes, or the technology of twentieth-century American warfare. Over in a ruined Schmidt, the German machine guns took up the challenge, bursting into high-pitched, hysterical life, as the men plodded across the wet fields to their date with destiny, like animals being led to the slaughter—tamely.

19

Up north everything was going wrong now. The rain (it would pour down solidly for nineteen interminable days) had turned the battlefield into a swamp. The one main highway, used by the Anglo-Canadian Army, had been flooded, creating a monumental traffic jam that would go on for days before it was finally sorted out. Montgomery was now forced to supply his isolated troops, marooned on patches of high ground, by boat or armored amphibious trucks. The Canadians quipped that they had been renamed the Water Rats, a pun on Montgomery's famed Desert Rats, who had fought with him throughout the Desert Campaign. For the Canadian infantry were being forced by the floods to make their assaults by boat instead of by vehicle or on foot. And all the while they were taking tremendous casualties, the equivalent of two battalions of infantry a day, as Field Marshal Model threw in more and more of his elite paras in a desperate attempt to stop Montgomery's breaking through to the Rhine and final victory in the west. The Boy Marshal knew that all would be lost if he didn't stop the Western Allies now before Germany's last great natural bastion, the River Rhine. It would mean the end of Hitler's vaunted Thousand-Year Reich, and there would be no future for him in a defeated Germany, a man who had been branded as a war criminal by the Russians.

Still not involved in the great attack, Simpson was plagued with doubts. Montgomery had by now drawn off the great bulk of the First German Parachute Army, and he was faced by only very weak enemy formations. But dare he risk attacking on the Tenth? Could he chance crossing the Roer in force only to have the river flooded, perhaps isolating his forward unit on the other side of a mile and a half of water?

In his despair, Big Simp polled his corps commanders. What should he do? It was a strange measure to take for an army commander, but he knew his corps commanders had had more experience of battle than he had. Their opinion was valuable. In essence, Simpson wanted to know whether he should postpone his assault. If he did, and Huebner's Corps succeeded in capturing the dams in time, thus preventing the Roer from being flooded, then it might well mean the end of his career. Eisenhower wouldn't take kindly to an army commander who had hesitated at the very last moment, when victory was in sight. But on this February 9, 1945, a tortured Simpson was more concerned with the fate of the men under his command than his military future. By early afternoon he had their replies. All his corps commanders, save one, urged a postponement of the Ninth Army's assault on the River Roer; it would be too risky under present circumstances.

Now Simpson realized that the ball was well and truly in his court. It was up to him. Only *he* could make the fateful decision. Again the tall, skinny commanding general agonized and vacilated, as his impatient staff awaited his orders. His twelve divisions were already in place, ready to move out. Soon the first assault parties carrying their rubber boats would be moving down the muddy left bank of the river and the bridging units were already hidden behind the dikes, ready to throw across the first temporary bridges for the second wave. God in Heaven, what was he to do? In the end, he told his staff as the rain fell outside in a steady gray, miserable stream that he would give them his final decision by five o'clock that afternoon. They filed out and left him to it, the agony of high command, with the fates of countless nameless young men, whom he would never see, now in his big capable hands.

The night before, Hodges, the commander of the U.S. First Army, had finally lain it on the line to Huebner. That day Huebner had thrown in General Gavin's 82nd Airborne Division in order to speed up the capture of Schmidt and the dams beyond. But still the obstinate Germans held out in what was left of the hilltop township, forcing the men of the 78th to fight for every shattered ruin. Hodges now rasped over the telephone that he couldn't understand why, with forty battalions of artillery at his disposal (a massive 780 guns), Huebner couldn't blast a road from our frontline positions straight to the dams![1]

Huebner blustered. But Hodges, who looked like a mild-mannered schoolteacher, was unusually abrasive—for him. "I have to have them [the dams] by tomorrow," he warned Huebner.

At that moment General Craig of the 9th Infantry Division, which had seen so much of the Hurtgen fighting, chanced to walk into V Corps HQ on a routine visit; his division was currently "resting." Huebner's sallow broad face lit up when he saw the other general. Parker's 78th Division, he knew, had run out of steam; they would never take the dams at their present rate of progress. Suddenly inspired, he snapped, "I've got to use the Ninth Division."

Hodges, under just as much pressure as Huebner, didn't hesitate. "I want the dams in the morning," the army commander snorted. "How you get them is *your* business," and with that he slammed the phone down.

Huebner turned to a mildly surprised Craig, who realized that his casual stopover to shoot the breeze was turning into something else, and asked how long it would take him to move one of his regimental combat teams, approximately three thousand men, toward Schmidt in order to attack the dams from that direction.

Craig, the veteran of the Hurtgen fighting, didn't hesitate a single instant. Confidently he replied, *"Immediately!"*[2]

"All right," Huebner commanded. "Move your div HQ, too."

Craig knew what that meant. In essence, the corps commander was giving him control of the 78th's two assault regiments, the 309th and 311th. In Huebner's eagerness to take the dams before Hodges relieved him of his first corps command, military protocol was being thrown out of the window (for General Parker was not consulted on the matter till later).

Craig took off like a shot for Schmidt, where finally the weary survivors of the 78th were mopping up the last-ditch defenders, aided by the Shermans of the 744th, which had recovered after the panicky flight on the hill. He immediately called his command post from there and ordered his first regiment—the 60th, which had been in on the Hurtgen fighting right from the start—to move up at once. In spite of the casualties the 60th had suffered before in the Death Factory, it moved with surprising speed. Indeed, by the time Craig left the Schmidt area, it was already on its way, eager for the new battle in the Forest, where, back in what seemed now another age, it had experienced 100 percent losses.

The last drive for the vital dams could commence.

But despite the renewed vigor injected into the attack by the newcomers and General Craig's forceful leadership, the going was still slow. Although the two regiments of the 78th (the 309th and 311th) were now supported by Craig's veteran 60th Infantry, they made little progress toward the dam. In the lead was the 311th, advancing along the northeast bank of the Roer reservoir, clearing the ground so that its sister regiment, the 309th, could jump off for its attack on the dam itself. But the 311th didn't secure its objectives till nightfall when it handed over the assault to the lead elements of the 309th.

Now, in the glowing early-winter darkness, the men of that formation grew nervous. They had split into two groups: one to capture the top of the dam, the other to reach the lower level and capture the powerhouse there before the Germans blew it up. Both groups, especially the one on the lower level, were exceedingly apprehensive. They knew that as soon as the handful of Kraut defenders became aware of their presence on the dam, these defenders would blow up the whole of the great concrete structure while there was still time.

Then all hell would be let loose. The dam held back a massive 81,000 acre-feet of water. Tons of concrete and reinforced steel would be flung into the air with the impact of a gigantic bomb bursting, and thousands of tons of water would come cascading down in a tremendous flow that could well swamp and carry away the whole battalion in a flash. It could be a terrible, man-made disaster worse than any created by nature.

Thus while the Top Brass, ranging from a nervous chain-smoking Supreme Commander himself, right down to General Craig, the last to be given the hot potato of Hurtgen, fumed and waited apprehensively and nervously, the progress of those reluctant heroes moving along the face of the giant dam in the wet darkness grew ever slower and slower.

Big Simp had long suffered from stomach ulcers—indeed, they would end his military career prematurely before he achieved the coveted four stars that were his due as an army commander. Throughout the campaign he had kept it concealed from most of his staff (Eisenhower himself would not learn until after the war that one of his four senior army commanders suffered from a serious disability). Only Simp's personal physician knew. This day, however, as he agonized on what he ought to do about the assault across the River Roer, he did not attempt to hide the pain that racked his skinny body.

His long, haggard face was drawn and pale. The telltale lines on each side of his thin, tight mouth were etched deeper than ever. There were dark circles below his eyes. He had almost made his awesome decision: one that none of his fellow commanders had been forced to take throughout the campaign in Europe, perhaps throughout the whole war.

When two of Patton's corps commanders, for example, had declined to attack outside Metz in 1944 due to weather and other factors, the Third Army commander had offered them the opportunity to write out their resignations then and there. Predictably, the attack on Metz continued, even if it did end in failure. But the Third Army had been seen by the world to be *attacking*! That was the important thing as far as old Blood an' Guts was concerned.

Now all of Simpson's corps commanders, save one, had recommended that the Ninth Army should not attack on February

10. If he concurred and postponed the assault over the Roer on the morrow, all his old friends from the Point, his cronies, his superiors in Washington would be confronted by the prospect of a whole huge American army deciding *not* to go into its first offensive—not because of the *enemy*, but because of the *weather*. Back in June 1944 when Eisenhower had been told the weather for the cross-Channel assault was not favorable, he had decided to go ahead, writing out a pre-prepared statement to the effect that if the invasion of Europe failed, he personally was to blame. Could he take that kind of irrevocable decision upon himself?

As it grew darker, a staff officer came in bearing news of the river. The Roer was still rising, albeit slowly. Sitting there in his big office with the rain pattering down outside in the February gloom, he pondered the latest news. Was it the damned rain that was making the river rise? Or were the Krauts already beginning to flood it from the dams? What was he to do? Should he take the calculated risk, just as Eisenhower had done at Portsmouth on the evening of June 5, 1944? His career would probably be over, he knew, if he called off the attack and the Roer did not overflow its banks.

He could never recall later how long he continued to sit there alone—agonizing. Suddenly, a voice in the back of his head told him, *"Postpone the attack!"* Big Simp vacillated no longer. He reached for the office phone.

It was midnight now. German tracer sliced through the darkness in angry white morse. Ducked low, the combat engineers of Craig's 78th raced across the top of the giant dam. The gaping mouth of the inspection tunnel lay ahead. Gasping for breath, chests heaving frantically, they slammed into the protection of the concrete wall, the slugs howling off the stone, splattering their red sweat-glazed faces with splinters. To their consternation, however, they found the tunnel was blocked after all. They'd have to find some other way into the interior of the dam. What were they going to do?

The officer in charge made a bold decision. In the darkness, taking impossible risks, they would slide down the whole 200-foot length of the steeply sloping face of the dam. If they managed to reach the bottom in one piece, they would enter the other tunnel located there and try to penetrate to the power room that controlled the dam and the waters.

Now the little band of combat engineers began their hair-raising descent. Foot by foot, clinging on to each other like grim death, they edged their perilous way downward, knowing that one false move would plunge them down into the icy waters below. Time and time again a man slipped in the darkness, stifling his yell of sudden fear, saving himself from certain death just in time.

By the time they were halfway down, all of them were lathered in sweat in spite of the biting cold and gasping for breath like ancient asthmatics. Still there was no sign of enemy resistance. Had the Krauts finally fled? Or had they some other devilish plan in mind? Were they about to blow up the whole gigantic structure with the engineers clinging to the outer face, doomed to a certain death if they did?

Whatever the engineers' gloomy forebodings were that long, wet, rain-swept night, they kept them strictly to themselves. There was no other alternative. They needed every breath and all the energy they could gather. The strain on their bodies as they came ever closer to the base of the dam was tremendous; they had to brace themselves constantly not to fall off the steep incline. Their bodies were afire with what felt like red-hot pokers plunged into pain-wracked muscles, their legs threatening to give out at any moment.

The first man hit the ledge at the bottom with a gasp of relief. He crouched there a moment sobbing for breath, doubled up, as if he had just run a great race. More and more followed him down. With fingers that felt like clumsy sausages they slung their weapons over their shoulders, legs trembling and rubbery, threatening to give way beneath them at any moment.

The officer in charge whispered an urgent command. In single file, pressed tightly to the concrete wall, their eyes strained in the thin yellow light as they entered the second tunnel. Nerves jingling electrically, they waited for the first shrill cry of alarm and they advanced on the tips of their toes.

A single, last-ditch Kraut machine gunner farther up in the warm gloom of the tunnel and they would be dead ducks. He could wipe them out instantly. But they were to be spared this day. There was no lone, last-ditch Kraut. The Germans had fled hours before. The tunnel was empty. All their effort, the sweat, the daring risks they had taken this long hectic night had been totally in vain!

Entering the powerhouse itself at the far end of the tunnel, the crestfallen engineers were confronted by smashed, wrecked machinery with empty schnapps bottles and half-eaten German Army rations littering the floor, together with broken glass. The engineers' opposite number, the German *Pioneere,* had done their work well. They had blown the valves that discharged the water from the dam. They had also destroyed the discharge valves on the penstock that carried the waters to a point of discharge beneath the Schwammenauel Dam. Obviously they had been in a hurry to get away and had failed to blow up the powerhouse sufficiently to create a major cascade of water. Simpson's staff had been right about the level of the Roer having increased significantly. Now there was a sufficient flow of water coming from the dam to keep the entire Roer Valley flooded for the next week, with the river at certain spots flowing a fast ten knots an hour: a speed that could make it very hazardous to launch a flimsy Army assault craft. In essence, after all the heartache and bloodshed in the Forest, Model's men had beaten the Americans!

Naturally, the official history of the campaign in Europe glosses over what was a defeat of the first magnitude. It states: "Allied commanders could breathe easily again" (after the capture of the dams). "The reservoirs that had directly and indirectly cost so many lives at last were in hand. It would have been better, of course, had the Schwammenauel Dam been taken intact, thus obviating any change in the Ninth Army's plan for crossing the Roer; but it was enough that the Germans had been forced to expend their weapons before any Allied troops had crossed the river downstream."[3]

The reality was different, very different. Admittedly, when Big Simp's Ninth Army finally did assault the Roer with four divisions in the first wave, his total losses were an amazingly low *one hundred men* killed and wounded. But the Ninth's exceedingly low casualties were achieved at the expense of the British and Canadians. For the U.S. official history does not take into account the slaughter that occurred farther north, where the Anglo-Canadian armies slogged it out with the Germans in a desperate battle for the Reichswald Forest, until finally the Ninth Army was in a position to attack once the floods on the Roer had receded.

While over three hundred thousand able-bodied young Americans of the Ninth Army stood by idly, shooting the breeze, playing cards, complaining about the weather, serving no useful purpose whatsoever (they did not even pin down a sizable number of enemy troops on the opposite bank of the Roer, for Model knew they were in no position to attack across the river), Montgomery's men fought and bled.

With Simpson unable to attack, General Horrocks, commanding Montgomery's assault corps of 200,000 men, was on his own, mired down in thick gooey mud of the kind he and his fellow commanders had once experienced as junior officers back in the dreaded trenches of World War I. At midnight on that February day when the engineers of the 78th Division discovered the dams were blown, Horrocks realized that his front was well and truly flooded. His Canadian and British infantry were now fated to fight one of the most grueling, punishing battles of the war, while the Americans stood on the sidelines as helpless, impotent spectators.

By the time Simpson's Ninth attacked at three-thirty on the morning of February 23, Horrocks had lost 770 officers and 9,660 men of his British contingent and 378 officers and 4,925 men of the Canadian one. It was the greatest total of British casualties of the whole campaign, higher than those suffered by the British at the tragic defeat of Arnhem the previous year.

By the end of the first week of March 1945, it was about all over and the Allies were firmly on the path toward the last bastion—the Rhine. The rubbernecks swarmed up from the rear to inspect the wasteland of the battlefield. Eisenhower paid a visit to Simpson's victorious Ninth Army. The Supreme Commander, the democrat par excellence, addressed three thousand infantry of the Ninth in a muddy field. As he turned to move off afterwards, he slipped and sat down hard in his best uniform in the muck.

The GIs roared.

Ike took it in good humor (at least in public). He struggled to his feet gasping, for he was totally out of shape, and, clasping his hands above his head, gave them the boxer's salute of triumph. The soldiers bellowed their approval.

Churchill followed: losing his false teeth (they later had to be special-delivered in a sealed box by a dispatch rider), having his military cap knocked off by the cannon of an armored car, and generally being awkward. But like Eisenhower he preserved his sense of humor. Reaching Ninth Army HQ, he asked a surprised Simpson how far it was to the Siegfried Line. Simpson told him that it was half an hour away. Churchill insisted he be taken to it. Once there, the Great Man descended from his vehicle followed by the Top Brass. Facing the dragon's teeth of the Line fumbling with his fly, he announced delightedly, a huge grin on his cherubic face, big cigar tucked in the side of his mouth, "Gentlemen, I'd like to ask you to join me. Let us urinate on the great West Wall of Germany!"

Remembering the photographers now aiming their cameras so excitedly, he wagged his finger at them and exclaimed, "This is one of those operations connected with this great war which must not be reproduced graphically."[4]

It was all great exciting stuff, splendid copy for the folks back home. Even Huebner, whose command of the V Corps in the last stages of the Battle for the Hurtgen had not been particularly awe-inspiring, joined in. Relaxing now and taking time off from his whittling (which he listed after the war as one of his two hobbies), he quipped to General Hodges about his 78th Division, which had borne the brunt of three months' combat in the

Death Factory, that he had "made him another good division."[5] What the cost of that particular action was in the dead and broken bodies of young Americans did not seem to concern the generals. They had their victory now—at last.

The fact that the Hurtgen had beaten them was conveniently swept beneath the carpet. That bold dash to the Rhine, which the Top Brass had been so confidently predicting ever since September 1944, had never come about. Field Marshal Model, defending the Forest, had stopped them dead. In the end, he and the Hurtgen had won. At enormous cost they had finally burst through the *Hurtgenwald,* only to find that the Roer dams, the only strategic justification for the six-month-long battle, had been badly damaged.

Although they conveniently forgot the defeat of the Hurtgen, the Top Brass still wanted their revenge. In their opinion, no one should be able to damage the prestige of the U.S. Army, as Field Marshal Model had done in the Forest, and get away with it. Before the dying Third Reich finally collapsed and surrendered, Model would have to pay for the defeat he had inflicted upon them in the Forest. Now the Top Brass wanted Model—*dead or alive!*

20

The Boy Marshal, as von Rundstedt had once called him so contemptuously, was now at the end of his tether. For two months now, ever since the Americans had crossed the Roer, he had been retreating with his army group, fighting a slow rear-guard action to the Rhine, then over it. For nearly two weeks he and his weary depleted army had been able to rest there on the eastern bank. Then Montgomery had attacked across the great river in full force. In a matter of thirty-six hours, it was virtually all over, and the Western Allies were thrusting on. In particular, the Americans were now causing him the greatest problems with Simpson's Ninth Army pushing north on his right flank and Hodges's First Army doing the same on his left flank.

The survivors of those divisions that had bled in the Hurtgen—the Big Red One, the Golden Arrow, the Lightning Division, and all the rest of them—were granting him no respite. All Model could do was to fight a little and then flee to the next position and start all over again.

On April Fool's Day 1945, Model learned that he had been cut off. Simpson's 2nd Armored Division and Hodges's 3rd Armored Division, which had played such a major role in the frontier battles, had linked up at the little German town of Lippstadt. Model was cut off with remnants of three armies, over three hundred thousand men, in what was first named the Ruhr Pocket and later the Rose Pocket, after General Maurice Rose of the 3rd Armored, who was killed by SS men while leading the link-up force.

Desperately Model pleaded with his superior, Field Marshal Kesselring, to be allowed to break out while there was still time.

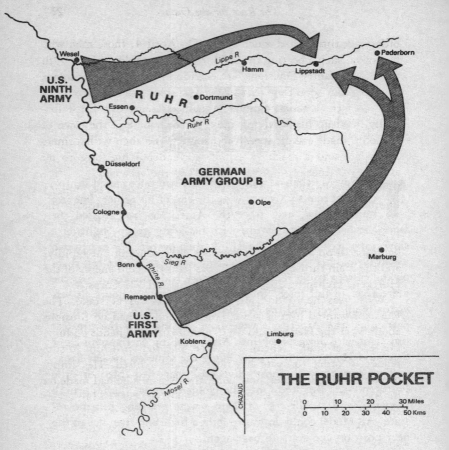

THE RUHR POCKET

0   10   20   30 Miles
0 10 20 30 40 50 Kms

He told the big bluff Marshal, "To continue the defense in this position is absurd, as such defense cannot even pin down enemy forces."[1] Model was wrong. His defense was going to pin down *eighteen* American divisions because General Bradley was determined to force his old opponent into surrender. Kesselring refused. On the Führer's orders, he told Model, Fortress Ruhr would be held to the last bullet and the last man.

Outwardly Model seemed to be his old self. He gave out orders for a last-ditch stand to all commanders and the local authorities. Swift drastic punishment was threatened to those who hid deserters or threatened to surrender to the *Amis*. But neither the orders nor threats had much effect. On April 4, those men who had taken such a beating in the Hurtgen, the soldiers of the 99th and 78th Infantry Divisions, attacked in force. At first resistance was stiff, but soon the Germans were surrendering in droves. In one instance, a tank commander named Lieutenant Ernst formally lined up his surviving tanks in the square of the town of Iserlohn, made a short speech to his men, and then with a smart about-face and a cracking salute, surrendered his force to an astonished American officer, *"korrekt"* to the very end.

By now even Model had lost the will to fight on. The Führer's Fireman, as he had once proudly called himself because in the past he had pulled so many hot chestnuts out of the fire for Hitler, knew there was no hope for his battered force. He was hemmed in on all sides, his supplies were running out rapidly, and the main thrust of the attack was led by his old enemy of the Hurtgen, Lightning Joe Collins with his old VII Corps.

What was he to do? His personal fate was at stake. The Russians wanted him as a war criminal and he had no illusions about what the Ivans would do to him if they laid hands on him. His Chief of Staff, General Wegener, pleaded with him to surrender in order to spare his men. Model refused. He simply couldn't surrender, even now, after the demands he had made on his men all these bitter years. How often in the past had he asked them to stick it out against overwhelming odds!

He continued to hold out, even achieving minor victories here and there. Once, a force of Gavin's 82nd Division crossed the Rhine into Model's territory only to be hit by a superior German counterattack. Of the 140 paratroopers who crossed the river, only 28 returned. The rest were all killed, wounded, or captured. But victories of that kind were mere drops in the ocean.

Model struggled with his conscience as the Americans pressed and pressed, containing what was left of seven whole German corps into an area of some 30 by 75 miles. On April 15, Model received, under a flag of truce, a courier from General Ridgway, who commanded the U.S. XVIII Airborne Corps. He bore a letter from the hook-nosed American commander. In it Ridgway stated: "Neither history nor the military profession records any nobler character, any more brilliant master of warfare, any more dutiful subordinate of the state than the American General Robert E. Lee. Eighty years ago this month, his loyal command reduced in numbers, stripped of its means of effective fighting and completely surrounded by overwhelming forces, he chose an honorable capitulation.

"The same choice is now yours. In the light of a soldier's honor, for the reputation of the German officer corps, for the sake of your nation's future, lay down your arms at once. The German lives you will save are sorely needed to restore your people to their proper place in society. The German cities you will preserve are irreplaceable necessities for your people's welfare."[2]

Ridgway's impassioned plea had no effect. Model was not interested in the airborne commander's interpretation of American military history. But on that same day Model did make a decision. He ordered all youths under the age of 18 and the older men of the *Volkssturm*, the German Home Guard, to be discharged officially from the *Wehrmacht* with immediate effect and sent home. Forty-eight hours later, he commanded all remaining ammunition and supplies to be distributed to individual units and left it up to local commanders either to fight on or to surrender.

It was too late to order surrender. Model's men were already doing so in their scores, hundreds, thousands. In one case, for example, one lone private of the 78th Division, which had been last to enter the Death Factory, set off to his battalion command post with 68 German prisoners. By the time he arrived there he discovered—to his astonishment—he had a staggering 1,200!

After the failure of Ridgway's gentleman-and-officer approach, Bradley tried a tougher approach. He promised the Bronze Star to any GI who brought in Model—*dead or alive.* But all his eager GIs brought in that same day was Model's Mercedes, a robin's-egg-blue affair with red leather upholstery, an appropriate color for a general who wore the crimson stripe of the Greater German General Staff on his breeches. Model had vanished.

In fact, the Field Marshal had abandoned the giveaway vehicle in order to slip through the American cordon. After finally dissolving his Army Group B, he had disappeared, together with three staff officers and five orderlies. As they slipped from one remote village to another, hunted by the victorious Americans all the while, Model's officers kept urging him to finally throw in the sponge and surrender.

Model had been disgusted in January 1943 when his fellow field marshal, Paulus, had surrendered his Sixth Army to the Russians at Stalingrad. He would never do that. He told his officers, "A German field marshal does not become a prisoner. Such a thing is just not possible."[3]

During his harassed wanderings, Model and his party came across Sgt. Walter Maxeiner, a three-times-wounded veteran of his disbanded army group. Maxeiner spotted the field marshal sitting on a gun carriage, his hands supporting his head as if he were in the depths of despair. Maxeiner recalled: "We went up asking what we should do. With great astonishment our young soldiers looked at the officers with the stripes on their pants and their medals. Never before had they been so close to the big brass."[4]

"When Field Marshal Model, for that is who it was, saw us, he beckoned us over, asked where our homes were, our age and military careers. For some time he discussed my tour of duty on the eastern front with me. It turned out I had been in a unit under his command at the time."

The veteran then asked the field marshal what he should do now. "He answered, 'Go home, boys. The war is over for us.' With a serious mien, he shook hands with me and said, 'Good luck on the trip home and tell your men not to lose courage and to continue to remain decent boys.' "

The time had almost come to bring his career to an end, Model knew. But there'd be no going home to mother, as the German soldier put it, for him. There remained only one honorable way out.

One day after Hitler's last birthday, on April 21, 1945, the

Model party reached a wood near the industrial town of Duisburg. His followers were weary and disheartened. Model's second adjutant, a colonel named Pilling, heard the field marshal ask in quiet despair, "What is left to a commander in defeat?" Model answered his own question. "In ancient times they took poison!"

Again one of his officers urged Model to surrender. Again Model replied, "I simply cannot do it. The Russians have branded me a war criminal and the Americans would be sure to turn me over to them—for hanging."[5]

Later that same warm April afternoon, resting in the shade of an oak tree, Model told Pilling wearily, "My hour has come. Follow me." Model then led his aide deeper into the Forest. Somewhere (for later only Pilling knew the exact location of the spot and he would never reveal it to Bradley's intelligence men despite a tough grilling by them) in one of the remoter glades, he drew his pistol and gave his final instructions as an officer whose army service went well back to the time before the Great War: "You will bury me here."

There was a muffled shot. While Pilling watched with a contorted face, Model sank to the ground, blood streaming from his shattered head, the pistol falling from his nerveless fingers. The Boy Marshal was dead, killed by his own hand: the Victor of the Hurtgen thwarting the Americans to the very end. Silently, Pilling picked up his shovel and began to dig a hole.

By now, however, the capture of their old enemy Walter Model no longer seemed so important to Hodges, Collins, and all the rest of the American brass who had fought him so long. He had disappeared* and that was that. There was still a little bit of mopping up to be done. But, in essence, they had won the war and their strategy was justified at last. When the final tally of the troops captured in the Ruhr Pocket was taken, the total came to 317,000 Germans—more enemy troops than had surrendered to the Russians at Stalingrad! The campaign, if that is what it can

---

* We shall see what happened to Field Marshal Model's body later.

be called, had cost Simpson's Ninth Army 2,500 men killed, wounded, and missing. Hodges's First Army had suffered about three times that number.

In their eyes, the thirty thousand young Americans who had been killed or wounded in the Forest had been avenged; their sacrifice had not been in vain. They had finally beaten Model and his men, who had opposed them for so long in the Hurtgen. Later, not one of them (save Gavin) would ever admit they had been wrong in starting the Battle of the Hurtgen Forest in the first place. Not one of them—from Eisenhower downward—would ever confess any sorrow at the terrible suffering of their men in the Death Factory. None of the Top Brass would declare their strategy (or the lack of it) had been confused right from the start. Later they would dream up the strategy of the dams. But even here, not one of them would ever take on the responsibility for failing to secure those dams in time and preventing the grievous losses the Germans managed to inflict on Montgomery's British and Canadians as a result of that failure. After all, ends justify means—*and they had won!* Hadn't they?

Indeed, after-events seem to show that America's Top Brass *never* did learn the bitter and bloody lessons of the Death Factory: the futility of throwing away young men's lives for the sake of their own prestige and that of the U.S. Army. Ten years after he had first attacked into the Hurtgen, supposedly in order to protect his right flank, Lightning Joe Collins, who had been the U.S. Chief of Staff, was sent to war again by his old Supreme Commander.

The now President Dwight D. Eisenhower sent four-star General Joe Collins to Vietnam as his special envoy. It was his task to convince the South Vietnamese generals that they should accept American military advisers to replace the recently beaten and discredited French. Lightning Joe succeeded all too well with some of his usual hard, tough talking, and the U.S. was involved in Vietnam.

Back home in that same year, a young brigadier general (who was the Regular Army's insider bet for the future Chief of Staff of the U.S. Army) was studying at the Harvard Business School. The man who had commanded the old 9th Infantry Division's artillery during the attack on the Hurtgen was grooming himself for his call to destiny. In 1964, a decade after his former corps commander, Collins, had involved the U.S. in Vietnam, that moment came. Gen. William Westmoreland, now aged a youthful 49, arrived in Saigon to take charge of the U.S. Army's presence in that ill-fated country.

Six months later two marine battalions waded ashore at Da Nang as the movie cameras whirred and pretty girls readied to present them with flower *leis*. More and more troops followed. It was the Death Factory all over again, throwing good money after bad. The Big Red One came, as did the Ivy Division, both veterans of that great slaughter thirty years before. By the summer of 1965 Westmoreland was pleading with the President for three hundred thousand men or more. Otherwise there would be a disaster in South Vietnam.

The same terrible war of attrition, with no apparent strategic purpose, save that terrible "body count," had commenced. It was Hurtgen's Death Factory all over again. Like the Bourbons, the Top Brass, who had been young captains and majors back in 1944, had forgotten nothing and learned nothing new.

In the end, it was left to a former corporal of the 84th Infantry Division, who, at the time of the Hurtgen Battle, had established himself nicely in the nearby village of Grotenrath, complete with red-haired German girlfriend, to sort it all out. "Uncle Henry," as his girlfriend (*Kraut Schatzie*) of that time had called him, did just that. As President Nixon's principal adviser, the now *Doctor* Henry Kissinger stage-managed the U.S. Army's withdrawal from that ill-fated country, leaving the erstwhile allies to the Cmmunist conquerors' revenge. Just like the Hurtgen, South Vietnam was an unmitigated disaster for American arms.

Right at the beginning, when the Top Brass realized what they were letting themselves in for, someone at the top should have blown the whistle and put an end to the pointless bloodletting. No one did. Twenty years after the fighting in the Hurtgen had ended, *Time*'s "Man of the Year," that former colonel of the 9th Infantry, now four-star General Westmoreland, told Assistant Secretary of Defense John T. McNaugton that "we are fighting in an escalating military stalemate."[6] But did his realistic assessment of the combat situation in Vietnam extend any further than that? Did he draw the obvious conclusion? Did he lay it on the line to the President? Did he threaten to resign if something was not done about the situation?

Of course, he did not. Just like those other generals back in 1944–45, whom he as a frontline soldier had obviously cursed more then once for being so knuckleheaded, he remained optimistic. That year he told President Johnson, "In the final analysis, we are fighting a war of attrition, . . . Defeat is not a real worry."[7] All he needed was more bodies. Time and men. At the then level of 470,000 troops in Vietnam, it would take him five years to beat the enemy. Give him another one hundred thousand troops and he would cut that time to three years. Add another one hundred thousand bodies *now* and he could possibly guarantee final victory by mid-1969.

It was the same old story as that of the Hurtgen. That one time 30-year-old colonel of artillery who, "athletic and affable," had seen his old division go into the Death Factory three times, to return shattered and broken, had learned nothing from the experience. So once again the sons of those men who had fought and died in the Hurtgen paid the same bitter price their fathers had done—in their own blood. A generation later the Top Brass had created another Death Factory. Let us hope it was the last.

Epilogue

Remember me when I am dead and simplify me when I'm dead.

> Lт. Kеiтн Douglas,
> *Royal Armoured Corps,*
> *killed in action, Normandy 1944*

Today the Boy Marshal, Walter Model, lies in Grave 1073/1074 at the Heroes' Cemetery, as the Germans call such places, in Vossenack, where so many young Germans and Americans died that winter. It had not been his wish to be buried among the men—so many of their graves without a name—who had died for him in 1944–45. Unlike Patton,* who lies with six thousand men of his Third Army just across the border, he left no orders on that score. But his son, a major in the newly re-created West German Army, had his father's body dug up from its hiding place in the Forest, where the field marshal had shot himself that April, and buried here.

It is a raw bleak place, especially in winter. The cemetery is exceedingly neat and well tended, of course, this being Germany. But there is little color and few flowers. Germany's post-war generations are ashamed of their soldier-fathers. Only the old ever visit these small, plain gray crosses, so many of them marked simply "an unknown soldier."

But the cemetery and those other Heroes' Cemeteries which dot the area are about all there is to be seen of that great battle that once raged among these rolling hills and wooded valleys. The villages that were so savagely destroyed that winter have all long been rebuilt and occupied by young people who weren't even born then. Here and there the shell-pocked sides of an old house or a garden shed, which on closer inspection turn out to be

---

* Patton is buried at Hamm Cemetery in nearby Luxembourg. For those interested in the ironies of history, no leading U.S. politician has ever visited Blood and Guts' grave. Even President Reagan, when he was a mere 20 miles away at Bitburg during his controversial visit to Germany, never took the half-hour journey to the grave of one of World War II's leading U.S. generals.

made of steel plates marked "105mm howitzer" and dated 1944,* indicate that something pretty terrible must have happened here once.

Stray away, however, into the woods (as thick as ever), away from those sterile, so-clean villages, strangely empty of children's laughter, for the Germans are a dying race—they have the lowest birthrate of any country in the whole world—and you stumble upon the rusting traces of that terrible time. Near where the 78th Division kicked off its last attack on the dams, there is a line of foxholes, each one complete with pieces of rotting GI blanket, just as the men of the Lightning Division left them.

The Kall Trail is still there too, running into the steep valley from Kommerscheidt, and just as difficult as it was when General Fleig led his Shermans up it in that desperate attempt at supporting the hard-pressed 28th. Here you can still see where the engineers blew away the rocks that terrible night so that the tanks could proceed. The slope to the side is still riddled with foxholes full of rusting junk that was once hard steel, the tools of sudden death. Halfway down, where the houses begin, bedded in stone now but still clearly recognizable, there is a length of Sherman tank track, rubber mounted in rusting steel. The last mementos of Fleig's attack.

What do the wanderers, those middle-aged Germans with their embossed walking sticks, leather knickerbockers, and red socks—well-nourished faces, red too, with the steepness of the ascent—make of it, one wonders? If they recognize the track for what it is, do they query how it came to be here in the depth of this peaceful forest? Do they recognize it as *Ami*, for they still use the word the *Landser* had used for his American opponent so long ago? But perhaps most of them pass by the unrecognized rusting reminders of that terrible time: just another piece of junk that litters the forests everywhere these days. The Germans are no longer so careful as they once were in their disposal of waste in our throwaway society.

---

* To house themselves immediately after the war, the locals made temporary shelters from the shell case containers left everywhere by the *Amis*.

But who now remembers those soldiers—German or American? Who still thinks of those thousands of young men who died—for what?—so long ago? Who recalls Colonel Petersen, twice wounded, out of his mind with despair, crawling down this same trail on his hands and knees? The abandoned litter station of the 28th, which Gavin came across at that corner there, packed with the young men who had been frozen to death as they lay untended and helpless on their stretchers? The blind soldier who saved his CO's life? The medics hiding the severed hand under the carpet? That reluctant hero—too old for infantry at 36—sobbing with fear before his first taste of combat? Private Sheridan, pistol in hand, winning his country's highest honor at 18, dead before he had begun to live? *Who remembers them now?*

Occasionally old men in funny caps make their way here to this remote border area after viewing the graves of those killed in the Hurtgen on the other side of the border near the Belgian village of Henri Chapelle (for no American soldier killed in World War II is buried in Germany). They wander around looking puzzled. Some of them find the old bunkers on Castle Hill where those two brothers of the 2nd Rangers died in each other's arms. But for the most part they are confused and disoriented. Someone has changed *their* battlefield and they go back to America to die sooner or later, remembering the times when they were young. For *those* memories are always with them, more vivid and real than anything that has happened to them in the long intervening years.

Seven times a year, according to the officials at Vossenack's Heroes' Cemetery, whitened skeletons are delivered to them. They are found regularly by the search teams still looking for batches of ammunition and the like dating from the great slaughter of 1944–1945.* No one knows anymore if they are German or *Ami*. So yet another victim of the Death Forest is laid to rest among his comrades of *both* sides.

"*Tote Soldaten sind niemals allein, denn immer werden treue Ka-*

---

* In 1985 alone, approximately one and a half million separate pieces of ammunition, etc., were picked up in the German state in which the Hurtgen is located.

meraden bei ihnen sein" ("dead soldiers are never alone, for loyal comrades will always remain with them") reads the memorial to the German division, the 116th Panzer, that slaughtered the 28th in November 1944 and made the last abortive attack out of Model's Ruhr Pocket.

Perhaps that sentiment, trite as it is, is about the only consolation for those who died so long ago and who are to die soon. Today, the survivors know that all their heartbreak, their suffering, their effort, their self-sacrifice were in vain. They fought and their comrades died in a battle without any real direction and which ended, in the final analysis, in defeat.

Surprisingly enough, however, of all the tens of thousands of young men who fought in the Death Factory and who went to their deaths so tamely, America today remembers only one single soldier. He died young too.

It is a bitter irony of history that the only one of these many who went into the Hurtgen who has entered the annals of World War II is the one who ran away—Pvt. Eddie D. Slovik, 3689415, Detroit, Michigan, Feb. 18, 1920–Jan. 31, 1945.

Source Notes

PART ONE *Into the Green Hell*

CHAPTER 1

1. Personal communication to author.
2. Ibid.
3. Joe Mittelman, *Eight Stars to Victory* (Washington: F. H. Heer Printing Co. and 9th Infantry Association, 1948).
4. Interview with author.
5. Ibid.
6. Ibid.
7. *BBC War Report* (Collins, 1945).
8. Carlos Baker, *Ernest Hemingway* (New York: Scribner's, 1969).
9. Ibid.
10. Joseph Collins, *Lightning Joe* (Louisiana State University Press, 1979).
11. Interview with author.
12. James M. Gavin, *On to Berlin* (New York: Viking Press, 1978).

CHAPTER 2

1. Mittelman, *Eight Stars*.
2. Ibid.
3. Ibid.
4. Ralph Martin, *The GI War* (Boston: Little, Brown, 1967).
5. Mittelman, *Eight Stars*.
6. Martin, *GI War*.
7. Charles MacDonald, *The Three Battles* (Washington: Office of Military History, 1952).
8. Ibid.

9. Frank Mack, *Yank—The GI Story of the War* (Duell Slona: 1947).
10. Gavin, *On to Berlin*.
11. Mittelman, *Eight Stars*.
12. Martin, *GI War*.
13. Dwight D. Eisenhower, *The Crusade in Europe* (New York: Doubleday, 1948).
14. Ibid.
15. Mittelman, *Eight Stars*.

CHAPTER 3

1. Mittelman, *Eight Stars*.
2. Walter Gorlitz, *Model* (Bensheim: Bastei-Lubbe Verlag, 1972).
3. Ibid.
4. David Irving, *The War Between the Generals* (London: Allan Lane, 1981).
5. Omar Bradley, *A General's Life* (New York: Simon & Schuster, 1982).
6. Ibid.
7. Collins, *Lightning Joe*.
8. Ibid.
9. Ibid.
10. Mittelman, *Eight Stars*.
11. Charles Currey, *Follow Me and Die* (Briarcliff Manor: Stein & Day, 1983).

CHAPTER 4

1. Mittleman, *Eight Stars*.
2. Wolfgang Trees and Ernst Hohenstein, *Holle in dem Hurt-genwald* (Triangle Verlag, 1980).
3. Letter to author.
4. Martin, *GI War*.
5. *Stars and Stripes* (October 20, 1944).

6. *History of 951st Field Artillery* (Germany: privately published, 1945).
7. Ibid.
8. Ibid.
9. D. Lavender, *Nudge Blue* (privately printed, 1968).
10. Ibid.
11. Letter to author.
12. Cornelius Ryan, *The Longest Day* (Collins, 1968).
13. Ibid.
14. Ibid.
15. William Huie, *The Execution of Private Slovik* (Signet, 1954).
16. Currey, *Follow Me*.
17. Letter to author.

CHAPTER 5

1. Irving, *War Between the Generals*.
2. Huie, *Private Slovik*.
3. Ibid.
4. Ibid.

PART TWO *The Death Factory*

CHAPTER 6

1. Currey, *Follow Me*.
2. Ibid.
3. Ibid.
4. Ibid.
5. Ibid.
6. Ibid.
7. Letter to author.
8. Ibid.
9. Currey, *Follow Me*.
10. Ibid.
11. Trees, *Hoelle in dem Hurtgenwald*.
12. Ibid.

CHAPTER 7

1. Currey, *Follow Me*.
2. Ibid.
3. Ibid.
4. Charles MacDonald, *The Siegfried Line Campaign* (Washington: Dept. of the Army, 1963).
5. Ibid.
6. *History of the 12th Regiment* (Washington, Infantry Press, 1947).
7. Ibid.
8. Ibid.
9. Ibid.
10. MacDonald, *Siegfried Line Campaign*.
11. Ibid.

CHAPTER 8

1. Mary Welsh Hemingway, *How It Was* (Weidenfeld & Nicolson, 1979).
2. Ibid.
3. Baker, *Hemingway*.
4. Bradley, *General's Life*.
5. *Stars and Stripes* (November 20, 1944).
6. Ibid.
7. MacDonald, *Siegfried Line Campaign*.
8. Ibid.
9. Ibid.
10. Baker, *Hemingway*.
11. Studs Terkel, *The Good War* (London: Hamish Hamilton, 1985).
12. Ibid.
13. Ibid.
14. Hoegh and Doyle, *Timberwolf Tracks* (Washington: Infantry Press, 1947).
15. Ibid.
16. Ibid.

17. Ibid.
18. W. Boice, *History of the 22nd United States Infantry* (Washington: Infantry Press, 1959).
19. Ibid.
20. Ibid.
21. W. Walton, "Hurtgen," *Life* (December 1944).
22. Ibid.

CHAPTER 9

1. MacDonald, *Siegfried Line Campaign.*
2. *Danger Forward* (Washington: Society of the 1st Division, 1947).
3. *New York Daily News,* November 11, 1945.
4. Ibid.
5. Ibid.
6. Ibid.
7. Ibid.
8. James M. Gavin, "Bloody Huertgen," *American Heritage,* Vol. 31: No. 1 (December 1979).
9. Ibid.
10. Letter to author.
11. *Life,* op. cit.
12. Jacobs, *Soldier* (New York: Norton, 1950)
13. Jacobs, *Heroes of the Army* (New York: Berkley Publishing, 1956).
14. Ibid.
15. P. Boesch, *Road to the Hurtgen Forest in Hell* (Houston: Gulf Publishing, 1962).
16. Ibid.

CHAPTER 10

1. Irving, *War Between the Generals.*
2. Ibid.
3. Ibid.

4. H. Butcher, *Three Years with Eisenhower* (London: Heineman, 1947).

5. Irving, *War Between the Generals*.

6. *History of 22nd Infantry*.

7. Ibid.

8. Boesch, *Road to the Hurtgen Forest*.

9. Ibid.

10. Ibid.

11. Ibid.

12. Ibid.

13. *History of the 1st Infantry Division*.

14. Boesch, *Road to the Hurtgen*.

15. *History of 22nd Infantry*.

16. Baker, *Hemingway*.

17. Ibid.

18. Boesch, *Road to the Hurtgen Forest*.

19. Ibid.

20. Ibid.

21. Ibid.

22. Ibid.

23. Ibid.

PART THREE *Dark December*

CHAPTER 11

1. Personal communication to author.

2. Ibid.

3. Ibid.

4. Ibid.

5. Ibid.

6. Ibid.

7. M/Sgt. Pogue, *Battle of Hurtgen Forest* (privately printed, 1945).

8. Personal communication to author.

9. Ibid.

10. Ibid.
11. Mittelman, *Eight Stars*.
12. Letter to author.
13. Ibid.
14. Pogue, *Battle of Hurtgen Forest*.
15. Letter to author.
16. Ibid.
17. Ibid.
18. *History of the Second Ranger Battalion* (privately printed, 1947).
19. Ibid.
20. Ibid.

CHAPTER 12

1. Letter to author.
2. Ibid.
3. C. Steinhoff, *The Last Chance* (London: Hutchinson, 1977).
4. Ibid.
5. Gorlitz, *Model*.
6. Ibid.
7. Ibid.
8. Ibid.
9. MacDonald, *Siegfried Line Campaign*.
10. *BBC War Report*.
11. Letter to author.
12. Ibid.
13. George Patton, *War As I Knew It* (New York: Ballantine Books, 1947).
14. Huie, *Private Slovik*.

CHAPTER 13

1. *History of Second Ranger Battalion*.
2. Ibid.
3. Interview with author.
4. Mittelman, *Eight Stars*.

5. Ibid.
6. *Paths of Armor* (Atlanta: A. Love Enterprises, 1953).
7. Ibid.
8. Ibid.
9. Ibid.
10. MacDonald, *Siegfried Line Campaign*.
11. Palmer, Wiley, and Keast, *The Army Ground Forces* (Washington: U.S. Army, 1948).
12. Ibid.

CHAPTER 14

1. *Lightning, the History of the 78th Division* (Washington: Infantry Journal Press, 1947).
2. Ibid.
3. *Paths of Armor.*
4. F. Nobecourt, *La Bataille des Ardennes* (Gallimard, 1953).
5. *Lightning.*
6. Ibid.

CHAPTER 15

1. Kay Summersby, *My Three Years with Eisenhower* (New York: Bantam, 1947).
2. Irving, *War Between the Generals.*
3. *History of Second Ranger Battalion.*
4. Ibid.
5. Ibid.
6. Mittelman, *Eight Stars.*
7. Charles MacDonald, *Company Commander* (New York: Ballantine, 1947).
8. Ibid.
9. Ibid.
10. *Playboy* interview (February 1978).
11. Charles MacDonald, *Battle of the Bulge* (Weidenfeld & Nicolson, 1985).
12. K. Strong, *Intelligence at the Top* (Cassell, 1968).

13. Bradley, *General's Life*.
14. Ibid.
15. Irving, *War Between the Generals*.
16. MacDonald, *Battle of the Bulge*.

PART FOUR *The Race for the Dams*

CHAPTER 16

1. Irving, *War Between the Generals*.
2. *Stars and Stripes* (March 18, 1945).
3. M. Modley, *The Invisible Soldier* (Wayne State Press, 1975).
4. Ibid.
5. *Stars and Stripes* (March 18, 1945).
6. Ibid.
7. Irving, *War Between the Generals*.
8. Modley, *Invisible Soldier*.
9. Ibid.
10. *The Last Offensive*.
11. Gavin, *On to Berlin*.
12. Ibid.
13. Ibid.
14. Ibid.
15. Ibid.
16. Ibid.
17. J. Giles, *The GI Journal of Sergeant Giles* (Boston: Houghton Mifflin, 1965).
18. Ibid.
19. Atwell, *Private* (Popular Library, 1958).
20. Ibid.
21. Ibid.
22. Ibid.

CHAPTER 17

1. Huie, *Private Slovik*.
2. Ibid.

3. Ibid.
4. Ibid.
5. Ibid.
6. *Selected Intelligence Reports,* Vol. 11 (Cheb, Austria: State Printing Office, 1945).
7. *Last Offensive.*
8. Gavin, *On to Berlin.*
9. Ibid.
10. Ibid.
11. Ibid.
12. Ibid.

CHAPTER 18

1. John Toland, *The Last 100 Days* (New York: Random House, 1966).
2. *The Battle for Germany.*
3. Ibid.
4. B. Horrocks, *A Full Life* (London: Leo Cooper, 1969).
5. *History of Second Ranger Battalion.*
6. Ibid.
7. Ibid.
8. Letter to author.
9. Ibid.
10. Ibid.
11. Ibid.
12. Ibid.

CHAPTER 19

1. *Last Offensive.*
2. Ibid.
3. Ibid.
4. Toland, *Last 100 Days.*
5. *Last Offensive.*

CHAPTER 20

1. Gorlitz, *Model*.
2. Charles Whiting, *The Battle of the Ruhr Pocket* (New York: Ballantine, 1970).
3. Ibid.
4. Ibid.
5. Ibid.
6. *The Sunday Times* (London: December 12, 1974).
7. Ibid.

Index

Aachen, x, xi, 9, 11, 15, 36, 163, 193, 218
Anderson, Colonel, 124, 127
Andrusz, Ed, 155
Army Air Corps, U.S., 183, 198
Arnold, Henry H. "Hap," 25
Atwell, Lester, 222–224

Barr, Robert, 167–168
Barton, Tubby, 12, 102, 119, 138, 176
Betts, General, 206
Black, Captain, 123–124, 134
Blaurock, Colonel, 37
Block, Dr., 148–149, 159
Blue Angel, The, 63
Boesch, Paul, 122, 123, 134–137, 139, 141, 142–143
Boice, William, 110, 143
Bond, Colonel, 48, 49, 177, 178
Bradley, Omar, 59, 91, 102, 192, 198–199, 200, 206, 207–208, 209, 210, 229, 234, 260, 262, 264
Briles, Herschel F., 54–55
Brooke, Alan, 128, 132
Brooks, Mel, 205
Brown, Lloyd, 58–59
Bulge, Battle of the, x, 131, 206, 213, 216, 217
Butch (PR man), 130–131
Butcher, Captain, 129

Call, Floyd, 231
Canham, General, 120
Carter, William, 188
Castle Hill (Hill 400), 151, 154–159, 172, 174, 201, 202, 273
casualties, xi, 51–52, 57, 64–65, 66, 96, 97–98, 142, 166, 168–169, 173–174, 179–180, 184, 222, 223, 256
Chicago Daily News, 140
Churchill, Winston, 132, 210, 213, 257
Clark, William D., 21
Colbaugh, Jack, 76
Collins, Joseph "Lightning Joe," xi, 14–15, 16–17, 42, 44, 45, 61, 69, 81, 101–102, 153, 163, 164, 165, 166–167, 176, 177, 180, 209, 261, 264, 265–266

combat fatigue, 24–25, 60–61, 75, 109–110, 223–224
Combs, Clarence Ed, 18–19
Condon, Lieutenant, 83
Cota, Norman, 59–62, 67, 68, 70, 75, 77, 80, 84, 86, 87, 90–92, 94, 95, 97, 218, 223, 225–226, 228–229, 231
Cothran, Harold, 215
Cox, William, 118
Craig, Louis, 21, 27–29, 34, 41, 42, 51, 176, 177, 250–252, 253
Cross, Colonel, 134
Crusade in Europe (Eisenhower), x, 29
Cummings, Father, 225

Daley, Colonel, 82
Daniel, Colonel, 114, 138
Davis, General, 81–82, 84, 90, 91
Death of a Division (Whiting), 184n
Dege, Wilhelm, 160, 161, 162
DeLaura, Anthony, 175
Dele, Elise, 190–192
Dickson, Benjamin Monk, 191–194
Dietrich, Marlene, 63, 99
Diven, Ralph, 10
Douglas, Keith, 269
Dunnett, Robert, 12

8th Air Force, U.S., 104
VIII Corps, U.S., xi, 191, 207n
8th Infantry Division, U.S., 98, 102, 119–120, 125, 132–133, 134, 138, 149, 151, 167, 174
8th Infantry Regiment U.S., 105, 107, 110
8th Parachute Regiment, German, 230–231
82nd Airborne Division, U.S., xiv, 17, 219, 221, 232–233, 249, 261
84th Infantry Division, U.S., 153, 174, 178, 187, 202–203
899th Tank Destroyer Battalion, U.S., 21, 40, 54
Eight Stars to Victory, 24
Eisenhower, Dwight D., x, 15, 17, 25, 28, 29, 42, 45, 59, 65, 81, 91, 128–131, 132, 164, 170–171, 198n, 199–200, 206–209, 213, 228, 229, 236, 252, 257, 265
Eisenhower, Mamie, 130, 199, 209

Ernst, Lieutenant, 261
Essame, General, 238

1st Army, U.S., 4, 11, 14, 44, 61, 63, 69, 92, 113, 164, 166, 191, 206, 209, 237, 249, 259, 265
First Canadian Army, 238
1st Infantry Division, U.S., "The Big Red One," xiv, 11, 27, 59, 98, 102, 113, 114, 115, 116, 119, 120, 137–138, 152, 176, 209, 217–218, 259, 266
First Parachute Army, German, 248
1st SS Panzer Division, 177
4th Cavalry Group, U.S., 31
4th Infantry Division, U.S., xi, 12, 29, 90, 92, 94, 95, 98, 99, 102, 105, 106, 107, 110–111, 118, 119, 120, 132, 138, 141, 153, 176, 178, 221
5th Armored Division, U.S., 9, 11, 69, 91, 92, 102, 124, 128, 132, 153, 174, 178, 180, 181, 187–189
5th Army, U.S., 183
V Corps, U.S., 44, 69, 101, 129, 153, 217, 218, 233, 234, 236, 237, 240, 250, 257
5th Panzer Army, 163, 166
5th Parachute Division, German, 164
15th Engineer Combat Battalion, U.S., 21, 22
15th Infantry Regiment, U.S., 181, 188
47th Armored Infantry Regiment, U.S., 155
51st Highland Division, British, 240
Fanny by Gaslight, 63
Fellman, Major, 226–228
Fleig, Lieutenant, 78–79, 80–81, 93, 272
Flood, Colonel, 76–77, 79
Francotte (Belgian gunmaker), 198
Freeman, Major, 117
Fuller, Earl, 74

Garcia, Marcario, 133–134
Gardner, Noble, 52
Gavin, James M., xiv, 17, 98, 219–221, 232–235, 236, 249, 261, 265, 273
Gerow, Leonard T., 61–62, 69, 70, 81, 90, 91, 97, 101, 119, 129, 153, 164, 166, 209, 217, 218
Gerow, Marie-Louise, 129

Gersdorff, Generalmajor von, xiv
Giles, Sergeant, 221
Ginder, Colonel, 139, 141
Goebbels, Josef, 5n, 165
Goering, Hermann, 117
Goforth, Major, 118–119
Gomez, Arthur P., xiv
Graff, Bob, 73
Grasett, A. E., 206
Green, John, 108
Grohé, *Gauleiter,* 7
Grotte, Ralph, 67

Hargrave, Pearlie, 130, 199
Harris, Arthur "Bomber," 8, 104, 239
Hatzfeld, Colonel, 74, 82–83, 84
Hays, Sergeant, 122
Heilmann, General, 164–165
Hemingway, Ernest, 12–13, 27, 63, 99–101, 104–105, 140
Henley, Captain, 118
Herrle, Lieutenant, 160–161
Higgins, Colonel, 203
Himmler, Heinrich, 193n
Hindenburg, Paul von, 103
Hirschfelder, Colonel, 203
History of the Second Ranger Battalion, 157, 242
Hitler, Adolf, 36, 37, 131, 132, 162, 163, 164, 167, 193n, 221, 263
Hodges, Courtney, 11, 14, 15, 38, 61–62, 69, 70, 81, 91, 92, 97, 101, 103, 113, 127, 164, 166, 177, 181, 191, 192, 193, 194, 198, 206, 209–210, 237, 242, 249–250, 257, 259, 264, 265
Hogan, Colonel, 176
Holbert, Captain, 179
Holzinger, Warner W., 9, 11, 160
Horrocks, Brian, 238–240, 256
Hostrup, Captain, 78, 93
Houston, Jack, 44
Howe, Albert, 76
Huebner, Clarence, 113, 120, 217–218, 219, 222n, 231, 232, 237, 233, 240–242, 243, 245, 249–250, 257–258
Hughes, Everett S., 45, 129, 130, 199–200, 209
Hurley, William, 126

Jeter, Colonel, 120, 124, 134
Jodl, Alfred, 131, 132, 163, 164

Johnson, Elliott, 105, 106
Johnson, Lyndon B., 267
Jones, Chester, 216
Jones, General, 184

Kaares, Kurt, 243–244
Kall Trail, 69–70, 77–78, 79, 81, 82,
    87, 88, 91, 93, 219–220, 272
Kampfgruppe Wegelein, 38, 48, 49
Kean, General, 103
Keate, Lieutenant, 54
Kee, Jack, 123
Kelch, Lieutenant, 53
Kelley, Jonah, 241
Kemp, Leroy, 216
Kenan, Tom, 101
Kesselring, Albert, 259–260
Kissinger, Henry, 266
Kluge, Günther von, 36
Koziak, Lieutenant, 226–227
Kraskin, Leon, 180
Kunzig, Colonel, 136

La Barr, Sergeant, 18
Lanham, Buck, 13, 99, 101, 105,
    111–112, 115, 118, 119, 134, 138,
    139, 140
Lavender, Don, 56–57
Lee, John C. H., 213–214, 215
Lee, Robert E., 262
Liebach, Colonel, 230–231
Life, 111, 118, 139
Lisko, Lou, 149
Luce, Clare Booth, 100
Luckett, James, 95, 96, 97
Luetgens, Heinz, 175

McAuley, Jack, 125–126
McAuliffe, Anthony C., 191*n*
McBride, Captain, 151
McCrone, Pat, 157
MacDonald, Charles, 204–205
McGraw, Francis, 114
MacKay, Walter, 76
McKeogh, Mickey, 130, 199
McNab, Robert, 189
McNaughton, John T., 267
McNeal, George, 10
Macon, General, 178–179, 180–181
Madden, Chaplain, 93
Majka, Benny, 126
Malloy, Spike, 76
Manteuffel, Hasso von, 163, 166

Marcikowski, Captain, 126
Marshall, George C., 42, 43–44, 166,
    216
Marshall, S. L. A., 183
Marzhauser, Bernd, 50
Maxeiner, Walter, 263
Medal of Honor, 55, 56, 114, 122,
    134*n*, 214, 241
Melton, Jack, 120, 121
Merode Castle, 176–178
Middleton, Troy, 191, 207
Miller, Graham, 116–117
Minick, John W., 120–122, 123–124
Model, Walter, 36–39, 113, 163–164,
    165–166, 167, 243, 248, 255, 256,
    258, 259–264, 264*n*, 265, 271, 274
Montgomery, Bernard, 37, 60, 132,
    209, 236, 237, 248, 256, 259, 265
Morgan, George, 111
Morrison, Private, 228
Moses, Albert, 21
Murray, Lieutenant, 133

9th Air Force, U.S., 104
Ninth Army, German, 36, 37
9th Army, U.S., 69, 218, 236–238,
    243, 249, 252–253, 255–257, 259,
    265
9th Infantry Division, U.S., xi, 18, 20,
    22, 23, 24, 25, 26–27, 29–31, 32,
    33, 35, 39, 40, 41–42, 44, 47, 48,
    51, 53, 54, 57–58, 61, 62, 69, 73,
    77, 98, 102, 115, 151, 153, 174,
    175–176, 202, 250, 266, 267
9th Infantry Regiment, U.S., 203
XIX TAC Air Force, U.S., 219
92nd Infantry Division, U.S., 216
99th Infantry Division, U.S., 203,
    204, 206, 209, 261
903rd Field Artillery Battalion, U.S.,
    200
942nd Infantry Regiment, German, 34
951st Field Artillery, U.S., 53, 54
Napoleon I, Emperor of France, 97,
    211
Needles, Edward, 68
Nellesen, Lene, 11
Nelson, Colonel, 87, 92–93
Nesbit, James, 83
Nixon, Richard M., 266

101st Airborne Division, U.S., 65

104th Infantry Division, U.S., 102, 107, 120, 153

106th Infantry Division, U.S., 183–184, 206

109th Infantry Regiment, U.S., 12, 67, 74, 90, 91, 93, 97, 225, 229

110th Infantry Regiment, U.S., 74, 75–76, 90, 92, 94–95

112th Infantry Regiment, U.S., 45, 74, 79–80, 81, 85, 87, 89, 90, 92, 97, 145

116th Infantry Combat Team, U.S., 59

116th Panzer Division, 81, 85, 95, 274

121st Infantry Regiment, U.S., 120, 124, 125

Oliver, General, 180–181

Otten, Manfred, 83, 84

Over the River and Into the Trees (Hemingway), 101*n*

Palmer, Chaplain, 180

Parker, General, 186, 218–219, 231, 232, 233, 240, 242, 243, 245, 247, 250

Patton, George S., 43, 45, 130, 131, 166, 169, 207, 208, 214–215, 217, 238, 252, 271

Paulus, Friedrich, 263

Peiper, *Obersturmbannführer*, 177, 210

Pershing, John "Black Jack," 15, 42, 43, 214, 216

Peters, Major, 116

Peterson, Carl L., 45, 74, 80, 81–82, 85–90, 91, 97, 273

Pilling, Colonel, 264

Pool, Frank, 125

Puetz, Hermann, 7

Pyle, Ernie, 26, 101

Quesada, Pete, 103, 198

Quinn, Chaplain, 108

RAF, 8, 76, 104, 239

Ramcke, General, 120

Ray, Bernard, 107

Reagan, Ronald W., 271*n*

Recknagel, Karl, 162–163

Ridgway, Matthew B., 261–262

Riley, John, 242

Ripperdam, Frank, 80

Ripple, Colonel, 78, 81, 86, 87, 92, 93

Road to Casablanca, The, 63

Robertson, General, 203

Roer River Dams, 44, 69, 192–193, 218, 237–238, 240, 242, 243, 245, 249–252, 253–256, 265

Rommel, Erwin, 26, 36, 201

Roosevelt, Franklin D., 31, 42, 191, 210

Rose, Maurice, 259

Rudder, Colonel, 150, 151, 155, 158, 159, 229–230

Rufiange, Robert, 189

Runstedt, Gerd von, 1, 35–36, 167, 193, 259

2nd Armored Division, U.S., 259

2nd Infantry Division, U.S., 203, 204, 209

2nd Ranger Battalion, U.S., 90, 98, 147–151, 154–159, 172–174, 201–202, 229, 242, 273

Sixth Army Group, U.S., 229

6th SS Panzer Army, 166

7th Armored Division, U.S., 210, 219, 231

7th Army, German, xiv, 164

VII Corps, U.S., 14, 15, 61, 69, 101, 153, 154, 261

16th Infantry Regiment, U.S., 114, 119

60th Infantry Regiment, U.S., xi, 20, 21, 22–23, 29, 34–35, 42, 57, 151, 176, 251

70th Infantry Division, U.S., 183

78th Infantry Division, U.S., 183–184, 185–187, 188, 194–195, 196–197, 200, 201, 202, 218, 222, 230, 233, 240–241, 242, 243, 250–251, 253, 256, 257–258, 261, 262, 272

709th Tank Battalion, U.S., 196

744th Tank Battalion, U.S., 179, 243, 245–246, 251

746th Tank Battalion, U.S., 21

761st Tank Battalion, U.S., 215

Salinger, J. D., 101*n*

Schmidt, General, 49

Schneller, George, 242

Schwartz, Stanley, 121

Searles, James, 115–116

Secor, Sergeant, 173

Seely, Colonel, 74, 94, 95

Seiler, Gus, 87, 88–89

Seitz, Colonel, 114, 138

Sheridan, Carl V., 55–56, 273
Shogren, Kin, 51, 151–152, 153–154, 168
Sibert, Colonel, 95–96
Sibert, General, 206
Siegfried Line Campaign, The, x
Simon, Lieutenant, 81
Simpson, William, 69, 236–238, 243, 245, 248–249, 252–253, 255–256, 257, 259, 265
Slanger, Second Lieutenant, 102–103
Slovik, Eddie D., 67–68, 109, 170–171, 225–228, 229–230, 274
Smith, Walter Bedell, 128, 130, 207
Spellman, Francis J., Cardinal, 20
Stalin, Joseph, 132
Stars and Stripes, 53, 102, 194, 215
Steinhoff, Colonel, 162–163
Stimson, Henry, 216
Strickler, Colonel, 74
Stroh, Donald, 102, 119, 120, 124, 142, 176
Strong, Kenneth, 198*n*, 206
Summerfield, Lawrence, 126
Summersby, Kay, 65, 129, 130, 131, 199, 206, 229
"Swede," Captain, 111, 118–119

3rd Armored Division, U.S., 102, 153, 174, 176, 259
Third Army, U.S., 14, 166, 169, 208, 214, 252
3rd Canadian Division, 240
3rd Parachute Division, German, 115, 152, 153, 176, 177
10th Panzer Division, 201
12th Infantry Regiment, U.S., 90, 92, 94, 95, 96, 120
22nd Infantry Regiment, U.S., xi, 12–13, 99, 100, 101, 105, 110, 111, 118, 119, 133
25th Infantry Division, U.S., 14
26th Infantry Regiment, U.S., 113–114, 116, 117, 137, 138
28th Infantry Division, U.S., 12, 29, 45, 57–58, 61, 63, 67, 68, 69–70, 73, 76, 77, 80, 87, 90, 91, 92, 95, 97, 141, 145, 146, 191, 203, 220, 225, 229, 230, 231, 233, 272, 273, 274

28th Infantry Regiment, U.S., 149, 152
29th Infantry Division, 59
XXX Corps, British, 238, 240
39th Infantry Regiment, U.S., 29, 34, 47, 48, 49, 50, 176–178
246th Volksgrenadier Division, 153
272nd Volksgrenadier Division, 243
275th Fusilier Battalion, German, 34
275th Infantry Division, German, 16, 49, 50
309th Infantry Regiment, U.S., 196, 201, 231–232, 250, 251–252
310th Infantry Regiment, U.S., 185, 195, 196, 201, 231–232
311th Infantry Regiment, U.S., 245–247, 250, 251
353rd Infantry Division, German, 16
TAC Air Force, U.S., 104, 173, 177, 195
Tankey, Private, 67–68
Task Force Davis, 90, 91
Task Force Hogan, 176
Task Force R, 81
Tempel, Captain, 179
Tex (record keeper), 129
Thomas-Weiss, Hannalore, 9
Thrasher, Captain, 53
Time, 267
Time-Life Group, 100
Trusty, Private, 121

U-507, 160, 161–162
Ultra Secret (Winterbotham), 228*n*

Vipond, First Lieutenant, 9, 10

Walton, William, 111, 118, 139
Weaver, General, 138, 142, 151, 154
Wegelein, Colonel, 38, 39, 49, 50–51
Wegener, General, 261
Wellington, Duke of, 145
Welsh, Mary, 99–100
Welter, Pastor, 11
Westmoreland, William C., 42, 265–266, 267
Wharton, James E., 59
Wilck, Colonel, 36
Winterbotham, F., 228*n*

Yank, 20
York, Colonel, 179

Zera, Maxie, 115
Zienke, Lieutenant, 122–123